Goodbye,
Mr. Christian

Books by Richard Dougherty

GOODBYE, MR. CHRISTIAN
WE DANCE AND SING
DUGGAN
THE COMMISSIONER
A SUMMER WORLD

Goodbye, Mr. Christian

A PERSONAL ACCOUNT
OF McGOVERN'S RISE AND FALL

by Richard Dougherty

DOUBLEDAY & COMPANY, INC., GARDEN CITY, NEW YORK, 1973

The quotation from Yeats from Collected Poems by W. B. Yeats © 1906 by
the Macmillan Company. Renewed 1934 by William Butler Yeats. Reprinted
by permission of The Macmillan Publishing Company, Inc., and the Macmillan
Company of Canada, Ltd.

ISBN: 0-385-01546-1
LIBRARY OF CONGRESS CATALOG CARD NUMBER: 73-79743
COPYRIGHT © 1973 BY RICHARD DOUGHERTY
ALL RIGHTS RESERVED
PRINTED IN THE UNITED STATES OF AMERICA

*For George McGovern and the thirty million voters
who wanted him to make America
a strong, just and merciful country*

Goodbye, Mr. Christian

CHAPTER *1*

MY FATHER, no stranger to disappointment in a hard life, used to tell about a lumberjack who worked three full years in the woods, saving every penny of his wages and never leaving camp. Finally he packed his bag and came into town where he checked into the best hotel. As he started to go upstairs to his room he passed a gaming room and decided to stop a moment just to try his luck. In minutes he was broke. "Well," he said as he watched the last chip raked away, "easy come, easy go."

I told the story to George McGovern at some point in the dying days of his ill-fated campaign for President when the handwriting was already on the wall. He, poor valiant bastard, laughed. I like George McGovern and admire him greatly, but I was never fonder nor more admiring than at the end of his presidential dream and of his agonies. The crushing defeat he suffered was, I believe, chiefly attributable to Senator Thomas Eagleton; but it was also partly due to bad luck and partly to McGovern's own mistakes. Still the stylish way in which he took the beating, the way in which he—with the support of an admirable Eleanor McGovern—walked down the gantlet of those final days was a mighty achievement and his alone. To my mind, because I put a high value on style, it constituted a kind of victory. It also, however odd to say, brought me a sense of personal victory. I had worked for him for a year and the experience had not always been happy. But now, as he walked away from the debacle with his head up, so could I. I could be content that my judgment of him as a good man was right.

In fairness I should warn the reader that this book is concerned as much with Dougherty as McGovern, perhaps more so. It is a memoir, but it is more particularly a fragment of autobiography written by one of the lesser players in the McGovern presidential drama. It is not a polemic, although it is unashamedly partisan, specially as it argues a defense of McGovern and his conduct of the tragic Eagleton affair. I won't be dismayed if scholars find the book little more than a gossipy, belowstairs account of what went on in the course of my service.

It is an intensely personal book, which some may find too revealing, but I am a man with few secrets beyond an occasional—and increasingly rare—fantasy which I'd not like to see in Macy's window. I write it because I am a cheerfully vain fellow who is incapable of believing that others are not as interested in him as he is in himself. And I write it because I am convinced that McGovern deserved better than he got—both from the gods and the American voter.

It is my hope to portray McGovern as a more dimensional man than he was commonly credited with being. It was often said that he was decent: too decent, according to some, to be President. Well, he is a decent man but not all that decent. He is also bright, slightly profane, responsive, good company; and he is the opposite of these, too, being nicely endowed with all the paradoxes that flesh is heir to. But I am a Stendhalian and what interested me most about him—and heightened my feeling of kinship with him—was his ambition. I know a climber when I see one, and when I, having been born and raised in the little town of Bolivar, New York, find myself associated with George

McGovern, a product of Mitchell, South Dakota, I know I'm dealing with a climber of my own breed.

I know how smart a smart rube can be, how tough, how cunning, how indomitable, how self-sufficient and self-sustaining. I know what went into the long hard climb from a humble Methodist parsonage in Mitchell to the stately chambers of the United States Senate. I made a less dramatic, but in many ways equally difficult, climb from my poverty-ridden origins in Bolivar to a good life among the oligarchs of Manhattan.

I did it by hard work, relentless optimism and that *sine qua non* of the climbing art, making friends who might be useful and then using them. I know that McGovern made it the same way. I know how the burden of guilt increases as one moves up, how the joys of success can, for a while, render the burden weightless. I know what a game the climb can be but also how a failure can hurt.

Aside from this, as it were, bond of kinship on which I'll lean in telling the story of the ultimate McGovern climb and my part in it, there were other things which attracted me. I shared his hatred of the war in Vietnam which I had always thought a hideous blunder. I liked the courage he had shown in speaking out against the war early on when to do so was risky. I liked him for being rather a maverick and a loner within the Senate "club." I liked his capacity for a biblical wrath in the face of injustice, bigotry, meanness and stupidity. I am an old-style New Deal Democrat of conservative instincts, and I am a snob; but I have never accepted the view that the so-called liberal holds a monopoly over social justice as a worthy and civilized concern.

So, when word came in the fall of 1971 that McGovern would like me to work for him, there was considerable appeal in the prospect. And the timing was good too, for I was feeling menopausal and mutinous.

I had turned fifty that summer. Earlier, in the spring, I published a novel—my fourth—on which I'd worked part time over a period of eight years. I was proud of the book and crushed by its failure to receive no more than a handful of reviews. Beyond this, however, I was no longer happy with the newspaper business. I had, as New York correspondent for the Los Angeles Times, a good job with a respected and prosperous paper. I should have been content. Instead I was increasingly bored and frustrated.

I had always found the peripheral character of newspapering somewhat unsatisfying. One is eternally the critic and never the artist. One stands at the edge of great events but plays no role in them. For the born newsman this is enough, but I was a novelist who used journalism to make a living. Too, when one is young it seems enough; or, if not, it is compensated for by the sheer fun of the trade and the pleasure of the company. But fifty is not young by any standard and it is quite old by the standards of reporting. I had stayed too long at the party.

Richard Wade was the emissary who brought the message from McGovern. He called one day late in October and said he wanted to talk to me. I suggested lunch and he met me at the Century Club. Wade is an old friend, a distinguished scholar and professor of history at the Graduate Center of the City University of New York. He is also a political buff of classic dimensions. He was a friend and early supporter of McGovern and was currently heading up the McGovern operation in New York State. McGovern was having problems with the press, Wade said. There was a McGovern press secretary, but he was young and his background was in television. The thinking of McGovern and Frank Mankiewicz was that the addition to the campaign staff of an established political writer could add weight to the candidacy and command more respectful attention. Was it possible, he asked, for me to get a leave from the paper. No, I said, but I might quit.

Subsequently I had a number of phone conversations with Mankiewicz. I had covered Robert Kennedy over much of his brief and tragic presidential race in 1968 and knew Mankiewicz, who had been the Kennedy press secretary, from then. Now he was McGovern's "political director," whatever that meant. I had several concerns. First, I didn't want the job of press secretary. I was too old, I said, to be shouting at cops and running for the buses. Couldn't I go along with the candidate as a kind of senior adviser? Mankiewicz said there would be no problem about that. Jeff Gralnick, who was the press secretary, would, Mankiewicz said, see to the care and feeding of the press. "You can just hustle the older guys in the back of the bus."

Second, while I was embarrassed at talking money, I had to be paid something in the neighborhood of what I was earning. He said he saw no problem there. Third, I was confused about the chain of command. All I knew about Gary Hart, the campaign manager, was that he was in his early thirties, and I could not conceive of taking orders from someone twenty years my junior. I knew that properly I'd be working directly for the candidate but still hierarchies could be sticky. "Frank," I said, "can you tell me: Will I be reporting to you?"

There was, I thought, a moment's hesitation at the other end of the line. Then Mankiewicz said: "Oh, sure."

There were small problems at home. Cynthia Dougherty is an enchanting and marvelous woman, but she has an extremely practical mind. She thought I'd gone slightly mad, although she was too kind to say so. "Nobody thinks he has a chance," she said of McGovern. "Well, I do," I said. There was, I thought, as much despair as affection in her eyes as she said: "Well, if you must, I suppose you must."

13

McGovern telephoned one evening when I was out of the house. "This is George McGovern," he said to her.

"Oh," she said, flustered. "How do you do, sir. What does one say in situations like this? Welcome aboard?"

"No," he said. "I'm the one who's supposed to say that."

My colleagues at the *Times*'s bureau gave a farewell party for me. It was supposed to be a surprise.

One of the guests was Tom O'Hara, from the old *Herald Tribune*. "A lovely day," I had said to him years ago when I was a green reporter and he a grizzled veteran. "That's right, kid," he replied. "You can see 'em picking their noses in Jersey."

Another was Mike Murphy, former police commissioner, a friend since the days when I was myself a deputy police commissioner and he a young captain. I published a novel about the New York cops once and when I asked him what he thought of it he said: "It's a great book for the Fire Department."

Dick Wald, another *Trib* alumnus, was now vice president of NBC News. "I need an adventure," I told him, explaining my move. "I need to set the blood racing."

"You need a sanity pill," he said.

Jack Tierney—a public relations executive for an oil company and former mayoral press secretary who once gave me a job as assistant to the hospitals' commissioner—brought a poster to put on the wall. It read: "Vote Dougherty—Unbossed, Unbought, Unqualified, and Uncompetent."

He also brought a cable from our mutual friend Les Slote, former press secretary to Nelson Rockefeller, now living grandly in London as a vice president of RCA International.

"Your superb qualifications: four disappointing novels, a Broadway flop, service in the most corrupt police department in the western world make you a welcome addition to PR ranks. I will sleep better at night knowing you are in the front lines."

It was an excellent party. Later a few of us wound up the evening at a Chinese restaurant. When it came time to pay the check I found I was missing a hundred-dollar bill. Could I have given it to a cab driver for a single? Cynthia looked at me and then looked away. When we got home the bill was on top of my chest of drawers. But by then I realized that I had somewhere along the way lost my treasured and expensive Briggs umbrella, bought more than ten years ago in London. I assured her of a by-now painfully patient expression that I would track it down in the morning. I could see she didn't believe it and time proved her right.

The next day Pete Hamill, writing a pro-McGovern column in the New York *Post,* had some nice things to say about me: "Dick Dougherty is not your ordinary reporter: He is a hell of a novelist (although his books never seem to sell); he is a first-rate reporter. When you hear that a Dougherty is willing to give up pensions, salary and the rest of the things that go with working for a paper like the Los Angeles *Times,* you know that something very serious is going on."

I lunched with Walter Lippmann and that serene and Olympian man admitted puzzlement at my having joined the McGovern cause. He agreed with the senator on most things, he said, and respected him for his early stand against the war. Yet McGovern struck him as "not strong," and he doubted he would be an effective challenger to Nixon. Lippmann's preference was Muskie, whom he called a good man. I said I had nothing against Muskie but he seemed to me rather a status-quo man and I thought the times too troubled, the discontent of people too deep, for the Democrats to nominate a middle-of-the-road type. What, I asked Lippmann, did he consider the central issue facing the country? "The credibility of our leaders," he said.

Later Jack Germond, Washington bureau chief of the Gannett newspapers, called and said: "What's a nice guy like you doing in a thing like this?" I said I had run out my string as a reporter and wanted to do something real. "He's a nice guy," Germond said, "but he's not going anywhere. He can't make news. He's too auto-lib, too predictable. Press a button and that's what Mc-Govern would say."

I said I still thought he had a shot at the nomination. "A damned long one," said Germond.

I had ideas about McGovern's failure to catch on. He was not, it was true, a great orator, but he was none the less a knowledge-able and effective speaker. He was not a flamboyant personality. But there was about him a sincerity, a calmness and dignity which got through to people. He had an appealing face too. I could not agree with those who attributed his troubles to per-sonality.

Nor could I attach much significance to his inability to capture attention in the press. News, after all, is seasonal. The press doesn't cover hockey in August or baseball in December, and to the extent that presidential politics is reported prior to the presidential season, the focus is almost exclusively on the front runners—in this instance Muskie and Kennedy. For the time being, then, McGovern was caught into a profitless bind. The press gave him minimal coverage because of his low stand-ing in the polls and he stayed low in the polls because of minimal coverage.

Also, aside from their unhappy effect on press coverage, it was difficult to take the readings of Harris and Gallup seriously. Polls taken at such an early stage, months ahead of season so to speak, are little more than measures of celebrity bespeaking no hard judgments on the public's part. To me the polls showed that George McGovern, the junior senator from a state with less than a million population, had little celebrity and, lacking that, inspired few positive responses from Democratic voters.

Not surprising this, and conceivably not all bad for McGovern in the long run. Clearly, to the degree that he was known at all it was for his opposition to the Vietnam war. There was nothing wrong with that. Also, being so little known, it seemed reasonable to assume that he was not the target of significant voter hostility. That could not be said of either Humphrey or Kennedy, both of whom had their haters.

Muskie appeared relatively free of hostility too, and yet his position seemed vulnerable to me. Once the presidential season opened he faced the prospect of having to prove himself with everybody watching, and watching him closely. A mistake—and all candidates make mistakes—that might merely embarrass someone far back in the pack could be seriously wounding to him. The Lindsay threat was a cause of anxiety among many McGovern supporters, but I found it hard to think that the mayor would get very far. The idea of capturing the presidential nomination of a party joined only months before seemed too crass.

According to my arrangement with Frank Mankiewicz, I was, before going to Washington, to spend a month or so in New York doing missionary work among the unbelievers at the newsmaga zines, the networks and the newspapers—particularly the New York *Times*. The *Times* has unusual importance not just because it is a great newspaper but because it is the paper read every morning by the decision makers of the other media. If the *Times* began to pay more attention to McGovern in its news columns, then it was predictable that *Newsweek, Time, Life,* CBS, NBC and ABC would start to pay attention too. Still, the other outfits were not run by robots and my intention was to talk with them all.

I had a simple enough message. First, if the autumn polls in a prepresidential year meant much of anything then the Republican front runner of 1967, George Romney, would now be in the White House rather than Richard Nixon. Second, out of McGovern's unheralded year on the hustings two things had emerged which commanded respect.

He had put together a first-rate grass-roots organization out of the young but seasoned workers of the Eugene McCarthy-Robert Kennedy campaigns of 1968. He had also established an impressive fund-raising operation, based on direct mail solicitation and small contributors, which had raised more than a million dollars. There were to be some twenty-three primaries in 1972 and, in primary elections where a very small percentage of the electorate bothers to vote, sound organization and steady money can spell the difference between victory and defeat.

I also planned to argue on another level that the mood of the nation was despairing, that people wanted a leadership which would bring about fundamental change, and that McGovern—critic not just of the war but of the whole moral tone of traditionalist politics—could provide that leadership. He spoke of an America which had lost its way, and it was my conviction that while he spoke the rhetoric of the left he would find sympathetic listeners in both the center and the right. I had no doubt that if he could win the Democratic nomination he would make Nixon the first one-term President since Herbert Hoover.

I got together with Dick Tuck for a drink over the weekend. He is a wise veteran of Democratic campaigns at all levels including a state Senate race of his own in California several years back. ("The job needs Tuck and Tuck needs the job" was a slogan that the voters declined to buy.) He is a legendary prankster, a gypsy and far nicer than most respectable people. Once during the 1968 Oregon campaign of Robert Kennedy,

18

a young wire-service reporter who had missed part of a speech asked Tuck if the senator had deviated from his text. "The senator," Tuck replied, "is not a text deviate." During the same campaign a garrulous driver of a press bus said: "I got Nixon coming in here next week."

"That's funny," said Tuck. "I had clap once myself."

Frequently during that campaign it was Tuck's duty to take Kennedy's dog Freckles out for his late-night walk. One night Freckles failed to make it to the street and deposited a dump in the hotel lobby. A couple of reporters came along as Tuck was cleaning up the mess and razzed him. "To you this is dog shit," he said with ill-concealed scorn. "To me it's an embassy."

"What do you think really, Dick," I asked him now. "Can McGovern make it?"

"It's a cinch," he said.

Monday, November 15, was my first day on the job. There was a card in the mail from my daughter Lisa, a twenty-year-old college dropout who was living an aimless life in Cambridge, Massachusetts. She is a darling and a worry. "Just a word to wish you luck," she wrote, "and to say I think you're very brave."

When I sat down at the phone the first Titan of the press I was able to reach was Dorothy Schiff, owner and publisher of the New York Post. A handsome and formidable lady, she said she had read about my move in the Hamill column. I said I'd like to pay a courtesy call on her and talk presidential politics. "Well," she said, cutting me down to size, "I usually reserve my time for the candidates themselves." She suggested I get in touch with editor James Wechsler. I said I would. An inauspicious beginning.

Tuesday morning I took a taxi downtown to Barney's to buy some clothes. When I told the driver I wanted Seventh Avenue and Seventeenth Street, he said: "Oh, Barney's, great place." I said I'd never been there but had meant to try it for years. The cabby was an unshaven, disreputable-looking character. "I go there all the time," he said. "You'll love the decor."

I had lunch with Roger Mudd and Gordon Manning of CBS. Manning, a fast-talking, round-figured type who looks like a John Held, Jr., cartoon, is vice president of CBS News and a friend from the days when I had a brief fling as a writer at *Newsweek* and he was a senior editor. They still tell a story about him and John Dennson when the temperamental Dennson was the editor of the magazine years ago. Dennson had a habit of grinding his jaws and making the muscles work in the side of his face. Manning took a new secretary along to a meeting with the editor one day and when they left the girl remarked on the odd mannerism. "I thought for a while he was chewing nuts," she said.

"He was," said Manning. "Mine."

Manning and Mudd were sympathetic listeners.

"We'll try to be helpful and fair, Richard," said Manning. "Send the money in small bills," said Mudd.

Wednesday I called on Mike O'Neill, managing editor of the *Daily News*. He is a gruff, plain-spoken fellow who over the last few years has quietly turned the *News* into one of the country's best newspapers. He was interested in the McGovern fundraising operation. He had recently been to a fat-cat lunch at "21," for a presidential hopeful he didn't name, and he had found it "rather demeaning." He thought in the long run McGovern would be better off with his small contributors. That evening Cynthia and I went to Teddy White's for drinks. "I'm counting on you to help me, you son of a bitch," said the champion chronicler of President making. I promised him I would. He didn't look convinced. "You're planning a book yourself," he said.

The party was a mix of politics and journalism. Cynthia went her own way and I wandered around with that semilost feeling one gets at cocktail parties. I talked with Mike Wallace about the possibility of getting a McGovern piece on his "60 Minutes" show. I talked to Jay Iselin who runs Channel 13, the public broadcasting station; to Eddie Costikyan who, when younger, was the head of Tammany Hall; to David Halberstam, my favorite advocacy journalist as well as critic: He admires my novels. I engaged in a bit of banter with Oz and Deirdre Elliott, friends of many years, and warned him of Halberstam's presence. Relations between the two had been cool since Halberstam blasted *Newsweek*, and inferentially Elliott, the magazine's editor, for treatment given one of its former Vietnam correspondents.

"I saw him already," Elliott said. "Big, isn't he?"

Arthur Schlesinger, Jr., was there, with Alexandra, his very tall wife. As I looked in their direction, a pretty, very tiny blonde came up to greet Alexandra. They shook hands, and the petite one rising on the tips of her toes while Alexandra bent down from her six feet four inches, managed kisses on the cheeks. Dick Wade appeared at my side: "Come meet Eleanor McGovern," he said.

I thought how doll-like she was. (Someone at *Newsweek* said in the course of the campaign: "If you tilt her back, her eyes close.") And, despite her chic, somehow old-fashioned. She might have been the ingenue in a production of *The Red Mill*. No, later than that: She belonged to the era of the big bands. She was the vivacious little number the fellows cut in on in the vast, music-filled spaces of some now-demolished casino.

I lost Wade in the process of getting to her. "I'm Dick Dougherty," I said.

21

"How do you do," she said. I could see nothing had registered. "I've just come to work for you," I said.

"Oh, *Dick Dougherty!*" she said. "Oh, yes. I'm sorry. I'm so glad to meet you." Later Wade and she, Cynthia and I and some others walked around the corner to Third Avenue and had dinner at P. J. Moriarty's. She and I faced each other across the table and had a chance to talk a little. George McGovern was, she said, "very down in his spirits . . . bored with himself and bored with his speeches." I said I would do my best to cheer him up.

Thursday morning I went to see my nose doctor. I have this chronic sinus thing that gets infected easily and makes me sick as a dog. Dr. Anne Belcher, a bossy little grandma, scolded me for not having come to see her sooner. I forbore to say that at her prices it was astonishing I came at all. It was sunny and pleasant when I stepped out onto Fifty-third Street and I decided to walk home up Madison Avenue.

Along the way I met Shirley Clurman. I'm fond of her because she laughs at my jokes. She even laughs when I'm not joking. I once recited the story of the disastrous opening night of my one and only Broadway play and by the time I finished she was rolling on the floor. Today she said how funny I'd been at dinner at the Elliotts' some nights ago. She said she called up Deirdre the next day and said: "Wouldn't you love to be married to Dick Dougherty?"

"What did Deirdre say?" I asked.

"She said no she wouldn't. 'He's moody.'"

In the afternoon I went down to the *Post* and had a pleasant talk with James Wechsler. He said he had no particular favorite among the Democratic aspirants, that he didn't think Lindsay was going anywhere. He said he wished Humphrey would "give up the dream" because he was so fond of him personally. "But

I'm afraid every time he speaks at a college now and doesn't get booed he thinks it's a sign of a Humphrey revival."

Cynthia and I were both up reasonably early Saturday morning. She was driving to Schenectady to visit her mother, an admirable octogenarian with an oddly negative approach to life's pleasures. I came in from tennis once and she looked at me brightly and said: "Did you get beaten?"

I took a cab to La Guardia through a morning that was gray as paste. On Capitol Hill I was briefly lost in the Senate Office Building before finding Room 362. Going past a mail cart I was amused to see the building referred to as Old SOB. In the Mc-Govern office I was greeted by a smiling Pat Donovan, the senator's personal secretary. She looked me over in one of my Barney's suits and said: "Very New Yorky!"

Gordon Weil, McGovern's executive assistant, appeared and gave me a cordial greeting. He asked for my home phone number. "Butterfield 8," I started to say. He broke in laughing and, rolling his eyes toward the ceiling, said: "Oh, no! I don't believe it."

McGovern appeared in the doorway of his private office, smiled and held out his hand. "Welcome, Dick," he said. "I'm glad to see you." I shook his hand and said: "Hello, George. I'm glad to be here."

CHAPTER 2

MCGOVERN HAD TO vote on a tax bill and suggested I go along to the Capitol with him; then we'd go somewhere for lunch. He led the way down to his car in the courtyard of the building. I had last seen him some nine months before when I had covered him—the only national reporter doing so—during a day and evening of politicking in Buffalo. He looked different now, it seemed to me, and as I fell slightly behind his brisk pace, I realized that he had let his hair get a good deal longer. We talked small pleasantries en route to the Senate. I waited in the car while he went in to vote. Talk of the campaign started when he was back behind the wheel and we drove to a small restaurant only a few blocks away. I told him he should not be discouraged by the difficulties of getting in the papers and on the tube. I said I was sure that when New Hampshire began to loom on the horizon, he'd find himself getting plenty of attention.

He said he was aware of that. "But it's still hard not to be depressed by the damn polls." He asked if I thought John Lindsay was going to announce and I said I did. "He could hurt us in Wisconsin," he said. When he pulled the car up to park he turned off the ignition and then sat still for a moment. "I don't know, Dick," he said and, making fists out of his extremely long, slender hands, began gently to pound the top of the steering wheel. "I don't know. But I just have a feeling we're going to carry this off."

"I think you will too," I said.

Inside the restaurant and seated at a rickety table with a dirty red-and-white-checked tablecloth he asked if I'd like a drink. I turned to the waitress, a bony, glum-looking blonde, and inquired if they served House of Lords gin. She shook her head. I said I'd take a Beefeater gibson then. McGovern ordered a bloody mary. "The food's supposed to be pretty good here," he said in a voice that lacked conviction. After we had ordered hamburgers—explaining to me that he might be called back for another vote—McGovern said to the waitress: "I'm Senator McGovern, in case I get a phone call." The woman appeared to understand, but I had the impression the name meant little to her. One could hardly blame him for being depressed if, after almost a year as a declared candidate for President, people didn't recognize him on Capitol Hill.

We talked about press agentry and he said he thought nothing was more important than press relations in a political campaign. Jim Hagerty, Eisenhower's press man, had always seemed to him the ideal press secretary, he said. That was why he was so heartened to have an "old pro" like me coming aboard. Also, and this was said almost plaintively, "It'll be nice to have someone my own age along." The problem with Jeff Gralnick, whom he said he liked, was, he feared, one of youth. "Sometimes when he doesn't have his own way he threatens to resign. Frankly I don't like ultimatums."

I expressed the hope Gralnick wouldn't resign in much the same way that I had expressed it to Mankiewicz. I said I was certain there'd be work enough for both of us; also that I didn't think news stories about staff shakeups were helpful to a campaign. McGovern nodded. "People are quitting or getting fired in the Muskie operation all the time," he said. "It looks messy."

Earlier I had given him a copy of a speech I had drafted. It contained a proposal for incorporating an occasional refund into the federal income tax system. Now, as he glanced over the first few pages, I urged him not to write it off immediately as a gimmick, although that was what it might prove to be. I was, I said, no economist. What I was attempting was to find a way for him to enlarge his constituency, to reach out beyond the peace movement and the ultraliberal community where his strength lay and awaken interest among working people.

"I'm sure you're right," he said. "But don't you think the big issue is still the war?" "Well, perhaps," I said, "but inflation and high taxes are very much on the minds of ordinary people."

He read through the memo accompanying the speech and, taking a pen from his pocket, underlined a sentence which read: "The weakness of the conservatives lies in the mistaken notion that the mass of the American people is as narrow and selfish as they are." I was disappointed that he didn't go on to underline what followed: "But they have no monopoly on bad judgment. For years the liberals have relied on the stick—forgetting the carrot—to force enlightenment on the people. It has ceased to work. The time has come for a bit of carrot."

"I think it's interesting, what I've read so far," McGovern said as he folded the speech and put it in his jacket pocket. "I'll finish it later." He asked if I was in a hurry to go back to New York and whether, if not, I'd like to join Eleanor and him and some friends for dinner. We could dine early enough to allow me to catch the last shuttle home at ten o'clock. "Eleanor said she had a wonderful time with you the other night," he added.

"She's a peach," I said, and that of course I'd stay.

"She's a terrific campaigner too," he said. "She goes out and speaks, writes her own speeches, works hard. She's a real asset."

McGovern had suggested that we meet at the Henry Kimelmans', so shortly after six I took a taxi to the Kimelman house on

California Street. It was dark by then but I could make out the facade of a sizable house that suggested sizable money. I heard the sound of bolts being thrown before a white-jacketed butler opened the door to me.

He led me into a small, handsomely furnished study and asked if I'd like a drink. I said I'd take a weak scotch on the rocks. Kimelman appeared to greet me and make certain I was comfortable. The senator might be late getting away from the Hill, he said, so there was a chance we would all rendezvous at the Jockey Club. Kimelman was, I thought, rather theatrical-looking for the businessman I understood him to be. He wore his thick black hair very full, the modish cut of his dark suit put my Barney's creation to shame. He had a strong and handsome face but a worrier's wrinkles in his brow. We chatted and he said how hopeful he was that I could get more "exposure" for the campaign; as finance chairman he was having a terrible time raising money. He excused himself, saying he wanted to "hurry Charlotte along." I sipped my drink and examined a couple of paintings. I thought them very ugly. "Aren't those marvelous?" Kimelman said, coming back into the room suddenly. "They were done by a young Israeli artist friend of ours." I said I thought they were very good indeed.

Mrs. Kimelman, a pretty woman in ruffles who seemed shy for one within her own domain, came downstairs. Kimelman announced that the McGoverns would join us at the restaurant, so we set off in their limousine. On the way I mentioned that I was going to have to eat and run and Kimelman said he'd have his driver take me to the airport.

McGovern, by himself, joined us as we were being seated by a deferential maitre d'hotel at the Jockey Club. As host he took charge of the drink orders and I was impressed as he gestured toward me and said: "And a House of Lords gibson for Mr.

Dougherty." Extraordinary people—politicians. I still have trouble remembering what brand of cigarettes my wife smokes.

Eleanor McGovern, looking smart in a blue velvet pants suit, came in accompanied by the Joe Floyds, friends from South Dakota. Mrs. Floyd, tall and handsome, seemed very reserved. Floyd, a pear-shaped man with a thin black mustache and a touch of Babbitt in his manner, gave me a bone-crushing handshake. The men, although deferring now and then to Eleanor, dominated the conversation, virtually all of which dealt with politics. There was, Floyd confirmed in response to a McGovern comment, trouble with the voters back home in South Dakota. The senator had not been back for some time and the people were, said Floyd, feeling neglected.

"I just can't see that," said Kimelman. "How can they possibly mind? They must be so proud to have their senator running for President."

"No, Henry," said McGovern, laughing.

"Don't kid yourself," said Floyd. "They say: 'Who the hell does he think he is?' That's South Dakota for you."

Mention was made by Floyd, who, it became clear, owned radio and television stations in South Dakota, about a television speech McGovern had taped a couple of weeks before and which had been shown nationwide at great cost. Everyone agreed with the candidate's own conclusion that it was a disaster. I said I had not seen it. Eleanor turned to me and said: "It wasn't good at all. They had George just sit there, stiff and awkward, and talk into the camera."

"I was tired and mad, doing the thing over and over," McGovern said. "I finally said: 'To hell with it. Run it as it is.'"

"I'm always saying George should use his hands more," Eleanor went on. "He has wonderful hands. Have you noticed them, Dick?"

29

The question struck McGovern as funny. I, responding to some primitive male sensibility, lied and said I hadn't. McGovern said: "Dick's not that kind of a guy, Eleanor."

There was talk of money and what might be done to improve fund-raising. Kimelman said: "We're still in the black, but just barely, and the costs are going up."

There was talk about the issues. Someone mentioned the "new populism" of Senator Fred Harris, the Oklahoman who had dropped out of the presidential scramble because of lack of funds. McGovern said: "I've talked to Fred about that—going after bigness, breaking up the big corporations. I don't think it's their size that's important. It's what they do that matters." I offered the comment that the word "populism" had unhappy connotations for me. McGovern said: "Racist. It has for me too."

McGovern told about inadvertently overhearing a conversation between Senators Kennedy and Tunney in the Senate steam room a few days before. It had taken a fit of false coughing on his part, he said, to let them know he was nearby. But in the meantime he had heard Kennedy predict a Muskie nomination and say: "George is a good man but his chances aren't good." Tunney, McGovern said, had asked: "What would you guess they are, Ted?" And Kennedy had replied: "About one in five maybe."

As dinner progressed I grew more conscious of how little the women participated in the talk. It made me feel far from home. The subdued female who sits silent and presumably attentive while her husband dominates the scene always strikes me as somehow rural. She is a very different creature from the women of New York. There, at least in the circles I inhabit, one battles for equal time with imperious women. But then, I reminded myself, I was in Washington which is pre-eminently hick. Of the several pleasing impressions I had of the McGoverns, not the least was how much—in looks, manner and style—they had liberated themselves from Mitchell.

When it was time for me to leave, McGovern walked to the door with me. He wanted to tell me he had finished reading my tax-sabbatical speech. "I kind of like the idea," he said. "We'll have to talk about it some more." He wondered, then, how much longer it would be before I'd report for duty in Washington. I said that Mankiewicz and I had figured on another two or three weeks of New York work but that could be cut short and that I would, in any case, go along on a swing into the Midwest with him week after next.

He said that was fine, adding as we shook hands, "I hope Henry didn't talk your ear off."

"No," I said, "I liked him."

Aboard the shuttle I reviewed the day in my mind and thought it had been good. I had found McGovern easy to be with and sensed he felt the same about me. I had learned certain things about the campaign, the most important possibly that Mankiewicz did not, in McGovern's mind, share equal power with Gary Hart. Mankiewicz was, as McGovern put it, "being a speaker and figure in his own right." I wasn't sure what that meant but clearly it didn't make Mankiewicz as influential as I'd thought him to be. This made me slightly uneasy but only slightly. It was midnight by the time I got home to an empty apartment. I missed Cynthia but I was quietly elated. I felt convinced I'd been right to enlist in the cause and I intended to do all I could to see that the cause prospered.

I hoped, in that connection, that McGovern was being more than merely polite in his reaction to the tax-sabbatical idea. I knew the country was full of apocalyptic nuts with gimmick solutions to the world's problems; I knew there was more than a touch of night school in my own intellectuality. But I also was convinced that—gimmick or no gimmick—the Joe Sixpacks of the nation would find it hard to go for McGovern's liberalism unless his package included something for them. Dick Wade had told me when I first discussed the sabbatical with him that the Mc-Govern staff was working on a tax-reform and welfare proposal called "Fair Share." It would, as he explained it, have the present welfare system replaced by a minimum income guarantee of one thousand dollars a year per person. This would be given to everybody theoretically but as a practical matter would be taxed away from those who didn't need it.

I had told Wade that, however good the idea might be, it would not do what I felt had to be done for the working stiff making thirteen or so thousand dollars a year. I had said that, to be blunt, that fellow had to be offered something the blacks on welfare weren't going to get. As I got ready for bed I decided I had been remiss in not advancing this admittedly crude argument to Mc-Govern. I was already working on a memo so, in the morning, I added a new pitch to it:

"I urge you to keep thinking about the tax sabbatical. You admit to being obsessed by the war. I am obsessed by the notion that the country is in peril because of the alienation of the yeomanry. A vast middle class, however ironical in Marxist terms, feels itself exploited by the very system it supports. The sabbatical would, while no panacea, inform these people that government at least recognizes their existence and honors their contribution. It would constitute the first tangible benefit they have received from government since the New Deal. It would help cool an increasingly dangerous temper. I am not pressing this because I think it would get you to the White House, although I believe it could. I am doing it because I am fearful that if a good man does not respond to this alienation with an appealing proposal, then a bad man will."

32

When I finished typing I put in a call to McGovern at home. I had been a little slow in getting the message, but it now seemed to me he had expressed more than idle curiosity in asking when I planned to get down to Washington full time.

When he came on the line I said that, on second thought, I was going to try to wrap up my New York efforts and get down there as soon as possible. "Yes," he said, "I was going to call you today and suggest that. I think it would be very helpful, Dick." I warned him that, at the risk of being a bore, I was sending him another memo regarding the tax sabbatical. "Fine," he said. "Eleanor looked at it this morning and thought it was interesting."

My friend Johnny Apple had what was to me a significant story in that morning's New York *Times*, even though it was buried well back in the paper. Under a headline reading "MUSKIE CAMPAIGN STILL LACKS SPARK," Apple wrote:

"Senator Edmund S. Muskie's campaign for the Democratic presidential nomination has moved him into so commanding a lead over his competitors that, in an ordinary year, he would be considered a winner already. But for a variety of ill-defined reasons, the party professionals don't think he has clinched the nomination yet and a small but apparently growing minority doesn't think he will."

Apple went on to support this lead with a number of quotations from unidentified party officers and elected officials around the country. Then he continued:

"Those sorts of comments, unfocused though they are, say something about Mr. Muskie's failure to generate any sense of excitement within his party. They also say something about the rest of the Democratic presidential field because no one has moved in to capitalize on many prominent Democrats' palpable longing for a new hero to lead them into battle in 1972.

"In the long run, many politicians across the country believe, the lack of deep-rooted enthusiasm for Mr. Muskie's candidacy (which also shows up in interviews with voters in many areas) means that if he starts slipping he will slip rapidly, because his support is mostly pragmatic, based on the idea that he might win."

Smart reporter that he is, Apple protected his flank by adding: "But as of today, the odds are that that will not happen because Mr. Muskie is in a strong position in both the early primary states and in some early nonprimary states."

This was very much in tune with my own sense of the Muskie fragility. If indeed his support among the party professionals was chiefly founded on the belief that he was a sure winner, any erosion of that belief, caused by weak showings in the first two or three primaries, could be devastating. This raised the distinct possibility that, riding high though he was at present, the big lantern-jawed Maine senator might well be the first of the major candidates to withdraw from the race.

These speculations prompted me to do still another memo to McGovern. I dated it November 24 and titled it "Looking Forward to a Muskie Withdrawal." I wrote:

"On the assumption that it is equally wise to be prepared for the best as well as the worst, I suggest that plans be made for a speedy and effective response to Muskie's dropping out in the wake of New Hampshire, or Florida, or Wisconsin. If such plans are already in the works, forgive me. If not, here is what I have in mind: The preparation of two lists, one with the names, phone numbers and addresses of his major financial supporters, and the other with the names, phone numbers and addresses of those major political figures who have supported him. Even at this early date it seems apparent that Humphrey is hoping a Muskie collapse will leave him principal heir to the estate. But I wonder about that. Here in New York, it seems to me, the Muskie element might more happily move in the McGovern direction.

"In any case it would do no harm and possibly a lot of good to waste no time in telling Muskie followers that you would welcome their support. I'm thinking of a telegram, written and ready to go within minutes. It would contain some suitably admiring words for Muskie, it would ask the recipient to join you, it would—for the major figures—say that you will be in touch with them by phone. The next day should indeed be spent on the phone. I suspect it would be a very profitable day. Even those who won't want to come aboard will be flattered and, I'd think, impressed with your professionalism.

"A good many of the larger Muskie financial people are known and I doubt that it would require much labor to put a list of them together. The same is true of the political leaders behind him, but it would also be well to get lists of the smaller fry—county chairmen, etc.—as they surface in the press. As I say, if this is already being done, my apologies to the troops."

Monday, and another week of proselytizing began. Conversations with Abe Rosenthal, managing editor of the New York *Times*. "Don't for God's sake get paranoid," he said. "All right, all right. I'm paranoid myself about the *Times*."

Mike Wallace: "Dick, you know he hasn't got a prayer."

Dick Wald: "Bring your candidate to lunch on December ninth with us big shots at NBC. We'll pick up the tab."

Walter Cronkite: "I wish some candidate would just stand up and explain—this is what we have to do, this is how much it will cost, here is how we do it."

Harry Reasoner: "I like George but he's sounding awfully whiny and negative lately."

I was very busy and full of myself. Gently, patiently, I explained to all these stars of journalism, and to anyone else who would listen, that Ed Muskie's enterprise was doomed, that the smart money was on George McGovern. It must have been trying on friends and loved ones. "Poor Mr. McGovern," Cynthia said at some point. "He thinks he's the one running for President."

CHAPTER 3

THERE IS AN appealing show-business quality, a suggestion of top banana, about Frank Mankiewicz. It is a legitimate quality: he is a son of the legendary screenwriter Herman Mankiewicz, and he was raised in the Hollywood of the golden days. On the short side and stocky, he displays no vanity in his rumpled attire. But there is an actor's vanity in the way he combs his steel-gray hair forward to cover a sizable bald spot. The effect is rather that of a wig. A touch of the actor is evident too when he turns on a considerable charm.

His heavy features are well molded and he has a big and engaging smile. He laughs outright rarely. He is a chain smoker of mentholated cigarettes and a telephone addict. No movie mogul, no mover and shaker in any field, was ever more linked to the telephone. Without one near to be touched, dialed, answered, it is almost as if the Mankiewicz personality was incomplete. Indeed the faintly oversized Mankiewicz head seems to tilt toward the right shoulder so accustomed is it to the cradled phone.

Dick Wade had given me advance warning and I quickly discovered on my own that communicating with Mankiewicz was difficult. When one called he was more often than not talking on another line and one had to choose between waiting or leaving a number to be called back. The first course was the better since a day could pass before there was a return call. On those

37

infrequent occasions when he came on the line immediately the conversation had to be hurried because callers on other lines were holding for him. Being aware of this and anxious to have a reasonably relaxed talk with him before taking off on my first trip with McGovern, I got him to agree to a lunch. The thing was that, aside from Wade, Mankiewicz was the one person I actually knew in the campaign hierarchy. I had never in Robert Kennedy days been on intimate terms with him, but I felt I could talk frankly with him and that he would talk frankly with me.

I needed guidance, really, about people and relationships in the campaign. I needed the kind of gossipy intelligence which would make me feel less like the new kid at school and which might spare me gaffs and embarrassments—not to say frictions.

Our lunch date was for Monday, November 29. Later in the afternoon there was to be a staff meeting at the senator's office, and the next morning we were to fly off for four days in the Midwest. When I arrived, Mankiewicz was meeting with some people at the campaign headquarters, a low-lying remodeled warehouse at 410 First Street, just off Capitol Hill. As I waited for the meeting to end I wandered around the place. It was humming with life. To the rear of a series of cramped little offices which housed Mankiewicz, Gary Hart, Henry Kimelman and other chieftains, there was a room perhaps half the size of a tennis court. It was filled with desks, mimeograph and mailing machines, and young men and women going about their chores with industry and zest. Phones were ringing, typewriters clacking. It had the chaotic yet businesslike quality of a big newspaper's city room as edition time nears. Certainly it bore none of the marks of a losing operation or of a candidate whose standing in the polls hovered around 4 per cent. When Mankiewicz was free and I walked into his office, he was, of course, on the phone. He put a strong tennis player's hand over the speaker long enough to say, "Hello." Then, continuing his conversation, he fished a memo out of some papers and handed it to me saying: "Take a look at that while you're waiting."

I read it very quickly. Addressed to McGovern, it was a long, single-spaced, thoughtful piece on organization and strategy. It had one or two tacitly critical comments on Hart's performance as campaign manager. But in general it was a review of the current state of the campaign with some recommendations on where to go from here. It seemed to me to make good sense and I said so when, his phone business over, we rose to go. Walking to the Congressional Hotel, less than two blocks away, Mankiewicz told me he had asked Chris Lydon of the New York *Times* to join us. "He's been assigned to us," he said. "And I figure the sooner you get to know him the better." I said that was fine. But I was disappointed that we were not to have the kind of talk I had hoped for. Lydon was late, so once we were seated in the hotel dining room, I had a chance to ask some questions.

The answers were not altogether satisfactory. Mankiewicz did caution me that McGovern's secretary, Pat Donovan, was difficult to deal with but said I wouldn't be having much to do with her anyway. Gordon Weil was inclined to be abrasive at times, as I'd discover in traveling with him, but that was nothing I wouldn't be able to handle. So it went. In effect, there were no problems; there was nothing special I needed to know. I felt slightly rebuffed. Was Mankiewicz one of those people who disdain to gossip? I was surprised. I have learned more about the world from gossip than any other form of communication. Ultimately Lydon, tall, gangly, talkative and likable, came to join us and the conversation was pure politics thereafter—with Mankiewicz visibly happier to have it so.

I didn't know quite what to make of the staff meeting in

McGovern's office in the afternoon. The senator, leaning back lazily in his chair behind his large desk, was—it gradually came clear to me—making substantial changes in staff assignments, even in rankings. But he was doing it at such a low key, that one might have thought the business entirely routine.

The theme of the meeting was, as he put it, to make sure that everybody's talents were being put to best use. There was no criticism of past performance; the new assignments would simply allow the greater flowering of a fellow's undoubted genius. Talking, so far as I could tell, without an agenda in front of him, he discussed the duties of each man in turn according to the random order by which we had seated ourselves in chairs and sofas around the spacious room. Gary Hart, whom I'd just then met, was told that from now on he should spend minimal time at headquarters and most of his time in the field. This was because of his remarkable organizational abilities. The Hamlet-like Hart, a lean young lawyer with a sensitive face and long hair, managed to conceal his joy at the news. Ted Van Dyk, whom I'd also just met, was to be freed of his fund-raising and allied activities at the headquarters and remove himself to his own firm's office downtown. From there he would be called on for his ideas and suggestions because his judgment was so highly valued. The bespectacled Van Dyk, who looks rather like a scholarly accountant, smiled wanly in reply to this accolade.

McGovern came to Jeff Gralnick, whom I'd met some months earlier in New York. Gralnick is a dark, good-looking fellow with modishly long hair and a brooding mien—not a man to wear the world like a loose garment. He, it developed—and here was news for me too—would henceforth concentrate his press efforts within the limits of radio and television. We had "a respected national correspondent in Dick Dougherty with us now," and Dougherty would take over responsibility for the writing press as well as do some speechwriting. I had the feeling my smile was as wan as Van Dyk's. I lacked the courage to look across the room at Gralnick. Kirby Jones, another young man of dark and lugubrious appearance, whose duties were unknown to me, was told baldly that McGovern had not yet figured out what to do with him. Gordon Weil, we were told, would go on traveling at the senatorial side. Mankiewicz would go on doing what he had been doing as political director. Were there any questions?

Hart had one. Had we now decided to run a fifty-state campaign or were we still planning to concentrate on a select number of primary states? Hart's rather thin voice carried an edge as it put the question, but there was no clear answer. Kimelman did not have a question but he had a complaint. It was the traditional complaint of campaign fund-raisers: The political managers were looking down their noses at the finance people and Kimelman found it irritating.

That, said McGovern, was distressing and we would have no more of it. The meeting stood adjourned. Back at headquarters, Mankiewicz and I were alone for a moment and he said: "Did you notice? He bought it." "Bought what?" I asked. "My memo," he said. It was late and the office was closing. I was staying at the Jefferson Hotel and I asked Mankiewicz if he would give me a lift downtown. I had two bags—one of those canvas carry-on affairs and a Valpac for suits and jackets—and I was concerned about being able to get a cab. He said he'd drop me off on his way home to suburbia. Kirby Jones also needed transportation, so the three of us got into the Mankiewicz convertible. Mankiewicz inquired where the Jefferson was and I told him Sixteenth and M streets. We came down from the Hill and turned north on Seventeenth Street, up past the old Executive Office Building at Pennsylvania Avenue to K Street and Connecticut. Mankiewicz turned left on K Street and, saying he was running late, asked if I'd mind his dropping me off there. "You're just a couple of blocks over," he said.

I said the walk would do me good. It was a pleasant enough evening for the end of November. I got my bags out of the trunk, said thanks and good night, and set off. I don't, in spite of the fact that I once lived there for two years, know Washington very well, and I bowed to Mankiewicz's superior knowledge. But I was troubled with the thought that Connecticut and K Street was a bit more than "a couple of blocks" from Sixteenth and M. And so it proved to be, my bags getting heavier at each step.

I was feeling the length of a somewhat bewildering day as I checked in at the delightful old Jefferson. I wasted no time getting down to the restaurant where I treated myself to two scotches with a martini as a rammer before dinner. I wondered what was going through the mind of Jeff Gralnick. It was true that I had come aboard to be helpful in dealing with the political writers; and it was true that Gralnick, with a background as a television producer of news and documentaries, was sophisticated about the mysteries of electronic journalism.

But this division of jurisdictions had from the first been left tacit and I was puzzled at McGovern's having chosen to spell it out. It made for an artificial and, to my mind unworkable, distinction between the network types and the print types, both of whom were, after all, reporters. And, in the absence of Mc-Govern proclaiming otherwise, Gralnick remained the press secretary. So where did that leave us? Gralnick had been, if not cashiered, then stripped of several buttons. And Dougherty? Nothing bad but beyond that I wasn't sure. And what about Hart and Mankiewicz? It seemed strange that the nominal campaign manager should be told to remove himself from head-quarters and go to work in the field. But there had been no suggestion that in doing this he would require a new title or suffer the loss of his present one. As for Mankiewicz, if he wanted to think his influence had risen—as I hoped it had—he was free to do so. But, on the surface, he seemed to have gone into the meeting as political director and to have emerged with nothing changed. Perhaps that was enough—to have held ground while Hart lost a little—but granting the brief time I had had to study McGovern, it didn't seem that way to me.

For all my bemusement I had to say that I was impressed by McGovern and his handling of the business. I began to discern a certain Chinese cast to the McGovern mind and to think that while no one else might know what he was up to he himself knew perfectly well.

I called home before I went to bed and Cynthia told me some stock I'd bought with most of the profit-sharing money I'd earned with the Los Angeles *Times* had gone down three points. Great, I said. She said she had been talking with John Goldman, my old *Times* colleague, and he had heard the bottom was dropping out of the stock. Johnny doesn't know what he's talking about, I said. I wished I felt as certain as I sounded. In the New York *Times* that morning had appeared the sad news of the death of Walter Maynard, not a close friend but an admirable man, a broker, an amateur horticulturist and rhododendron expert, and a gentleman of the old school. He had died of a heart attack, and Cynthia and I talked about what a crushing blow this would be to Augusta, his widow, whom we have known much longer.

Like ours the Maynards' had been an autumnal romance preceded by earlier marriages. I have come to know these are the best romances of all. Possibly they are the bravest too since all the heart's courage left over from past encounters is laid on the line. "Please take care of yourself," Cynthia said.

43

Next morning at the airport I took the first opportunity to tell Gralnick I hoped the division of press responsibilities had not upset him. He swore that it hadn't. I told him I didn't want to be press secretary, that I didn't want any title at all. I said I was certain he and I would hit it off and he said he thought so too.

McGovern, greeting me warmly, seemed in good spirits. When we boarded the chartered plane, an Ozark Airlines DC-9, I hesitated, waiting to see what form the seating arrangements would take. McGovern took the window seat of the first row on the first-class section's port side. Gordon Weil, following behind with a fat briefcase and a heavy-looking satchel, sat down next to him. I took a seat a row back on the opposite side of the aisle. A couple of rows behind me were Gralnick and his pretty wife. She seemed extremely nice and intelligent, although I had been given to understand that some in the campaign staff resented her coming along on campaign trips. The rear section of the plane was no more than half full of newsmen if it was that; but we were to have more join us in Chicago and the hope was there'd be enough to help cover the cost of the charter as well as to give the swing publicity. When we were airborne I walked back to talk. I had known most of them for a long time.

What in God's name did I think I was doing, they all asked in one way or another. I told them I was helping to put a good man in the White House. They laughed. Bruce Biossat said: "Dougherty, you're an idealist. I never suspected it."

There was a well-attended news conference at Chicago's Midway Airport with virtually every question involving Mayor Richard Daley, a proclaimed neutral in the presidential contest but thought by many to favor Muskie. Reporters in Chicago cover Daley the way *Osservatore Romano* covers the Pope. I thought McGovern handled the questions, all couched in such a way as to stir up trouble, with skill.

We flew on to Carbondale in the southern part of the state. A hundred or so supporters greeted us at the airport. McGovern spoke to them briefly in the terminal lobby, and we then headed by car and bus to the student center of Southern Illinois University. The crowd there was disappointing at first—we'd arrived before the time of class changes—but it built up rapidly. There were heckling questions from the partisans of Linda Jenness, the presidential nominee of a party called the Socialist Workers. Why wouldn't McGovern debate Linda Jenness? Two reasons, he replied: First, she was not a candidate for the Democratic nomination; and second, she was only thirty years old, which meant that under the Constitution she was not eligible to be President. It wasn't a bad answer but it didn't satisfy.

McGovern was using a technique in his appearances which I had seen other candidates use, notably Robert Kennedy in 1968, and about the wisdom of which I'd always had doubts. It was to speak for twenty or so minutes and then throw the meeting open to questions. The thinking behind this was sound in theory: It made for a kind of dialogue between candidate and voter; it let the candidate see what was on people's minds; and, finally, it gave him a chance to show how informed he was and how quick on his feet. However, underlying all this is the assumption that the questions put forward will be reasonably interesting and intelligent. That, alas, is not always the case. Instead the device serves as an invitation to windbags, bores and outright nuts to have a field day at the expense of a serious public man. Such people don't want to ask questions; they want to make speeches disguised as questions—to which, moreover, they already know the candidate's answer. They don't want enlightenment; they want to make the candidate squirm. I admired McGovern's pa-

45

tience with the eccentric and rude young troops of Linda Jenness—and I knew he was committed to the question-answer technique—but I wondered if the device was worth the trouble.

From Carbondale we flew to St. Louis, then Bloomington, Illinois. By then night had fallen. I was beginning to be depressed by the continuing distance between the candidate and me. I had expected that at some point he would ask me to sit with him for a bit. But each time we boarded the plane Gordon Weil sat down beside him. Weil was, of course, providing essential service: He carried the so-called trip book which was used to brief McGovern on the next stop—who would greet him at the airport, who were important political or community leaders, what were the special problems of the area. I understood this, and I understood that for the better part of a year Weil had often been his only traveling companion. Still, if this day's pattern was to be standard procedure, I was in for a vexing and unlooked-for frustration. How could I be useful to a man if I couldn't talk with him, discuss problems, offer ideas and counsel?

After we had taken off for Bloomington, McGovern put his seat back and stretched out for a nap. In a few minutes Weil got up and came to sit with me. I debated inwardly about mentioning my distress to him since he obviously took satisfaction out of his place next to the throne. Finally I figured, what the hell, nothing ventured nothing gained.

"Gordon," I said, "I know you have real business with him and that for the present I don't. But do you suppose I might sit with him now and then?"

He seemed to bristle. "Well," he said, "of course you understand that I have Senate matters to take up with him as well as politics. There are important things that must be discussed, decisions that must be made."

I said I understood that. "All I'm asking is that when there is some time I might have a little. Actually I'm asking because it would be helpful to me. I still don't know him as well as I need to. I'm not going to be able to contribute much until I feel closer to him and he feels easier with me."

He nodded slowly, but then said: "Also there are times when he simply doesn't feel like talking. I've traveled with him so much that I can sense that."

"Well, hell," I said, "I think I have wit enough to recognize times like that."

That was the sum of the exchange. I had, it was clear, rubbed him the wrong way, but I supposed it was better to have made my point and gotten it over with. I could only be grateful that he hadn't said—as he might well have: "I'm sure when the senator wants you to sit with him he'll ask you."

My knowledge of Weil was fragmentary. I knew he was thirty-four or thirty-five. It was evident that he was intelligent and well informed on a variety of subjects. I knew he was an economist and that he had done some work in journalism—briefly on the *Wall Street Journal* and as a stringer on economic news in Europe for the Washington *Post*. He had done some teaching on the college level. He came from one of the suburban towns on Long Island and had gone to Bowdoin. He had joined the McGovern staff two or so years earlier, originally as press secretary. That was about it. He had good features in a strong face, dark, slightly curling hair worn on the shorter side, businesslike steel-rimmed glasses, pink gums over white teeth. He was of medium height, well and powerfully made. He was conventionally, even drably, tailored, and a pipe smoker with the pedantic manner pipe smokers often have. He was not a figure to stand out in a crowd of Washington civil servants or the middle managers of the financial world in downtown Manhattan. Still, he was plainly a man of will and ambition.

47

There were two events in Bloomington: a reception with local party leaders and supporters and another campus appearance at Illinois State University in Normal. By the time they were over and we boarded the plane for Chicago we were running an hour and a half behind schedule and we still had an event in Evanston before calling it a day.

I had gotten up at 5:45 A.M. after a restless night. It was now fifteen hours later and I was bone tired. The reception at the Orrington Hotel in Evanston was, despite one's fatigue, a heartening affair. The big ballroom was jammed with people who had waited hours to greet McGovern. The roar with which they received him might have led one to think no other candidate stood a chance of the nomination. It was the classic antiwar crowd—a mix of the young and long-haired in their uniforms of affected poverty and of the middle-age, middle-class bulwarks of American liberalism.

I ran into Dick Cooper, an excellent writer and charming man who heads the Los Angeles *Times* bureau in Chicago. We found a corner in which to stand while McGovern spoke. It seemed to me—although my being tired probably colored the decision—that he spoke too long. By the time he had finished the crowd had slimmed noticeably. There were still several hundred people, however, and as he—with Weil trailing him—made his way to the exit he was surrounded by fans who wanted to shake hands or get an autograph. I told Cooper I'd meet him for a drink at a reception upstairs. Then, thinking I could be of service in getting the candidate through the crowd, I made my way up to him.

I took a position in front of him and started asking people to make a little aisle. I turned every now and then to guide him along, saying, "This way, George." Or, "Down through here." We began to make better, although still slow, progress. When

48

McGovern and Weil finally disappeared behind the exit door, I leaned back, half sitting, on the edge of a table and lighted a cigarette. I wanted desperately to go to bed but knew that I should keep my date with Cooper. As I wrestled with my conscience a young McGovern worker from Chicago approached me. He was full of zeal and ideas. As we talked I saw Weil bearing down on us wearing an angry expression. He posted himself directly in front of me and, ignoring the young man, said: "Listen, you are new around here and you still have a few things to learn."

"Oh?" I said.

"Yes," he said, removing his pipe from his teeth and stabbing the air with it for emphasis. "The first thing is that we never ever call the senator *George* in public." The young man began edging away. Weil continued: "I don't even do that in private, and I've known him a lot longer than you. The second thing is that he does not like to be touched. Not by you, not by me, not by anybody. The third thing is that he prefers to go slow through crowds. He doesn't like to be hurried. That is his way of campaigning. That is his South Dakota way."

I was shocked and chastened. He was, I understood immediately, absolutely right. I had barged in on procedures with which I had no familiarity. But I was taken aback by the savagery of the attack. I had never in my life suffered such a dressing down. It was hard to believe, yet here was this angry face only inches from my own and my ears were stung by the loud nasal voice. At length I said, with what I hoped was a measure of dignity, "Thank you, Gordon." He turned on his heel and stomped away. I leaned back against the table edge. My pulse was banging in my head.

I found Dick Cooper again but have no recollection of my conversation with him, although I remember having two strong

49

drinks in the course of it. I went to bed—it now being after midnight—in a state of shock. Then I lay, aching with weariness, unable to sleep, the scene repeating itself in my mind like something on film. It was all so out of balance. Yes, it could be that I had asked for it in making my seating request. But should that have provoked such a response? And was it so awful for a contemporary to call a United States senator by his first name? I was a year older than McGovern. I couldn't think so. Should I have punched my attacker in the nose? I couldn't think that either; he would have been on me like a tiger.

I had to acknowledge that Weil was spunky. Still, civilized men did not talk that way to each other. Certainly young men did not talk that way to men of my age. I wondered what kind of dark Dickensian corner I had wandered into.

In the morning I made a deliberate effort to give Weil a cordial greeting. It was returned stiffly but politely.

The big event of the morning was a courtesy call on Mayor Daley at City Hall. En route there from Evanston the car carrying McGovern made a sudden stop on the expressway—clear of all cars but our own motorcade, thanks to the mayor's police—and the press bus slammed into the back of it. No one was really hurt in either vehicle. McGovern, while admitting to some whiplash effects, made light of it. We proceeded on and McGovern spent forty minutes talking privately with the mayor. We were then allowed into the mayoral office to let the photographers take pictures of Daley—pink-faced, blue-eyed, blue-suited and gracious—and his visitor.

At an impromptu news conference outside the mayor's office McGovern told reporters that he and Daley had had a friendly talk. No, he had no intention of filing delegate slates in Cook County and thus challenge the organization. He accepted the Daley pledge of neutrality. He did, however, plan to seek delegates in the rest of the state, had told the mayor that, and been told in return that Daley expected all presidential candidates to do so. McGovern reminded the newsmen that Daley had testified in favor of primaries at the hearings of the McGovern Commission on party reform.

Milwaukee was next on the schedule and we were airborne only minutes when Weil asked me if I'd like to have his seat. I thanked him and joined the senator. Weil's manner in making the gesture had been casual and that was a relief. McGovern, still suffering the effect of whiplash, talked about his meeting with the mayor. It had been fine, he said, the only disconcerting thing being that, on top of a headache, "almost every time I looked at him I saw three Daleys." He added: "I'll tell you something that would shock my supporters, Dick. I kind of like him." I said I rather admired him too.

McGovern had a prepared text for his speech in Milwaukee to a group of businessmen supporters. It was updated New Deal in viewpoint, offering a sharp indictment of the Nixon administration's economic policies, particularly the deliberate increase in unemployment, and it was well received. Afterward we flew to Eau Claire for a campus appearance at Wisconsin State University. It was evening when we left there to fly to Minneapolis. Weil came to sit with me in the course of that flight.

It was as if the previous night's unpleasantness had never happened. We talked idly about any number of things. Both of us, it developed, were victims of early-morning insomnia. We discussed books and writing. He had, I learned, published a book on gold. He was self-mocking about it, promising to read one of my books if I would promise in turn not to read his. He asked where I was staying in Washington. I said at the Jefferson but that I intended to find something cheaper when I came down from New York full time. He said that if I ever found myself

51

stuck for a room I'd be welcome to stay at his house. I thanked him. It was obvious that this was as close as he could bring himself to an apology. But that was what it was and I was delighted.

Word had come that the Senate was going to vote the next day on Nixon's new nominee for Secretary of Agriculture, and it was decided to interrupt our schedule and return to Washington late in the evening. McGovern felt he must be on hand to vote against the nominee Earl Butz, whom he regarded as a partisan of the corporate farm and the big milling companies and a threat to the family farmer.

So, following the visit to Minneapolis—memorable for a golden full moon shining through a snowstorm with flakes the size of feathers—we headed back. At some point en route McGovern told me that he and Eleanor were going to the Kimelmans' place in the Virgin Islands for the Christmas holiday. Would I, he wondered, like to join them the day after Christmas? I, assuming that Cynthia was included in the invitation, said I'd have to check with her but that I thought we'd love to. At another point something prompted me to tell him the story about the two mice on the cellar stairs who were looking up through a crack and studying the legs of a young woman in the room above. They argued back and forth in the manner of connoisseurs, the one mouse insisting that the girl's legs were exactly like Marlene Dietrich's, the other that they were more like Marilyn Monroe's. Finally a third mouse came along and they turned to him to settle the argument. He said he was sorry but he couldn't help them because "I happen to be a titmouse myself." It is a silly story but I had never before seen McGovern laugh so hard.

With the Midwest swing aborted and no indication that the press people would reassemble for that part of the schedule McGovern might be able to honor the following day, there was little reason for me to remain in Washington. I slept late in the morning and then, after a brief talk on the phone with Mankiewicz, flew home. I would be glad to get there. I was exhausted and catching a cold. It had been a confusing and rattling three days. I was pleased by the McGovern invitation to the Virgin Islands but I remained shaken by the encounter with Weil. And I thought again about Walter and Augusta Maynard. Walter had been, I guessed, in his early sixties. Not all that much older than I. I remembered Eddie Mathews, a long-time friend of the Maynards and their neighbor on Beekman Place, telling me once about the first time he met the lovely Augusta. He was taking an early-morning walk along the beach on Maryland's Eastern Shore when he heard the sound of a horse galloping on the sand. Suddenly out of the mist and into the soft light came "this beautiful girl with the *vin rosé* hair." She called good morning to Mathews, pulled the big beast to a halt and, patting its neck, said: "This horse is a son of a bitch."

A beautiful girl with *vin rosé* hair. What a charming image. Now no longer a girl, and now a widow.

I thought that Cynthia was probably right to frown on this quixotic adventure of mine. One could joke about time running out and the days dwindling down to a precious few, but the awful truth was that time did run out—and at a merry clip to boot.

CHAPTER 4

TEDDY WHITE HAS a mind like a woodland pond—busy with movement and sound: bird song, bugs, the whir of wings, snaps in the underbrush, fish jumping. Sometimes there are clouds overhead: gloom and rolls of thunder; sometimes theoretical mists descend: ideas flash like lightning, insights strike like hailstones. My God, of course, why had he not thought of that before? The beaverlike figure sits up, the bright eyes widen behind thick lenses, the mouth opens in unabashed admiration of the mind's fecundity.

This day as he and I sat at lunch in a Lexington Avenue saloon around the corner from his house the mood was cloudy. He felt badly about McGovern. He liked him, although they differed on foreign policy. He much preferred Nixon's approach to foreign policy. Still, he liked George and was sorry that the guy just wasn't going anywhere.

"You can have your kids," he said. "George Meany and the big guns of labor aren't going to let him get within a mile of that nomination."

"Theodore," I said, "you're old and out of touch. Labor is going to be lucky if it even gets to the convention much less to stop anybody."

White is a goodhearted man. "Well," he said, "I hope you get a book out of it."

Another political writer and friend whom I thought to be

nearer the mark about our problems was Bruce Biossat. I didn't agree with him any more than I agreed with White that the cause was hopeless. But I thought he was right to look beyond the old guard—the party regulars and the union chiefs—to the ordinary working people and to argue that here was where McGovern faced fundamental difficulties. Writing in his column in the Washington *Daily News* a few days after our shortened Midwest trip, Biossat called McGovern's swing a "success that didn't help him much." McGovern got good crowds, Biossat wrote, and handled them "with polished ease," yet: "Most of the time he was talking to people who have already taken their McGovern vows."

The amnesty issue, Biossat thought, illustrated as much as anything the difficulty the senator faced in attempting to widen his support: "Senator McGovern knows full well that it turns off workers even as it reinforces him with students. . . . He offsets the amnesty call with urgings to give compassionate aid to returning Vietnam veterans . . . [but] this doesn't even seem to register with workers and others who dislike his amnesty stand. Nor is it clear that if it did they would see it as a real offset to proposed forgiveness for behavior they really hate."

Biossat noted that McGovern tried more for "balance" in his speeches than he used to. "He hacks at the Vietnam war with undiminished vehemence, but he's for security and is no pacifist. He talks of slashing $30 billion yearly from defense but gives no comfort to kids who want to drop the Army in the ocean. He deplores police excesses, but voices great sympathy for the too-numerous burdens laid upon them. Yet, almost certainly, the offsets are lost in the shuffle. He is seen by large numbers of Americans as a near-extremist, as soft and permissive, as Mr. Nice Guy going nowhere."

Jeff Gralnick circulated copies of this column among the staff with the comment that "maybe we shouldn't try so hard to get Bruce Biossat on our planes." Gralnick couldn't have been more wrong. Some of my own impressions of the Midwest swing had not been all that different. Before I had read the Biossat piece I'd written a memo to McGovern, with a copy for Mankiewicz, touching on, among other things, the problem of enlarging the McGovern constituency:

"You asked for a thoughtful criticism—the impressions of a fresh observer—on your speaking performances. Let me start by saying that I think you're an extremely effective speaker. You convey an impression of unsanctimonious decency. You know a good deal about a good many things and discuss them with authority. I would urge you not to fret, as I suspect you do in moments of self-doubt, about the theatrical aspects of yourself as a campaigner. You are a reserved, calm-surfaced man. Be true to what you are and don't worry about whether to move your hands, or raise your arms or any of that.

"I see two weaknesses or inadequacies and I think both are correctable. First, you have the teacher's habit of talking too long and becoming too detailed. This is less apparent in the speeches than in the Q and A. I noticed several times when a question was put to you there was a delighted reaction when you said simply: 'I'm for it . . . (or) I'm against it.' But then you would go on to explain why, and the excitement in the audience would dissipate. The short pithy statement on where you stand is really all most audiences want to hear and I recommend you try to resist the pedagogical impulse and leave it at that.

"The other problem, which we have discussed, is that of the peroration, the final appeal for help, for a sense of urgency which matches your own. I urge you even if it goes against the grain initially to start using the first person singular instead of the first person plural. Currently, even as you talk of the need for leadership, your reserve, modesty, call it what you will, prevents you from manifesting the qualities of leadership. Say to the people: 'I care about this . . . I want to correct this . . . I want this to be a better country . . . I ask you to join me.' Then you can proceed with the 'together we can,' etc., etc. These are terrible times, everyone senses the fact, and virtually everyone knows we must be led out of them by a strong man. You should give up muting what I think to be your considerable strength.

"Re asking for help: I'll repeat what I said to you: It is enormously flattering when a man in high position asks ordinary people to help him. It makes them feel important, as it should, and they like the feeling. Far from being a show of weakness, it is a show of wisdom and sensitivity.

"On another matter:

"The problem of predictability is frustrating generally and specially so in terms of making news. You come out for amnesty for the draft evaders and the reaction of the press is ho-hum, McGovern's on the side of the underdog again. Beyond the press and among the folks it is similar. You bear the stereotype of the Pavlovian liberal and it has you boxed in. If one must be stereotyped this is an honorable one. Still, it is hurtfully limiting your ability to generate interest outside your basic constituency. Good crowds and all, we are still, I'm afraid, talking to each other in this enterprise, and that's not enough.

"The tax sabbatical: Here I am again. Frank tells me he has read the proposal and rather liked it. I'll try to avoid repeating myself and discuss the idea with reference to the problem of predictability—of breaking the stereotype and capturing the interest of a broader constituency. Your offering evidence of concern for the man-in-the-middle, a concern which gave him hope of a sabbatical respite from a punishing tax system, would excite interest. You would no longer be summarily dismissed as a known quantity—a one-issue dove, a champion of welfare folks over working folks, a 'Goo-goo,' as Robert Moses used to say. The man, that is to say, who can come up with an idea which could mean a fifteen-hundred-dollar or two-thousand-dollar tax rebate every seven years can't be all bad.

"You said that your first reaction to the idea was that it was gimmicky. Well, it is; but it is a gimmick in the same way tax withholding is a gimmick. Withholding had the effect of making huge tax increases less onerous, indeed almost less real. This would have roughly the same effect by providing the illusion of a tax cut when, in point of fact, it would serve to make high tax rates—or the continuation of them to meet our great needs— more bearable."

There was a lot of hard sell in the memo obviously, and I thought as much as I wrote it. But three weeks had passed since I put the idea of the sabbatical forward and, so far as I knew, it had caused hardly a ripple. My concern was less for the idea itself—maybe it was a crackpot notion—but for the need, an imperative need I believed, for us to get consciously to work on finding ways to expand the McGovern support among average run-of-the-mill Democrats. The McGovern "kids," as Teddy White called them, and the middle-class idealists of the peace movement could provide a committed nucleus around which to build toward victory in the primaries. All the same I was convinced they could not win a primary by themselves and certainly not a general election. That, it seemed to me, was what Biossat was telling us.

Another concern lay behind the memo. It was a fresh and cresting wave of distaste for Richard Nixon and his administration. Over the weekend that outfit had had the gall to denounce India's invasion of East Pakistan.

One adapts, one learns to live with almost any misfortune by putting it out of mind. I have had weeks go by without once thinking that Nixon is President of the United States. Now here he was in all his Tartuffian splendor assigning virtue to the genocidal junta of Pakistan and the criminal rampage it had conducted in East Pakistan for months, while condemning a properly outraged and put-upon India for aggression. "Few things said in the name of the United States lately," wrote Tony Lewis in the New York *Times*, "have been quite so indecent . . . the comment matched Uriah Heep in sheer oleaginous cynicism about the facts of the situation and about our own moral position."

Well, as I saw it, with Nixon and the morally impotent Henry Kissinger we had no moral position—not in India or Pakistan, not in Vietnam nor anywhere. Under a leadership of charlatans and bullies this great Republic clumped about among the nations like a lout, feared by most, respected by none. Nor were things much better at home where a thinly disguised racism was in the saddle, the people's worst instincts were appealed to, and the noble sentiments of patriotism were reduced to the cliché of the bigot's bumper sticker. It was time to send the Nixon crowd packing, and I wanted George McGovern to be the man to do it.

McGovern came up to New York on December ninth for a full, indeed overfull, day. He started with a morning visit to the editors of the *Amsterdam News* in Harlem and finished up near midnight at a dinner of the Ben Franklin Reform Club in the Riverdale section of the Bronx. Between the two he spoke to a rally at Hunter College, lunched with the hierarchs of NBC News, taped a half-hour women's talk show, and went to two fund-raising cocktail parties. In the course of one of these he took a crack at John Lindsay, telling a questioner that if the mayor decided to enter the presidential race and run on his record at City Hall he would be in "rough shape." This was bound to ruffle feathers at the Hall but I couldn't get upset about it, as I believed Mankiewicz and Gary Hart were certain to do. I'd had talks with both about our relations with the Lindsay troops, as the mayor obviously inched toward a declaration of candidacy. Dick Wade only a few days before had earned the Hart-Mankiewicz displeasure by telling a *Times* reporter (Wade thought he was off the record) that the Lindsay administration was guilty of "a scandal a day."

I had, at Mankiewicz's suggestion, called up Dave Garth, the mayor's communications adviser, and, in effect, apologized. Garth said he thought Wade's saying that New York was "Lindsay's Vietnam" was "a bit much, on or off the record." I said that was probably so and promised that, while we were going to fight them all the way, we'd try not to draw blood. The Hart-Mankiewicz theory was that we shouldn't cut the mayor up in the approaching struggle because the Lindsay people would come around to our side in the end. I could see that. But my own judgment was that the mayor, failing in his own efforts, would be more inclined to support Muskie. Also I did not think that McGovern would suffer greatly in the eyes of most New Yorkers if he came to be viewed as anti-Lindsay. The mayor's stock was low in the city and particularly among the Joe Sixpacks of Brooklyn and Queens, precisely the voters we needed to start bringing aboard.

I ducked the political dinner in the Bronx that evening because Cynthia and I were having a dinner party for Doug Kiker, a friend from my days in the Washington bureau of the *Herald Tribune*. It was a small attempt to acknowledge our indebtedness to him for sheltering us in Rome for a week the previous September.

He was NBC's Rome correspondent then and had now only

just returned to the States to help cover the presidential campaigns.

It was a delightful party—only the Gordon Mannings, the Dick Walds, Kiker and us. In tribute to our Roman holiday, I made fettucine alfredo and it was excellent. The wine proved to be indifferent but Kiker pronounced it superb. I asked Manning at one point why he had never offered me a job at CBS. He asked, taking me seriously, if I had ever done any television. I said a little and that I was terrific at it. "He is too," said Cynthia, "and, you may not believe this, but what comes through is sincerity."

Next morning she and I exchanged preoccupied goodbyes as she hurried off on some errand and I prepared to go to Washington and on to California the following day. The McGovern jibe about Lindsay's performance as mayor had indeed touched a nerve at City Hall. Tom Ronan, writing in the *Times,* quoted Lindsay's press secretary Tom Morgan as saying: "Senator McGovern obviously knows better. Mr. Aurelio has set up a Lindsay-'72 office for only a few days and there is already this evidence of panic in the McGovern ranks."

Mankiewicz and I discussed the flap as soon as I got to his office in the afternoon. I advanced the view that, while I wouldn't want to see it carried too far, a McGovern-Lindsay feud could help us a good deal more than hurt us. I argued that the Reform Democrats who had been largely responsible for the mayor's re-election as an independent in 1969 had gone sour on him. They were now chiefly in the McGovern camp, with a small group still holding out, hoping for a resurrection of Gene McCarthy. In any case the risk of alienating the Reformers was slight while—as I'd suggested before—the chance of profit among the blue collars of Queens and Brooklyn was considerable.

Mankiewicz appeared convinced. He seemed weary and, I

thought, low in spirits. I wondered what he wanted for himself out of this admirable but still madcap adventure. That there was a full measure of idealism in him I had little doubt. He had given up what I'd always understood to be a promising career as a young lawyer in Los Angeles and spent a year at Columbia's Journalism School—a romantic if not plainly altruistic move—and he had been among the pioneers of John Kennedy's Peace Corps. All the same he was too forceful, too talented a man not to have ambitions for himself quite aside from those he had for the candidate.

This was the first chance I'd had to talk with him at length since the Midwestern trip and I took the occasion to tell about my unsettling scene with Gordon Weil. He listened sympathetically except to interrupt me on the point of calling the senator by his first name. "Gordon's right," he said. "We don't do that."

I said that was fair enough. Then I went on to tell him that Weil had subsequently made tacit apologies. I thought things were going to work out all right, I said—thinking as I said it that I was beginning to talk like Mankiewicz—but, still, it wasn't easy.

"You'll be okay," he said. "Hang in there."

I checked in at the Jefferson late in the day, called Cynthia and got no answer. I called Lisa in Cambridge and got no answer there either. I went downstairs and dined alone, feeling fragile as a moth. There is nothing like a solitary hour in a hotel room to take the stuffing out of me. All the cockiness turns to dust. I see myself as an aging waif.

I called home again in the morning before heading for the airport. Cynthia had gone to the Walter Lippmanns' for drinks the night before and then on to dinner somewhere. She had got

63

loads of political advice at the Lippmanns', she said. "An awful lot of people feel that your man is just not forceful."

"That's helpful," I said.

"I'm afraid it's true though, that people think it. Mary de Liagre knows a voice coach in Hollywood who, she says, could set things right in ten minutes."

"We'll look him up," I said.

Flying west McGovern told me a story relating to his occasional difficulties in remembering names—a cardinal failing for any politician but specially so in the small-town culture of South Dakota. It was in 1962 while he was still in the White House as President Kennedy's director of the Food for Peace program, but making plans to return home and run for the Senate. One of the Kennedys—McGovern thought it was Robert—had told him of the success they had had in drawing crowds through mass mailings of engraved invitations. There was something apparently about the engraved card which made it more effective than newspaper ads or phone calls. McGovern decided to try it.

"We went through the Rapid City phone book and sent out several thousand invitations saying come to a reception at the high school and meet Eleanor and George McGovern. Damned if the whole town didn't turn out. The reception line ran out of the building and down the street for blocks." For weeks prior to this, McGovern said, the predominantly Republican press in the state—getting ready for his formal entry into the Senate race—had been cutting him up, implying that he'd been corrupted by the Kennedys and their fancy eastern friends and had turned his back on his own kind.

"The editorials were saying that I'd been away so long I'd forgotten South Dakota and everybody in it. That was sort of on my mind as Eleanor and I got into position for shaking hands and the line started to move. The way it was I was going to greet people first and then introduce them to Eleanor, saying: 'Eleanor, you remember Mrs. So-and-so.' Well, the papers weren't altogether wrong about my having been away awhile. I was seeing a lot of familiar faces but I couldn't put names to them, and some were people I really knew quite well. I began to get into a panic. Eleanor was no help. She saw what was happening and started saying: 'Who are these people coming up, George? Be sure and introduce me.'

"Finally, as I was looking desperately down the line hoping to remember somebody's name I saw Bob Cook who had been a county chairman of the adjoining county and whom I'd known for years. I could hardly wait for him to get to us. When he came up, I said: 'Hello, Bob,' and, 'Eleanor, you remember Bob Cook.' I felt like embracing the guy, and to keep him from moving right on, I said: 'How's your wife, Bob?'

"He said: 'I lost her.' I had to think fast. I knew he was a druggist and a prominent man in his community and that there must have been something in the papers about Mrs. Cook's death. I said: 'Oh, of course, Bob. I'm so sorry. Eleanor and I read about it.' He started shaking his head to stop me. 'No, no, no,' he said. 'I mean here—in this damned crowd.'"

We landed in San Francisco in midafternoon, and thereafter, by small chartered plane and car, campaigned deep into the evening—in Sacramento, Oakland and Berkeley. It was midnight—three in the morning our time—when we checked into the Holiday Inn in San Francisco's Chinatown. Sunday was more of the same including a return to Berkeley where Assemblyman John Miller, a black legislator and important supporter, was sponsoring a bazaar in the Berkeley High School.

It was a faintly depressing collection of booths featuring the usual handicrafted junk. McGovern went through the thin crowd shaking hands and stopping now and then to buy some trinket. Somewhere in the course of these wanderings he was asked to sign a petition demanding that bail be granted Angela Davis. Miss Davis, the beautiful black-militant philosophy teacher and admitted Communist Party member, was being held for trial as an accomplice in the kidnaping and murder of a Marin County judge in August of 1970. McGovern signed the petition.

I was not with him at the time and I didn't learn of the signing until evening as I was having dinner in the St. Francis Hotel with Bruce Morton of CBS. Morton, a reserved, bright fellow, asked in his dry fashion if I knew what had prompted the senator to sign such a thing. I said I didn't because this was the first I'd heard of it. "Rather risky," he said. Inwardly I agreed, but I tried to sound casual about it. I did, in the course of a little more discussion, get the impression that Morton had been the only newsman to observe the signing. That was a relief. Chris Lydon was also traveling with us and if he had witnessed the scene we could have been sure the New York *Times* would carry the story the next morning.

Morton obviously intended to report the incident but he was without a television crew and thus confined to radio reporting. That wasn't so bad because it is a curious fact that practically nobody in the news business pays attention to radio news.

McGovern and Gordon Weil were spending the night at the home of a supporter in Palo Alto. I put a call through to him as early as possible in the morning. I wanted to tell him that Morton had the story and to prepare him for questions about it in case he was approached by reporters before I rejoined him. Had he actually signed the petition, I asked? "Yes," he said— the voice sounding sheepish—"I got kind of trapped into it. I was surrounded by blacks. But, Dick, shouldn't everybody have a right to bail?"

I said my understanding was not in a capital offense. But, I added, even if that were true the crime Miss Davis was charged with was so ugly, so outrageous in the public mind that the thing was political dynamite.

I suggested that if he was asked he should acknowledge that he had signed the petition, but explain that he had done so because he had been told the young woman's health was failing as a result of months of imprisonment. I said I had read something to that effect in the papers a few weeks earlier. He agreed that might be the best way to handle it. We had scheduled a news conference for the end of the morning at the San Francisco Press Club. It was for the purpose of having Willie Brown, chairman of the State Assembly's Ways and Means Committee and an influential black political leader, publicly endorse McGovern's candidacy. This was a good news story for California and for the black community in general. It was not, for certain, a story one wanted to see topped by Angela Davis.

As the time of McGovern's arrival approached, I came out of the conference room and posted myself by the elevator. I wanted to reiterate my concern and, at the same time, tell him that so far the newsmen assembled had not indicated that they had heard the Morton report. When the senator emerged from the elevator with Weil at his side, it was immediately apparent that Weil not only didn't share my feelings but was ready to make a public fight out of the incident. "What's all the excitement? What's wrong with it?" he asked. "Isn't bail guaranteed by the Constitution?"

"Not in all cases," I said, "but that is beside the point."

"How is it beside the point if she's being denied her constitutional rights?" he demanded.

"Look, Gordon," I said, "I'm not a lawyer and neither are you. Neither is our candidate. What is most to the point here is that the question of bail for Angela Davis should not be made an issue on which we campaign for the presidency. This was a terrible crime. Whether she's proved guilty or not, it is a fact that the guns used were guns she had purchased; and it is a fact that a judge was blown to bits by one of the guns. I'm not talking law. I'm talking politics and public relations. Believe me. I've been around a few years and I know what I'm talking about."

"I think Dick's right, Gordon," said McGovern softly. That settled the matter. Luckily Bruce Morton's report never did get picked up by the rest of the press. Later on Miss Davis was freed on bail—ultimately to be found innocent of the charge by a jury. But the incident was, I thought, a close call and I remained distressed by Weil's obtuse response to it. His appetite for argument and confrontation seemed to extend to everything. However admirable that might be in other fields, it seemed to me a dangerous trait in politics.

Good news greeted us that afternoon as we flew into Los Angeles and somebody shoved a copy of the New York *Times* into McGovern's hands. It was a story reporting that, at long last, a dent had been made in the Gallup poll. While the lead was to the effect that Nixon would defeat any of the four leading Democratic contenders (with Muskie or Kennedy giving him a "close race"), the new survey indicated that: "For the first time Senator McGovern of South Dakota, while trailing Mr. Nixon by a considerable margin, has moved up into the category of a credible candidate."

The Gallup figures, the story went on, were based on a late November survey, and gave Nixon 49 per cent of the vote, McGovern 33 per cent, Alabama's Governor George Wallace 12 per cent, with 6 per cent undecided. However: "This put Senator McGovern a close fourth among the Democratic candidates, only 4 points behind the 37 per cent showing for Senator Hubert

68

H. Humphrey and 8 points below the 41 per cent figure that both Senators Muskie and Kennedy scored.

"It was the first time that the Gallup poll had tested Senator McGovern against the President. Until last month, the Gallup organization explained, the number of voters who recognized Mr. McGovern's name was relatively so small that a match-up against Mr. Nixon would have seemed unfair."

There was no doubt but that it was a turning point. Campaign workers in Los Angeles and across the country reproduced the *Times*'s story by the thousands for distribution. Our often mournful-looking candidate took on the aspect of a man who'd just come into an inheritance. The lift in spirits carried us through Tuesday in Los Angeles and environs; then on to Kansas City on Wednesday where a convention of the National Farmers Organization, the most liberal of the farm groups, gave McGovern a rousing reception. It was a fitting end to what had to be counted a heartening five days on the trail.

Exhausted and fighting still another sinus infection, I split off and flew to New York that evening while the others returned to Washington. I was so tired that I couldn't help but wonder if that was what a five-day swing did to me, what would happen when we hit the road full time? When I got home and dragged myself into bed, Cynthia looked at me and said: "What am I going to do with you?"

"Shoot me," I said.

In the mail next morning was a memo from Gary Hart addressed to Mankiewicz, Gralnick and me. It said: "We should move the story, in whatever mysterious ways such stories are moved, that the Muskie campaign is urging committed McGovern supporters to switch to Muskie to stop Hubert Humphrey. Humphrey is being used as the villain to encourage 'liberals' to rally around the Muskie candidacy. We should drive this wedge deeper and to tighten Muskie in such a way as to increase Humphrey's determination and displeasure with Muskie."

I read the memo, then read it again and still again. What in the world was Hart trying to say? Muskie people were urging McGovern people to switch to Muskie, otherwise they might all wind up with Humphrey as the Democratic nominee? All right, I've got that. But then we McGovernites should respond to this tactic in ways which would increase Humphrey's determination to get into the race? I guessed that was it. Humphrey's entry presumably would take strength away from Muskie and thus improve our prospects. Well, that was fair reasoning if you felt the long-range contest was between us and Muskie—as Hart apparently did. But what if you felt, as I did, that Muskie was weak and that our ultimate match would be with Humphrey? Then, it would seem, we'd be better off to discourage Humphrey from joining the fray too early. In any case I could see that I was not thinking along the same lines as the campaign manager. And I was puzzled, as I've been many times, at the widespread failure of lawyers to learn to write.

Later in the morning I got a call from Mankiewicz: Jeff Gralnick was quitting. "Oh dear," I said, "was there no way we could change his mind?" "No," he said. "It looks like you're it." Not long afterward there was a call from the candidate. "How would you like to be press secretary?" he said with a little laugh. I said: "Fine. But when we get into high gear I'm going to need an energetic assistant. I can't keep the pace every day. I'm too old."

"Oh, come on," he said. "You're not that much older than I am." So that was that. I was press secretary as of January 1, whether I wanted to be or not. I should have seen it coming.

70

I supposed I probably had and preferred to ignore it. Anyway I had the faint feeling that I'd been taken.

The following week was Christmas week and the only press activity scheduled was lunch with the editors of the Washington *Post*. I flew down from New York for that. Kay Graham, the attractive widow who presides over the *Post-Newsweek* empire, was a gracious but unexcited hostess. She yawned several times as McGovern answered questions from the fifteen or so editors around the luncheon table. I thought he was doing well in an atmosphere which was, if not unfriendly, then subtly condescending. One fellow said at some point that all he'd heard from the senator so far was "generalities." McGovern replied: "Well, you've only been asking general questions."

There was a subject, however, on which he became, if anything, too specific. That was the plan for tax and welfare reform which had not yet been made public. My heart sank a little as he outlined what was, in effect, the "fair share" idea. It still centered around a grant of a thousand dollars a year to everybody, with those not needing it returning the money in tax payments. I was distressed because, for one thing, I was hearing the death knell for my tax sabbatical, and for another I would have preferred a different way to announce such a complicated proposal to the world. The entire colloquy at the table was being taped and the *Post's* intention was to run the full text in the Sunday paper. I had supposed—and I assumed everyone else had—that when the tax-welfare package was completely finished, as it apparently wasn't as yet, we would make a production out of the announcement, with distinguished economists standing at the candidate's side to sing the praises of the plan. Now that expectation was dashed as McGovern doled the proposals out as an exclusive for the *Post*. Since it was the only thing of news value to emerge from the interview, I wasn't surprised when, at the end, Dick Harwood, the editor who'd run the show, asked if they might use that part of the tape for a separate story in the next day's paper. McGovern said he saw no reason why not and neither Mankiewicz nor I raised an objection. I didn't know what Mankiewicz was thinking but I figured—the damage being done—that it couldn't make much difference.

I had made a date with Jeff Gralnick and we met later at the Congressional Hotel and talked over a beer. It was a less than cheering experience as Gralnick unburdened himself of his disappointments in the McGovern service. He liked McGovern, he said, and wished him well, but had found working for him one of the great frustrations of his life: "McGovern is obstinate, self-centered and unheeding; he won't even communicate in anger. I sat up there in his office the other day trying to get him mad, calling him every kind of dummy, and he just sat there nodding agreement. I tell you Eleanor McGovern is the one who ought to be running for President."

Gralnick warned me about Weil, for whom he had nothing good to say. "He'll try his damndest to isolate you from the candidate," he said. I replied that I'd already had some experience of that. We wished each other luck—he was returning to television with ABC News—and I went back to campaign headquarters. I was saying goodbye and Merry Christmas to Mankiewicz when there was a call from McGovern. Mankiewicz was only a minute or two on the phone, saying: "Sure, sure, we'll take care of it." Then, putting down the phone, he said: "He wants to have a press conference tomorrow. Don't you worry about it. Gralnick's still here. We'll handle it."

"But what's he want a press conference for, Frank?" I asked.

"Open government," he said.

This was a list of high-sounding pledges a McGovern administration would abide by in informing the public and which stood in contrast with the secretiveness of the present White House operation. Most of the pledges were fine, although one—to open Cabinet meetings to the public now and again—struck me as both phony and naive. Anyhow the statement had been sitting around for at least two weeks and could sit awhile longer. I asked Mankiewicz if he thought it made any sense to hold a news conference on the thing the day before Christmas Eve. He shrugged: "He wants to do it. It'll get some space."

I flew home feeling disquieted and annoyed. Was that how decisions to call press conferences were made? Did our candidate not bother to consult his press secretary—more accurately his press secretary designate—about the wisdom of calling in the press? Did he even seek advice from Mankiewicz? He hadn't appeared to in this instance. If I had been asked I would have said the open-government proposals didn't have enough weight to warrant a news conference, that they might better be incorporated in a speech. But I hadn't been asked, and that bothered me more than anything. If McGovern looked on press secretaries as men, who merely batted out news releases on orders from above, then he had picked the wrong man in me.

As I fumed I was vaguely aware that something else about the business troubled me, but it was not until later, when I was getting ready for bed, that I realized what it was. The morning Washington *Post* would, of course, be carrying its exclusive story about the McGovern tax and welfare plan. Reporters would be a lot more interested in that than in the open-government promises; they would ask about it and write their stories on it while open government went into the wastebasket. Also, one could wager, the stories—because of the *Post's* exclusive—would only be catch-up stories, therefore, short, oversimplified and misleading. What chance might have remained for presenting the plan to the public in its best light and under the best auspices would be totally down the drain.

I wondered if I should call McGovern and Mankiewicz and suggest that the news conference be canceled. It was a bit late for that. And, in truth, was it appropriate for me to offer advice on a decision in which I'd not been invited to play a part anyway? It didn't seem so. It was depressing.

I did my Christmas shopping the next day, deliberately putting the campaign out of my mind. I was delighted to find what I thought to be a perfect present for Cynthia—and for myself: a big handsome book containing all the lyrics of Cole Porter. "I would gladly give up coffee for Sanka/Even Sanka, Bianca, for you." Who in this heavy and hirsute age could write like that? Mr. Porter would remind us of how left behind we were—and how happy to be there.

Christmas Eve we went down the block to Dave and Mary Lou Ryuses' for drinks. Among the guests were the John Lindsays, the mayor looking handsome but tense. We had a short, I felt somewhat strained, conversation. We agreed that the Democratic race was still wide open. I knew he was on the brink of announcing but no reference was made to that. I said finally that I wished him luck no matter what his decision. He thanked me and wished me the same. We had our Christmas dinner that night and Dick Wade joined us. It was a small but jolly gathering—Cynthia's Kathy and Andrew, and my Lisa. In the morning we opened presents and played carols on the record player. At one point Lisa said: "I feel very Catholic at Christmas." A wave of guilt struck me: The poor pagan was never raised in any church.

At noontime she and Andy got ready to leave, he having volunteered to drive her to her mother's far down on Long Island in Amagansett. I stood at the window and watched them get into the car and pull away. I thought back over the Christmases—sixteen at least of the twenty-one she had known—that Lisa had split the holiday between her mother and me. I thought of the scores of times over the years that I had watched her go away, specially the times I had taken her into the gloom of Penn Station and put her on the train for Amagansett. I wondered if there was a sadder sight in the world than a little girl getting on a train alone.

I was sinking into the annual Christmas *Weltschmerz*. I attempted an assessment of where I was and what I was doing there. Where, really, did I stand with George McGovern? Did his notions of me and my value coincide at all with my own? Sometimes I thought so, sometimes I didn't. It was interesting, and a little strange, that the invitation to the Virgin Islands had never come up or been referred to again. I presumed that was because I had mistakenly assumed that Cynthia was included. But if there was a problem of room, or if he had been thinking in terms of a strict working holiday, why hadn't he said so?

A basic speech which I had drafted and handed in two weeks before had elicited nothing beyond acknowledgment of its receipt. The tax sabbatical was dead. There had been no reply to my memo on the need to widen our constituency. And, of course, there had been the ill-advised, or rather non-advised, open-government news conference about which my fears had been fully confirmed.

But I had to be on guard against paranoia and self-righteousness. He was a busy and properly obsessed man engaged in a great and awesome undertaking. Advisers buzzed around him like insects; memos came in floods. He already had more than enough staff people given to sulks. I would do well to blunt my own perhaps neurotic sensibilities and plug along like a good soldier.

Besides, I had motives in all of this which were not entirely noble. I had wondered about Mankiewicz's private ambitions in the McGovern cause. It was only fair to throw a harsh light on my own. It was all very well to tell people I had enlisted for the sheer adventure of the thing, or for the worthy purpose of putting a good man in the White House, or the less worthy purpose of writing a book. All of these explanations were true. But there was more to it than that.

I wanted to be touched by the brush of history. I wanted to be a close adviser to a President McGovern. I wanted to have some effect on the world's events instead of having them always affect me. I wanted, if not fame then celebrity, if not my picture on the cover of *Time* or *Newsweek* then a nice fat side bar in the front of the magazine. I wanted to be recognized by more people than a couple of waiters and Charley Miller, who runs the hardware store in Quogue, Long Island. I wanted to savor the long shot's joy at upsetting the handicappers. I wanted to pull rugs from under pontificators. I wanted that rarely acknowledged prize of every climber—a private revenge on the favored ones of the Establishment, on the kids back in Bolivar who flashed five-dollar bills and drove off in the new cars their dads had bought them while I sat on the steps of the Bolivar Hotel with nickels in my pocket, no car and nowhere to go if I had one.

Hell, why not a picture on the cover of the newsmagazines? Why not the President's *closest* adviser? Hereafter, when I questioned my relationship with McGovern, I would do well to remember that he offered me a possible taste of all these worldly sweets. It was a reassuring thought. It was both a strength and a weakness, I decided in a sudden rush of affection for myself, that even at fifty my fantasies were rarely earthbound and the well of invention seldom ran dry.

CHAPTER 5

THE ART OF protest was in bad shape in America. Logically our command of the art should have improved over the long course of the Vietnam war, of the black "revolution" and the various liberation movements. But with the possible exception of an improvement in the lot of women, almost the opposite seemed to have happened. Little had been gained in the cause of justice and nothing in the cause of peace. What had gone wrong? More precisely, why had the war in Southeast Asia been allowed to rage endlessly and mindlessly on?

The question rose in connection with a small incident which occurred in Washington the Tuesday after Christmas. I was going up Pennsylvania Avenue in a taxi when we were stopped momentarily by the police to allow a group of two or so hundred Vietnam veterans to pass by. Nixon had escalated the bombing again and the veterans—carrying banners and chanting "End the war . . . stop the killing" and the like—were obviously en route to the White House.

They were a wild-looking bunch—combat boots, assorted and tattered fatigues, bandanas around the foreheads, beards, tangled masses of hair blowing in the wind. As I watched them march past in ragged order I caught the eye of a young man with a flaming red, specially curly beard. I nodded and, I thought, smiled sympathetically. His reaction was to raise a clenched fist and glower at me. To be fair it may be that he thought my

77

smile one of mockery and perhaps I looked to him like the stuffiest Establishmentarian. But wasn't it also fair to ask: What if I did? Isn't protest aimed at public opinion in a democratic society? Isn't the idea to win converts to one's cause, to encourage doubts and second thoughts in the minds of one's opponents? How did a clenched fist bring recruits into the peace movement?

I think what had happened was that, in a cruel accident of history, peace as an objective of the peace movement had proved to be of secondary importance to the act of protest itself. The means somehow came to be—however unwittingly—more honored than the end.

How else did one explain techniques and tactics which were so self-defeating, which played so neatly into the hands of leaders like Richard Nixon? Did anyone believe Nixon could have kept the war going if the young legions of the peace movement had looked like David and Julie Eisenhower instead of the Manson family? Wasn't the termination of that terrible war a goal of sufficient worth to warrant a few modifications in one's—that appalling phrase—life style?

I suspect that peace and the peace movement became a kind of cover, a spurious *raison d'être,* for the mutiny of the young which swept through American society in the last half of the 1960s. Their hearts may have been in the right place but their minds were addled. Repelled by an imperfect world, offended by its disciplines, they sought to build—and succeeded to a considerable extent—an antiworld.

It was a simple-minded, Rousseauist world of noble savages, monosyllabic conversations, sexual license, drug fads, mooching and bad manners. It was a gigantic and elitist nose thumb. Lacking humor, most of the young took it seriously and so, unfortunately, did most of the bourgeoisie as this mass of spoiled

78

babies took to the streets to persuade a free electorate that the war must end.

Persuasion was hardly a part of what ensued. How could it have been since so much of this vanguard was a community—a counterculture—already at war with the status quo. Thus did these warlike Harrys offend and frighten every tax-paying square in the nation. Peace in the mind of the ordinary citizen became linked with dirt, drugs, promiscuousness, radicalism and hatred rather than love of country. Peace became un-American, God help us all.

So here we were in the fourth and, once desperately hoped, last year of Richard Nixon's presidency, a people universally sick to death of the war, with a President who had promised to bring peace but had not. And was he suffering for his failure to deliver? The contrary: His stock was never higher. Within the bored and dwindling ranks of the peace movement, and the members of the antiworld in general, there was no problem in fixing the blame. The blame lay with the red-necked bovine mob which was the American people. It was safe to say that Mr. Nixon knew better. Wasn't he the man who had got up on his car in San Jose a year or so earlier and, raising his own version of the clenched fist, said: "This always gets 'em." Mr. Nixon learned very early what every unappealing politician must know if he is to survive: The way to win friends is to pick the right enemies. Just as he had used the Commies to get within range of the White House in years past, so—we could depend on it— would he use the Visigothic hordes of the peace movement to keep the bombs falling and perhaps, however ghastly the notion, win another term into the bargain.

Or so, in a fit of middle-aged bile, it seemed to me as I tried to guess the age of the young man with the belligerent manner. My guess was that he was around four or five in 1954 when,

In the wake of the French defeat at Dien Bien Phu, the then Vice President Nixon wanted to send our bombers into Vietnam. I thought that was madness even then. Who was this red-bearded adolescent to shake a freckled fist at me?

I spent two days in Washington doing nothing very much but handling some of Mankiewicz's phone calls. I was amused to see that a certain pecking order obtained in the handling of newsmen. If a call was from a relative unknown at, say, the Newhouse papers, Mankiewicz would ask me to take care of it. If the caller was a Johnny Apple of the New York *Times*, Mankiewicz would say: "I'll take that." He rubbed me the wrong way one morning when, as I walked in, he tossed a couple of sheets of paper across his desk and said: "Get releases out on these, will ya? And quick. Hmmm?"

No matter how I tried to get through to Mankiewicz I remained at arm's length. I was about to leave off trying, but it puzzled me. That evening, with McGovern still in the Virgin Islands and not due back till after New Year's, I thought up some now forgotten excuse for going home.

The following night in Manhattan I got a phone call from Jay Iselin, general manager of Channel 13 and an old friend. Was there, he asked—Iselin picks his way through words the way people step over cow slops—any chance of lunch soon? There was, he said, this new kind of news show forming up at Channel 13 which would require a sort of managing editor—anchor man; and he was thinking that maybe, just maybe, I might be the guy for the job.

I said that was flattering but I didn't see how I could be a candidate. He said, well, wouldn't I at least get together with him so he could tell me more: "Really damned exciting." I said okay and we made a date for lunch. I met him on New Year's Eve day at a little French restaurant on Fifty-seventh Street. Iselin is an attractive character. He is not much bigger than a jockey, very smart, energetic, a good salesman with a well-born accent that approaches but does not reach what used to be called Episcopal throat. Channel 13 had this substantial sum of foundation money to set up an experimental news show, he said, and he was looking toward a package which would appeal frankly to a literate and socially conscious audience. What he needed was an anchor man who was "a sophisticated party who knows the city and the country, who knows politics and government." Wouldn't I, at least do a run through, a kind of screen test, to see if I liked the camera and it liked me?

"I couldn't walk out on McGovern, Jay," I said. "Not now anyway."

"Can't you be a bit of a rat?" he said.

"Not that much," I said. "After the New Hampshire primary maybe, but not before."

"We've got to get going before that," he said. He asked if I could think of others who might do and I proposed a couple of names. "Think television," he said as we parted. I went home feeling low in spirit.

In the evening Cynthia and I went to Will and Mary D. Kirsteads for dinner. It was the familiar, comfortable New Year's Eve crowd: Oz and Deirdre Elliott, Hank and Fanny Brennan, Bill and Sisi Cahan, Dave and Mary Lou Ryus. We are all roughly contemporary and products of that life in the 1930s and 1940s which was, in turn, a holdover from the 1920s. We are romantic remnants of the Depression and the New Deal—snobbish, but liberal in our politics; given to a tongue-in-cheek nostalgia. Names—names of books, plays, people, songs, places —trigger special and shared emotions: *The Great Gatsby, Pal Joey, Private Lives* (Very big, China. And Japan? Very small.) Noel Coward, Groucho Marx, W. C. Fields, James Thurber,

81

Artie Shaw's "Begin the Beguine." We are readers. We are gossipy. We are always on the watch for that quick line which will leaven whatever the threatening lump and bring laughter. We are parochial, self-congratulatory and perhaps a little brittle, a breed for whom the music began to stop around 1960.

The Seventy-second Street residents—the Ryuses, Elliotts, Doughertys—left together at 2 A.M. and walked the few blocks up Lexington Avenue, slightly tight but lucid. At home I fixed myself a weak but entirely unnecessary nightcap, sat down in the living room and stared at the wall. Cynthia looked in at me after a while and said: "Don't be sad."

I have cause to be grateful to the Lord for many things but I am, by the widest margin, most grateful to Him for my wife. She is virtuous in the classical sense but not so much as to be boring. She is—as she resents my telling people—a year older than I, but she is one of those favored beauties in the presence of whom time has been corrupted. She has a high-cheeked, faintly Oriental face with an elegant little nose, a strong chin and a sweet mouth. She has the figure of a young girl. Her walk is from the hips and has an easy swing to it. She has the fanny of a drum majorette. Dancing, she is so liquid as to be weightless in one's arms. She is a flirt, although the years and a Presbyterian decorum have brought restraint. Once before we were married I told her I'd been offered a job in West Africa. "Run away with me," I said.

"Can't you find something on the East Side?" she replied.

She has a kind and loyal nature, and a conscience which is all out of proportion to her capacity for sin. If she were to use me ill—which is not conceivable—she would feel so wretched that I'd think myself to blame.

She can be annoying. She is a worrier and a natterer: Did you call your brother? Have you booked a table? For me a bottle is half full, for her it is half empty. She is a list maker and meticulously checks her bank statements. I gave her an adding machine for Christmas once and she couldn't have been more pleased. She is my friend and companion. She tolerates my eccentricities, enriches my life and thinks I'm funny. A divine woman. An almond-eyed enchantress.

What, I asked myself, as she turned and went down the hall to our room, had I been thinking of these last troubling days? To whom was I indebted—George McGovern or Cynthia Dougherty? In the one universe I was the sun around which virtually everything revolved. In the other I was a small and distant planet whose absence from the firmament would hardly be noted. Or would it? I didn't know what to do.

Monday, January 3, I took the shuttle to Washington in preparation for a trip into New Hampshire. I had a lunch date with Dick Tuck and joined him at the Carroll Arms, across the street from the Old Senate Office Building.

For all the merry madcap that Tuck presents to the world, he is a capable and proud man. I assumed that, through an arrangement with Mankiewicz, he was on some kind of retainer, but it was evident that, up to now, he had stayed on the outer edge of the campaign. "I give Frank ideas, suggestions. He says: 'Hey, great!' and that's the end of it. I don't hear anything more, so I don't do anything more." He said that, from his view, I hadn't seemed to grasp "the handle" on things either. I granted as much. "You ought to grab the ball and run with it," he said. I said that I didn't know whether I wanted to. "Remember the immortal words of old Joe Kennedy," he said. "When the goin' gets tough, the tough get goin'."

We had scheduled a news conference for early afternoon so that McGovern could comment on some rather spectacular lies about the war and the American prisoners, which Nixon had told Dan Rather in an exclusive CBS interview the previous day. As I got up to go and get ready for the conference, Tuck told me about a broker friend of his in San Francisco who wears Brooks Brothers suits and drives a big Mercedes to work. It seems that the Mercedes broke down at an awkward place on an express highway one morning and the fellow decided to thumb a ride to a phone. The first vehicle to come along was a Volkswagen bus jammed with hippies.

As it sped past, one of them leaned out a window and shouted: "Get a job, ya bum." Tuck is always a comfort.

McGovern hadn't yet come in when I got to his office. I sat down and waited at an unoccupied desk in Pat Donovan's office which directly adjoined his. I glanced at the Washington *Post* and made a phone call. At length he arrived, sun-tanned from the Caribbean holiday and looking dapper in a new suit. I rose to shake hands and offer a belated Happy New Year, but by the time I was up he had said a quick "Hello, Dick," and walked briskly on into his office. I walked down to the end of the room and stood near the private office door. It was open and I heard him say to Pat Donovan: "That's too bad about Eleanor and the 'Today' show." After a bit Pat came out and sat down and went to work at her desk. I remained standing where I was and pretended to read a pamphlet I'd picked up from another desk. I looked at my watch from time to time: five minutes passed, then ten, then fifteen. I had been puzzled by McGovern before, impatient with him several times, disappointed in him once or twice, but this was the first time he had made me mad.

So much, I thought, for Jim Hagerty and the importance of the press secretary. Did this gawky rube from Mitchell think that presidential candidate Eisenhower had left Hagerty to cool his heels outside an office? If so, then he knew little about either Eisenhower or Hagerty. And who did he think I was? Some broken-down rewrite man recruited from the National Press Club bar? Some forelock puller who was awed by the marbled majesties of the United States Senate? Fuck him. I am a haughty man. I had had enough from this odd grab bag of hayseeds and neurotics. I was mentally rehearsing the way I'd pick up my coat, say goodbye to Pat Donovan, and get out of there when Gordon Weil appeared at the door of the sanctum sanctorum and signaled me in. I went. "How are you, Dick?" said Mc-Govern cheerfully. "Fine," I said. But that had torn it.

I'm hardly an old Washington hand but I've observed enough United States senators to know that the Senate does something to their heads. The Senate is often called the most exclusive gentlemen's club in the world. Leaving aside the gentlemen question—some of them are, some aren't—the fact is that it is not a club at all. It is a confederation of a hundred baronies—dukedoms might be nearer the mark. Their domains are not impressive—a half-dozen rooms behind the towering office doors. The demands on their executive talents are pitifully small—a dozen clerks and a mimeograph machine; somewhat more if they happen to head up a committee or subcommittee. Their duties are what they want them to be. Mainly they lean to making speeches and showing off at public hearings. A few of them work very hard: the leaderships and the important committee chairmen. The Senate half of the Capitol is a delightful place—steam rooms, sun lamps, massage, dining rooms. With advancing seniority there are small, charming offices hidden under stairways, which no one is supposed to know about and where one can retire from the pressures of the day. All in all, Senate life is an exhilarating fraud and the senators themselves con men of a high order.

They are aware of what a good thing they have going for them and they labor instinctively to protect it. They defer to

each other, they invest each other with august qualities of mind
and character until in time each becomes a very Cicero. It is an
intoxicating process of mutual self-deception, but it preserves
the collective illusion and the world is prevented from becoming
the wiser. Enter then the senatorial staffs to complete the brain
scrambling and spark imperial visions in the mind of even the
most down-to-earth personality. The kowtowing, the flattery
are not to be believed. It is enough to spoil even so nice a man
as George McGovern. It was enough certainly to make him
misread my nature and my mission. I knew my station well
enough. But I also knew my worth. I was not designed to be a
batman—nor to be treated like one. Still, for the time being, I
held my tongue.

That evening we flew to Manchester, New Hampshire, in a
small chartered plane. We rose at six the next morning and
drove to Concord, the capital, to file for the March seventh primary. Three newsmen flew up with us: Bruce Morton, David
Broder of the Washington *Post* and Carl Leubsdorf of the Associated Press. Several more joined us in Concord, so the
coverage of the filing—swelled by three camera crews from Boston stations—was good. The filing statement was no great shakes
as literature, but it dealt with the things that the occasion required and was aimed at working people: taxes, inflation, im-
port quotas which raised the price of fuel oil, government
secrecy, special privilege. There was only an oblique reference
to the war. There was a light jibe at the candidates who were
ducking New Hampshire—Humphrey, Lindsay, Senator Henry
Jackson. The competition was challenged to debate and also to
make public the sources of their campaign funds—a dig at
Muskie.

"I know," McGovern said, "that the political pros automati-
cally concede this state to your neighbor, Ed Muskie. But I don't

86

think New Hampshire men and women give anything auto-
matically."

There were some tense minutes for young Joe Grandmaison,
the head of the campaign in New Hampshire, when it developed
that the filing fee had to be either a cashier's check or cash. A
roly-poly fellow with the face of a cynical cherub, Grandmaison
finally came dashing in from a bank with the cash.

In the evening I took a break from campaigning in order to
see Muskie's long-awaited official announcement of candidacy.
It was poor. The speech was old-fashioned and flowery; and
technically the thing was embarrassing—Muskie sitting bolt upright and stiff in a wing chair built for dwarfs. Dave Broder and
I watched it together. I asked Broder, one of the more gracious
of our journalists, what mark he gave it. "Maybe a C," he said. I
thought that was about right. I didn't think Muskie had been
hurt by it except in the sense that in his peculiar position as
front runner anything that didn't help was a kind of setback.

Next day was another exhausting—and cruelly cold—one. I
started to get signals that the sinus infection was back again.
There was a modestly amusing moment as we stood outside the
gate of the General Electric plant at Somersworth at six in the
morning to greet workers. It was snowing hard and McGovern
was bareheaded and getting soaked. I suggested to Weil that
we ought to get him a hat. "He never wears hats," said Weil. "He
hates anything on his head."

At that point McGovern left off handshaking and walked
over to us. He pointed at my imitation fur and said: "Dick,
could I borrow that hat of yours?"

Weil, I must say, laughed as hard as I did. There were times
in the course of the day when I wondered if McGovern had not
sensed that I was sore at him. At breakfast he left a table where
he had been sitting with Grandmaison and Weil to join Ted

Van Dyk and me. Van Dyk complimented him on the new, rather bold plaid suit he was wearing. "Thanks," he said. "That's my Dougherty suit." Flying to New York in the evening he said to Weil: "Gordon, would you get Dick's speech out of my bag. I want to read it." He nodded several times as he looked through the speech—one I'd given him before Christmas—and said: "I like it, Dick." At another point, he smiled at me and said: "You still keen on your tax moratorium?" I said no, I'd about given up on it. "It's really not a bad idea," he said.

At La Guardia he and Weil hurried to make a flight which would take them to Milwaukee where, next day, they would join Charles Guggenheim to make a series of television spots. I took a cab and got home at about ten o'clock. It had been a seventeen-hour day. I was rotten tired and sick.

I went to see Dr. Belcher in the morning. She flushed out my head, gave me a prescription and a lecture. At home I went back to bed and slept through most of the afternoon. When I woke up I made a cup of tea and called Jay Iselin. Did he still want to give me a screen test? "Sure," he said. "How about tomorrow?" I hesitated, then thought: why not? We made a date for the afternoon. I showed up at the studio on Ninth Avenue wearing a blue shirt which someone had told me years ago was required for television appearances. The run-through consisted of my reading some news copy and then talking extempore with a pair of young reporters about stories they'd worked on. I didn't think I was bad as I was doing it and I didn't feel specially nervous. But when I saw the thing played back I had to admit that I simply wouldn't do. Iselin said: "No, no. It was great." But, vain as I am, there was no getting away from the fact that I came over looking rather like an Irish frog under a fright wig.

I'd been trying to decide whether I should submit my resignation to McGovern or Mankiewicz. In the strict sense,

Mankiewicz was the superior to whom I ostensibly reported and it was with him I had dealt in the hiring process. But I was quite aware that in following that line of reasoning I was rationalizing myself out of a face-to-face with McGovern. I had made up my mind to offer ill health and the weight of years as the reason for my decision—and there would be a measure of truth to that. But I knew that if I tried to tell McGovern such a story he would look at me with his sorrowful hound-dog expression and see me for a liar. I decided to take the coward's way and late in the evening I called Mankiewicz at home. "Frank," I said, "I've decided I'm too old for the job. I've got to get out."

"Whaaaat? What do you mean?"

"Just that. I've decided I'd better quit. I've the feeling I'm sort of a peripheral figure in the operation anyway."

"No you're not. Not at all."

"Well . . . but that's beside the point. The fact is that I just can't take these seventeen-hour days. I have this damned infection, and I ain't got the stamina."

"But, Jesus, Dick," he said, "this is the best media week we've ever had."

I don't know why the remark struck me funny, but I had to struggle not to laugh. Perhaps it was because that here—in submitting a resignation—I had at last got through to Mankiewicz.

His surprise, I could not doubt, was genuine. That was a surprise to me. Was he unaware of how consistently he had made me feel like an *Ausländer?* In any case I saw nothing to be gained in bringing that up or, indeed, in offering any complaints. I told him that my overriding concern, which I was sure he shared, was that my departure be carried out in such a way as to cause no embarrassment, no hurtful news stories, to the campaign. I said I would hang on while we searched for a replacement in the press job and then drop, if not entirely out, then down. I said I staunchly believed McGovern was going to win and that I wanted to continue to play a part in the effort.

"Well, look," Mankiewicz said, "think it over, will you? I'll bet we can work something out." I said I would and hung up with a feeling of relief.

"It's done," I said to Cynthia. She said: "I hope you're doing the right thing."

"So do I," I said.

It was January seventh and almost thirty years to the day since that cold morning in 1942 when I said goodbye to my mother and father in Bolivar and set off into the great world. No child ever had more loving parents. They were poor and getting old. I, with my job in the post office as a substitute clerk and mail carrier, was an essential contributor to their support. Still, not yet being twenty-one I had gotten them to give their consent to my enlisting in the Army Air Corps in the wake of Pearl Harbor. I argued that by enlisting I could be assured of a relatively safe ground crew job, and that the alternative—to wait for the draft—would almost certainly see me land in the infantry where the odds for survival were infinitely shorter. It was a sound argument, but it was only part of the truth and they knew it. The more painful truth was that I wanted to be free of them. I hated Bolivar. I loved them but I resented them for having failed in show business and taken up refuge in Bolivar. I resented them for being poor and, through their poverty, entrapping me into what loomed as a life of servitude in what they themselves called "the small time."

So, however absurd to say, the advent of World War II was for me little more than an excuse for running out on Jack and Elizabeth Dougherty. They survived. My mother at sixty took a job in the school cafeteria; my father found work in the shipping room of a plant in a neighboring town. I arranged to have part of my pay sent to them every month. But this was meager compensation for what I'd done and ever since the guilt of it had been a hard rider.

Were my complaints about McGovern valid or was I picking small slights, disappointments, humiliations merely to make a case? Was I—because I was bored, because I wasn't getting things my way, because the appetite for the adventure had declined in near exact ratio to the rise in physical fatigue—simply running out on somebody again? There was no real analogy between my relations with my long-dead parents and my relations with George McGovern, but what I was examining was me. In that sense the connection stood. Was I doing the right thing, as Cynthia put it, or was I, in Jay Iselin's phrase, being a "bit of a rat?"

And was this not fair to ask: that I had expected too much of McGovern? Had I not freighted him with altogether too many of my own hopes, fantasies? Had I a right to do that?

Was there, back in the mind's attic among the Freudian baggage, the notion that I—as Cynthia had teased—was myself the presidential candidate? There is a would-be dictator in every poet. Or, a worse crime by far, was it that I, coming up from Bolivar, had fallen short of ambition's mark while McGovern, coming up from Mitchell, had hit the jackpot, and thus, lurking somewhere in me, was the resentment, the—however elaborately disguised—envy of the loser? A depressing thought, but I could not discount it altogether.

In Washington next morning there was no indication that Mankiewicz had passed word of my resignation to anybody. I'd flown down early for a hastily called news conference—still another about which I'd not been consulted. Joe Floyd, the South Dakota television tycoon, greeted me cordially when I arrived at the Senate office. I could hear McGovern in his private office rehearsing his statement—a call on Nixon to set a date for the withdrawal of our forces from Vietnam, not exactly hot news coming from him. Floyd told me he had just come from the big caucus room down the hall where the conference was to be and that everything was in readiness.

I thanked him and sat down to exchange a few pleasantries with George Cunningham, my favorite among the Senate staff and McGovern's administrative aide. He is a rotund, droll, dedicated man who has been McGovern's chief lieutenant forever. He was also, significantly perhaps, involved hardly at all in the presidential effort, concentrating instead on his boss's obligations and duties as the senator from South Dakota. In a little while Gordon Weil came in and, addressing the office at large it seemed, said: "Dick, I've just done some of your work for you. I checked the conference room." I said: "That's very decent of you, Gordon. You're all heart." Cunningham choked on a laugh as he puffed at his pipe. As though by magic, all doubts about quitting were swept from my mind. I felt almost indebted to Weil for making the course so clear again.

On Sunday, back at home, I half waited for a phone call from McGovern. But none came and I wondered if Mankiewicz was delaying telling him in the hope that I would yet have a change of heart. Following the news conference Mankiewicz had said again how "flabbergasted" he was, and urged me to think it over for a week. I'd said no, my mind was made up.

Sunday night I went back to Washington and stayed at a motel near National Airport in preparation for a near-dawn departure on a western campaign swing. When I arrived at the designated American Airlines gate it developed that an economy-class reservation had been made for me. "We only have first-class for the senator and Mr. Weil," the young lady told me. So Weil had struck yet another blow for stoutness of resolve. I made up the fare difference with a credit card.

Shortly after we were airborne Weil vacated his seat and McGovern beckoned me over. "Frank's told me of your wish to leave, Dick, and the reasons why. I'm awfully sorry but I can understand. It is a crazy business." I assured him that it was the press job that I was quitting and that I didn't intend to divorce myself entirely from the campaign. I said I'd work on a voluntary basis with Dick Wade in New York and continue drafting speeches and offering ideas. He said he'd appreciate that. He said Mankiewicz had suggested Wade or Pierre Salinger as possible press secretaries. I said I doubted if Wade could be spared from New York but that Salinger, a former White House press secretary, would be wonderful. Privately, I doubted that Salinger would do it.

We talked about the punishing schedules of the trips, and he said he found them as killing as I did and was going to do something about them. He said he supposed "home" might have played a part in my decision. I said Cynthia had been a good sport about it but, yes, in a way. He said: "I know how that is. Politics is really terrible for a woman. I wouldn't have blamed Eleanor if she'd taken a lover years ago."

He asked if I thought Weil might be able to do the job. I said I didn't, that he had enough to do as it was. I wondered if the question was an invitation to discuss Weil further but I let it pass. Throughout the conversation McGovern wore an expression which was at once regretful and fatalistic. His tone was matter-of-fact. At no point did he indicate that he was surprised, yet I suspected he was. At length he said: "I guess there's no chance you'll change your mind?" I said I was afraid not. "Yes," he said, "yes. Well, I'm darned sorry." He looked down between his bony knees as if he'd seen something on the floor. Then, after a pause, he said: "I just like the hell out of you, and so does Eleanor." I found myself, a rare thing, lacking words. Finally I said: "Likewise."

CHAPTER **6**

I BEGAN TO enter limbo. On the one hand I was free of
the enterprise, on the other I wasn't. I was *there* still but one
wasn't sure for how long; and I was there on my own terms. I
was not happy about it but I was happier than I had been. Mc-
Govern, who seemed more and more to me to have a taste for
ambiguity, appeared content. It was hard to tell about Mankiewicz. I had the feeling he was down on me. I thought that, from
his viewpoint, he had reason to be. But he gave no sign of it.

At some point in the trip Gordon Weil took me aside and said
he was "really sorry" about my decision and asked if it was final.
I said it was, but that I hoped to be helpful on a part-time basis
and I thought it was "probably better this way." I think in a
sense he actually was sorry. He and I did not always rub each
other the wrong way. I couldn't but think what an uneven bundle
of gifts he was: so bright about many things, so obtuse about
others; at times witty, at others barren of humor. I wondered if
he realized that I saw him as a bully, or if he ever stepped back
to gain detachment and saw himself that way?

I knew he was not without self-awareness. "Somebody has to
say no around here," he said to me once. "I don't mind being the
heavy. I don't mind being the spook at the door." A heavy. A
spook. His vision of self could admit those definitions, and rather
proudly. But a bully? Something balked at that, and whatever
it was it doubtless accounted for his occasional puzzlement at

the extent of his unpopularity among the campaign staff. It was as if he wanted to be feared and liked at the same time—a combination which, I'd imagine, had eluded bullies down through the centuries. The other side of this might have been that his opinion of others around him, including me, was so low that he didn't give a damn what we thought. But that was hard to believe. He was neither that insensitive nor that invulnerable.

Two incidents remain in my mind from that trip, an unusually brutal one even by our scheduling standards. The first occurred late in the evening of Tuesday, January 11. We had arrived at the old St. Nicholas Hotel in Springfield, Illinois, having risen at six in the morning in Los Angeles, flown to Seattle for nearly a full day of campaigning, then to Chicago where we switched from the scheduled airlines to a small charter which carried us downstate to the capital city.

Despite its being almost midnight there was a reception awaiting us at the hotel. Among the perhaps two hundred smiling and sweaty people jammed into a room off the mezzanine were four or five "McGovern girls," pretty young things in straw hats, white blouses over which blue sashes proclaimed the candidate's name, and hot pants. They were natural subjects for the news photographers and in minutes McGovern was standing in the midst of them posing for pictures. When the picture session was over and McGovern was circulating through the room, I fought my way to the bar and got a drink. I was looking around for a place to sit down when three young women appeared in front of me.

"Are you Dougherty?" asked one of them. I nodded. The tone was not friendly. They were dressed almost identically in the granny style—skirts to the floor, cardigan sweaters. One of them asked: "Are you responsible for him posing with those women in the hot pants?"

"Well, no," I said. "Except that the photographers asked us to pose, and we did."

"Don't you realize what an insult that is to the women's movement? Don't you know how offensive women like that, sex objects like that, are to women like us?"

"Yes," I said, "I'm aware of that, and so is the senator, but we have a free press, you know; and we're trying to run an open campaign. It's hard to say no if the press asks for something." I resisted the temptation to say this was also a free country and if pretty girls wanted to show off their legs they had every right to do so. But that would not have done. These three were deadly serious.

"We don't give a damn about the press," the woman said. "We either have a candidate who is committed to our goals or we don't. We don't want some chauvinist who is putting us on."

"Oh, good Lord," I said. "Nobody is more committed to justice for women than George McGovern. Haven't you heard? Just now, within minutes of our arrival, he rejected fourteen out of seventeen delegate slates proposed by our people here in Illinois. He rejected them because there weren't enough women on the slates. Isn't that more important than hot pants?"

"Not to us it isn't," she said. "The movement is the only reason I'm running as a McGovern delegate."

"You're being rude to us," said another one. "You wouldn't talk to us this way if we were men."

"Rude?" I said. "I'm sorry. I didn't mean to be. I . . ."

The first cut in on my stuttering with a parting shot. "You'd better tell him to get rid of those McGovern girls around the country, or he has lost the movement." Then they were gone—as though by broom.

The second incident, rather less dramatic, came two nights later in Madison, Wisconsin. I had asked Gene Pokorny to sit down with Bruce Morton and Paul Hope, political writer for the Washington *Star,* to give them a briefing on Wisconsin. Pokorny is an extraordinary man of twenty-six, a Nebraska farmer with a Harvard education. Slender, almost frail, with steel-rimmed glasses that tend to slip down his nose, he looks even younger than he is, and there is an occasional crack in his voice that makes one wonder if it may not still be changing. If you were casting him he could be the high school valedictorian or maybe the newly arrived biology teacher; but never what he actually is—a politician nonpareil.

He, as head of the McGovern campaign in the state, was telling Hope and Morton how victory could be put together in Wisconsin. The one proviso was that McGovern make a respectable showing in New Hampshire; this would mean that he'd come into Wisconsin as a viable candidate no matter what happened in the primaries immediately following New Hampshire—Florida and Illinois.

Where, Hope asked skeptically, were the McGovern votes going to come from since, as of now, Muskie seemed far out in front? Pokorny tapped the tips of his fingers together and proceeded to answer. There would be so-and-so many new voters, more than one hundred thousand of them on campuses and two thirds of these in thirteen towns where the McGovern operation was fully organized and working. Pokorny thought 60 per cent of this constituency would be McGovern's. There were the farmers, numbering two hundred thousand or more, who knew McGovern as a good farm senator and who were unhappy with the price of corn. Republicans among them could cross over and vote Democratic ballots. Hubert Humphrey was strong with this group too, but Pokorny had already got a mailing out to almost one hundred thousand rural box holders and he thought the farm help could be significant.

Then he guessed that in historically progressive Wisconsin there were roughly one hundred thousand committed liberals, the "true believers," as he put it—antiwar, passionately anti-Nixon, even antiparty regularity. Add to them forty-six thousand schoolteachers and thirty-five thousand union members where pro-McGovern feelings were known to be strong. The result, over-all, should be a McGovern vote of around three hundred thousand which, Pokorny estimated, would amount to 30 per cent of the vote, and 30 per cent should be enough. It was likely, he concluded, that Humphrey would run ahead of Muskie to take second place.

This paraphrase is inadequate, maybe even inaccurate. The impressive thing was the performance of Pokorny. It was without guile and in the unadorned presentation of facts, figures, guesses, there was the ring of authority. When he finished there was a moment's silence. Then Hope, shaking his head as though to dispel a trance, slapped his notebook shut and said only partly in jest: "Jesus Christ! George McGovern's gonna win."

I recall these two scenes because to my view they illustrated both what was best and worst about the coalition McGovern had put together in his quest for the presidency.

By her own testimony, the "movement" was the *only reason* the militant female of Springfield was running as a McGovern delegate. One could respect her candor but exactly how desirable was support of that nature? Better than nothing, one would have to say, but how much? The significant thing about her and her two friends was that they were exclusionary. The choice they offered McGovern was clear: It was either them in their granny garments or the McGovern girls in hot pants. Take it or leave it.

Within such a context, of course, the rigidity of the women seems comical. But suppose the subject at issue were not hot pants but, to pick a thorny one, abortion? Would the choice

99

offered McGovern then be between women's lib and millions of practicing Catholics? In so far as the dogmatic trio from Springfield was concerned, I'm afraid it would.

Let me say that these three were not typical of the majority of women activists in the McGovern organization. However, they were representative of a significant minority. Let me say too that this, for lack of a better phrase, *purist factor* was to be found in fair abundance and in varying degrees of intensity throughout the McGovern coalition: among the Reform Democrats, the peace movement forces, the civil libertarians, the environmentalists, the blacks, the Chicanos, the liberal Irish, the liberal Jews, whatever. No distinctive grouping was free of it.

So these were the troops McGovern had assembled for his march on the White House and what a bigoted and nitpicking collection they were. The difference between them and a Gene Pokorny was the difference between ideological man and political man, between a partisan of the issues and a partisan of the candidate. The labors of Pokorny were aimed at electing a President; the labors of the purists were directed at electing an agent with a specific set of instructions—a lobbyist, as it were.

It is, of course, fitting for people with special concerns to work in the political process on behalf of these concerns, supporting candidates whose views they share and opposing those whose views they dislike. But a candidate for President of the United States is different from candidates for any other office. Just as— as Dwight Eisenhower was fond of saying—the President is President for all the people, so is a presidential candidate a candidate for all the people.

The President can never meet the requirements of the purist factor in any so-called movement; he cannot be the agent of any so-called movement. And neither can a candidate for president.

I submit that if this principle applies to both the President and the would-be President then issues, as issues, ought to be of a secondary order of importance in the presidential selection process. The significance of issues lies in the extent to which they offer insights into the intelligence, ability and character of a candidate. The issues, and the stands taken on them, should help us to the chief business before us as voters: to make a judgment of a man who aspires to be our leader. But the issues are not the chief business themselves.

In the end we are voting for a man, not a packet of position papers; and, as a man rather than a computer print-out, a presidential candidate should be allowed, indeed encouraged, to cultivate that near-Olympian overview which is unique to the presidency. The main thing demanded of a great prince, the Duke of Urbino contended, was *essere humano,* to be human. It is to the humanity of the man that we should look when choosing a President rather than the purity of his views on a given issue. Most of us, I think, do that instinctively. Gene Pokorny—and thousands of other McGovernites—did so. But to the Springfield trio, and I fear thousands like them, this was false doctrine; and the question for McGovern was whether the idealistic but practical Pokornys could keep the purists from dragging his candidacy under.

My hunch was that they could, but there was no denying that for a candidate whose greatest need was a broadening of his constituency, McGovern had a hospitality problem in his own camp. If girls in hot pants were not welcome among his legions, how much chance was there for a cop or plumber?

New Hampshire was now less than sixty days away. *Newsweek,* in its issue of January 10, had published a state-by-state survey which made things look as if the show was over before it began. Muskie was given twenty-nine states and McGovern one —his own South Dakota. Hubert Humphrey was also given one

—his Minnesota, Representative Wilbur Mills, chairman of the House Ways and Means Committee, was granted his native Arkansas. Scoop Jackson was given his state of Washington plus Oklahoma and Tennessee.

"How do the top Democratic contenders stand as the Presidential sweepstakes get underway?" asked *Newsweek*'s editors. "No delegates have yet been picked. And as a result of recent reforms, the delegate selection process will be more unpredictable than ever. Still, by gauging local sentiment, it is possible to get a first reading on the race. For this survey—the first of a series— *Newsweek* correspondents talked with Party leaders and workers in every state.

"The survey plainly documents Senator Edmund Muskie's lead for the nomination. Indeed, if Muskie ultimately wins only two thirds of the delegates from the twenty-nine states in which he is now favored, he will have the nomination all but sewed up. At the same time, the preference for Muskie in many states is based on his front runner's status. Should he falter in the early primaries, much of this support might fade."

CBS News also did a survey to estimate the probable first-ballot support of the candidates at the July convention. Some five hundred sources—party leaders and local political reporters —were questioned and the conclusion was that Muskie would go to the convention with 1,199 delegate votes or only 310 short of the 1,509 needed for nomination. Humphrey ran a poor second in the survey, Jackson was third, and McGovern was fourth with 164 votes. The, to us, heartening Gallup match-up of the candidate with Nixon seemed not to have impressed anybody; indeed, the latest regular Gallup poll still showed McGovern as the first choice of only 5 per cent of the nation's Democrats.

But life was only just beginning to stir in the presidential creature and some of the stirrings were at odds with the surveys. *Newsweek*'s editors, for example, gave Massachusetts to Muskie with this comment: "With Kennedy out, power goes for Muskie; Lindsay a sleeper here."

Yet on January 15, only days after this was published, the Massachusetts Citizens Caucus, the mother ship of Reform Democrats in the Bay State, gave its endorsement to McGovern with a third ballot vote of 62 per cent of the 2,600 Reformers participating. This, as had been agreed to prior to the convention in Worcester, pledged all the Reformers—a significant element in the peace-conscious state of Massachusetts—to unite behind McGovern in the presidential primary. It was a devastating blow to the eccentric candidacy of Gene McCarthy, whose people had helped organize the caucus and had confidently predicted a McCarthy victory. It removed any lingering doubts as well about McGovern's having pre-empted virtually all the peace movement—once the exclusive turf of the poet-politician from Minnesota. Representative Shirley Chisholm, the black woman from Brooklyn, ran second in the voting with 23 per cent. McCarthy was third with 13 per cent. But "Lindsay a sleeper" in Massachusetts? He won only a fraction of the remaining 2 per cent of the vote.

Lindsay looked better two weeks later in Arizona where, in the first step toward the selection of that state's twenty-five delegates, he edged out McGovern 23.6 per cent to 20.4. Muskie was first with 37.8 per cent of the votes cast. Scoop Jackson was not in the running at all, although *Newsweek* again had said of Arizona that Muskie had the organization but "Jackson rates a strong second."

The same day in the mayor's own New York a convention of the New Democratic Coalition, the largest and most powerful Reform organization in the country, endorsed McGovern with a third ballot vote of 60 per cent, Lindsay who had enjoyed the Coalition's support in winning re-election as an independent in 1969, received 1.4 per cent of the vote. At least 60 per cent of the vote was required to win endorsement and McGovern would have had that on the second ballot except for some petty challenging by disgruntled McCarthyites which brought his vote down from 60 to 59.8. Another long and boring ballot was taken for the sake of two tenths of a per cent. New York Reformers would rather wrangle than eat. Indeed at one point there was a dispute over whether the rules allowed an adjournment for lunch. It was already midafternoon and they might have lunched twice in the time it took to fight it out; but on they went. Mankiewicz, who had flown up from Washington for the occasion, turned to me and—paraphrasing the old song—said: "Every little meaning has a movement all its own."

Finally, in Iowa, another early starter in the presidential process, precinct caucuses showed what Jim Flansburg, the able political writer of the Des Moines *Register and Tribune,* called surprising McGovern strength. While Muskie ran first with 36 per cent of the vote, McGovern won a respectable 23 per cent. The indications were that these percentages would ultimately be translated into nineteen of the state's forty-six delegates for Muskie and fourteen for McGovern, with the rest uncommitted.

So while it was early in the game, there was reason to think— even if one was not a McGovern partisan—that the junior senator from South Dakota was more a contender than the experts realized. Throughout this period, of course, there had been a steady succession of front-page stories announcing personal endorsements of Muskie by governors, senators, state chairmen and other party leaders. But by and large these gentlemen and ladies had few if any votes to deliver beyond their own.

Johnny Apple's New York *Times* report on Arizona spoke to

the point: "Perhaps most important," Apple wrote, "the Arizona voting constituted a stunning triumph for the Democratic Party's reform rules in their first significant test.

"Designed to open the party to broad public participation, they did just that as rank-and-file voters chose students, blacks, Indians, Mexican-Americans, peace activists, justices of the peace and a nun as delegates.

"In 1968 five prominent Democrats met in a series of closed meetings to name Arizona's delegation to the Democratic National Convention; yesterday more than 35,000 people went to the polls to take part."

I made a two-day trip to New Hampshire with the candidate in mid-January. Then, at his suggestion, I had stayed home and tried to be helpful to Dick Wade in connection with the convention of the New Democratic Coalition. Kirby Jones, who had been doing some political work in Pennsylvania in addition to acting as a Mankiewicz assistant, was called on to fill in at the press job. With the New York NDC convention over, a silence settled between Washington and me although I called Mankiewicz once to inquire about Pierre Salinger and when he might be coming aboard. "Pretty soon," Mankiewicz said. I wondered aloud if some announcement to that effect shouldn't be made. I said Teddy White had told me there was gossip that I was leaving because I thought the thing was a losing proposition. "We could scotch that sort of stuff with a Salinger announcement," I said. "Yeah," said Mankiewicz, "I'll do something about that."

It wasn't until a week later that I was summoned to duty again through a call from Mankiewicz who wondered if I'd go to New Hampshire for a few days. I said I'd be glad to, but reminded him I was off the payroll and that it was essential I get expenses reimbursed once in a while. He promised to do something about it. I hoped he would: They owed me almost a thousand dollars.

I flew to Boston the morning of February 9 and met McGovern and Gordon Weil at the airport. We drove to a little neighborhood health center in Fenway for a press conference at which McGovern offered proposals for the improvement of emergency medical facilities everywhere in the nation. Crews and correspondents from Boston's three network stations were there along with reporters from the papers and wire services. They weren't very interested in the medical proposals. Nixon's H. R. Haldeman had said the evening before in a television interview that the President's war critics were "consciously aiding and abetting the enemy of the United States."

It was a treason charge, in effect, and McGovern was delighted to respond along the line that this was the old Dick Nixon surfacing with his well-remembered smear tactics. The newsmen liked that for its news value and one could be sure that the story would be given a good play on the local news shows that evening and in the *Globe* and the *Herald Traveler* the next morning.

I was good for two days of campaigning and then I got sick again. It was an encouraging two days however. McGovern was working the factories hard, in a day as many as seven or eight small ones—usually shoe factories—and it was evident that he was making progress. Fred Emery, a correspondent of *The Times* of London, followed McGovern through the work benches for part of a day and conducted a random survey of those who'd shaken the candidate's hand. His findings gave McGovern a batting average of better than .500. McGovern, as the one who looked directly into the faces and felt the responses to his handshakes, was in a better position to detect change than anybody and he was becoming ebullient.

At the end of the first day he called Gary Hart and Joe Grandmaison into a meeting and ordered that the schedule be tightened up so that he spent less time traveling and more time in the factories. "I should be shaking eight hundred to a thousand hands a day," he said. The polls at the time were showing us at about 18 to 20 per cent with the primary less than a month away. McGovern's instinct told him this was wrong. He asked Hart and Grandmaison what percentage they guessed he might end up with. Twenty-five, they both said. He was suddenly angry. "Christ almighty," he said, "what am I knocking myself out for? If that's the best I can do I might as well give the whole thing up right now."

He was still mad when, after an uneasy interval, Hart and Grandmaison withdrew. "I tell you I think I can win this damned thing, Dick," he said. "I can see it in people's faces." I felt sorry for Hart and specially Grandmaison, who'd been visibly startled by the outburst. I was sure they had held their estimate low to keep his hopes a bit nearer the ground and thus guard against disappointment. I told him as much, but it was a while before he cooled down. What had happened, I suspected, was that over the last couple of weeks he had put all his chips—emotional as well as political—on New Hampshire. The Florida primary, next on the calendar, had by now emerged clearly as a disaster area with George Wallace riding the "busin'" issue over the bodies of every other candidate in the field. Illinois, next in line, had never been too promising and of late had looked less so. In order to be strong going into Wisconsin, therefore, and McGovern believed he had to win Wisconsin—he needed to give Muskie a real race in New Hampshire. I began to wonder if he did not think he had to win New Hampshire. That was aiming too high, I thought, but if that was what he believed then it explained the rare display of temper.

Next day his spirits were up again. We were riding along at some point gossiping about a friend in Washington, a rather renowned swordsman who had recently married an extremely rich widow. "Did you hear what Sandy Vanocur said about that?" McGovern asked. I said I hadn't. "He said: 'Fred has followed his cock right into Fort Knox.'"

It was almost ten days before I got to New Hampshire again. By then it was obvious that things were moving in McGovern's favor, and rapidly. Muskie, responding to steady needling, had agreed to a television debate. I conducted a survey of my own at the Daven Division of McGraw Edison Company, an electrical components plant just outside Manchester, and more than half of the twenty men and women I questioned said McGovern had their vote. The bigger guns of the press had begun to take second looks, and one sensed a slight uncurling of the journalistic lip.

One night over dinner McGovern asked me about a man who had been suggested for the press job. I don't know why but I had a hunch the suggestion came from Salinger. In any case I had to say I didn't think the fellow would do. "That settles that, then," said McGovern.

It had become apparent that Salinger was not interested in being press secretary, if indeed he ever was. He had arrived in the country from Paris some days before, and had already made a couple of speeches in the French-Canadian sections of New Hampshire. Salinger was, after all, a figure in his own right, a former White House press secretary to President Kennedy, a former United States senator from California. It never made sense that he should turn back the clock to a role he had played a dozen years ago. I couldn't understand why Mankiewicz had thought he would. In any event it was clear that no progress had been made in rounding up a capable press man and I found this depressing. If I had been rid of the infection in my head I'd have volunteered to take the job back.

At the end of the week McGovern left for a quick visit to Wisconsin, and I went home to New York. The following day Muskie, reacting to the poisonous treatment the Manchester *Union Leader* had been giving him, stood in front of the newspaper's offices and denounced publisher William Loeb. Overcome with emotion as he protested the paper's attacking not only him but his wife, Muskie appeared to shed tears.

The incident received more than a little attention in the press and there seemed no doubt that it had damaged the Maine senator politically. Republican National Chairman Robert Dole immediately proclaimed that Muskie lacked "stability." McGovern kept his mouth shut like a gentleman.

I planned to rejoin the candidate on Thursday, March second, and stay with him through the primary on the seventh. Mankiewicz called the day before I was to go, however, and said there'd been a change of plans. He and Kirby Jones would look to the needs of the press in New Hampshire while I, he hoped, would "mind the store" for him in Washington. I was disappointed and said so. "Christ, Frank," I protested, "I was looking forward to it."

"Well," he said, "somebody's got to be down here."

I said okay. I knew I was being a baby about it. My curious position—or nonposition—was after all of my own choosing. Still it would have been fun, and I felt as if I'd been bumped.

A great gloom descended on me and the rest of the week I hung around the house like mustard gas.

Cynthia worried about me. One evening she handed me a handwritten quotation from Yeats:

> *Bred to a harder thing*
> *Than Triumph, turn away*
> *And like a laughing string*
> *Whereon mad fingers play*

Amid a place of stone,
Be secret and exult,
Because of all things known
That is most difficult.

The lines were familiar but I couldn't remember the name of the poem. I asked her. "Never mind," she said. "That doesn't matter." As soon as I got a chance, without her knowing, I looked it up. The title was: "To a Friend Whose Work Has Come to Nothing."

Sunday was the day of the New Hampshire debate. Dick Wade came to the house and we watched it on television. It was a travesty with characters like Sam Yorty and Vance Hartke and an incredible young man named Edward Coll who waved a rubber rat around as a symbol of the nation's decay. I felt sorry for both McGovern and Muskie as they tried to conceal their bewilderment at being in such company.

Tuesday morning, as promised, I was at the Mankiewicz desk in Washington—taking phone calls and referring them to the headquarters at the Howard Johnson Motel in Manchester. I had a pleasant lunch with Art Buchwald, Russell Baker and Art Hoppe—a group which I'd guess might account for 90 per cent of the humor in Nixon's Washington. Over coffee Buchwald said it had just come to him why my man would never be elected President. "Why was that?" I asked. "Because he makes everybody feel ashamed of themselves," he said.

Late in the afternoon, before the polls closed, McGovern called me. He wondered if I had any ideas for what he might say after the returns were in. I had been working on a short statement, as a matter of fact, and I read it to him. He stopped me once or twice to make a note. Then, when I'd finished, he said: "Dick, I've been thinking. You know Kirby is a nice kid and he tries awfully hard, but he just can't seem to do the job. I was wondering how you'd feel about coming back full time?"

"Well," I said, "I've been thinking along those lines myself. I think so, sure."

"Let's talk about it more tomorrow then," he said.

"Fine," I said. "Good luck tonight."

The vote, when the returns were in, was Muskie 48 per cent, McGovern 37. It was an undoubted victory for Muskie but it was not the overwhelming victory which had, only weeks before, been universally expected. There was little question about it: The front runner had been slowed. George McGovern was in business. So, apparently, was I.

CHAPTER 7

THERE WERE GRATIFYING news stories and interpreters in the papers the next morning. "MUSKIE WINS, MCGOVERN 2D IN NEW HAMPSHIRE VOTING," proclaimed a three-column head line over the lead story in the New York *Times*. "Primary Victory Claimed by Muskie and McGovern," was the head over Johnny Apple's interpretive side bar. The mood at campaign headquarters was one of fiesta. McGovern was scheduled to fly down from Manchester, make a brief stop in Washington and then proceed to Florida. I was, as he had suggested the night before, to go along with him.

A news conference in Washington was in order. It would give us a new lead to put on the New Hampshire story and thus keep it going for another day. With Florida looming as a certain negative for us the more we could downgrade it and capitalize on New Hampshire the better. I had made this point to Mankiewicz by phone late the previous night and received his okay to set the conference up.

Sometime around noon, when the press had been notified and everything was in readiness, I asked one of the girls in the office to pick up my advance money for Florida. She came back with an odd message.

Mankiewicz, it seemed, had been on the phone with Marian Pearlman, the campaign controller, and told her to tell me that I should not go to Florida with the candidate until I saw him.

He, it developed, would not be coming down from New Hampshire until some time after McGovern.

I thought it a little strange that Mankiewicz should be passing cryptic messages through third parties since I'd been in the office and reachable all morning. It was strange, too, that Marian Pearlman, whom I liked and who liked me, should pass the message through still another third party. But I was too busy to dwell on the matter and I figured that if that was what Mankiewicz wanted me to do, that was what I'd do.

The big room at headquarters was swarming with newsmen and camera crews when the McGoverns arrived about 2 P.M. I met them on the sidewalk in front and led them down a side passageway for easier access to the rear of the crowded room. Kirby Jones, scowling and unresponsive, was with them and I included him in my quick briefing before we went into the conference.

Jones is a rather beefy man of thirty or so. He has an attractive face with heavy dark brows. He wears his black hair fashionably long and thick tortoise-shell glasses. I attached no great significance to his sullen manner with me because he almost always appeared sullen. I had, however, learned from the girls in the office that he had taken to calling himself the senator's press secretary and I wondered if the candidate had told him that he was asking me to come back on the job. If so that could account for his seeming more lugubrious than usual.

In any case I, having set the news conference up, never thought of turning its management over to him. The management of a McGovern news conference, I should add, consisted generally of saying at the start to the cameramen: "Tell us when you're ready, gentlemen," and at the end: "Thank you, ladies and gentlemen." To be denied these functions was to be denied no great role. Be that as it may, it was immediately apparent that

Jones was offended. I was—just as immediately—sorry; and having already savored the privilege of asking the cameras if they were ready, I asked him if he wanted to close the show when the time came. His grunted response was something to the effect that since I'd started it I should finish it.

I have to say that while I was genuinely sorry at having been insensitive I was also astonished. It had not occurred to me that Jones took himself to be anything other than a willing worker who was filling in temporarily at a post for which he had no qualifications. He was, to the best of my knowledge, a political type of some experience. I knew that he had worked in other campaigns, among them the Senate campaign of Richard Ottinger in New York two years before, and that he had done a stint in the Peace Corps. But he had never worked as a newsman or at anything remotely connected with the press.

I stayed with the McGoverns as they made their way to the car through hosts of excited and jubilant campaign workers. At the car McGovern told me we wouldn't be leaving for Florida for a couple of hours and that he would see me at the airport. I was on the point of saying that I might be held up because Mankiewicz wanted to talk to me when Mankiewicz himself arrived The McGoverns pulled away. I walked over to greet Mankiewicz and congratulate him. That done, I said: "Frank, I'm a little confused by your message. Do you want me to go to Florida or not?"

His reply as he turned to go inside was: "*He* wants you to go." The emphasis on the *he* was unmistakable. And so, for a man not given to displays of emotion, was the unfriendly tone.

What had I done now?

After a moment I went inside and down the narrow hall to the press office which adjoined the Mankiewicz office. Kirby Jones was not at his desk and both doors to Mankiewicz's office were closed. I could hear Jones's high-pitched voice through the thin partition but I couldn't make out what he was saying. His secretary, Cissie Owens White, said: "Somebody's very angry." I said I gathered as much. Dick Tuck wandered in at that point; he too was going to Florida. I told him odd things were happening. He asked what else was new. At length Jones emerged, sat down at his desk and turned his back to the rest of the room. I reckoned that the sensible course for me was to retreat. I asked Tuck to wait while I got my coat out of Mankiewicz's closet; then we could take a cab to the airport together. I tapped on the office door and stepped in. Mankiewicz was on the telephone. He looked up and said: "Dick, would you mind?"

"I'm sorry, Frank," I said, "I just want to get my coat."

I stepped to the closet beside his desk, grabbed the coat and departed as speedily as I could. Mankiewicz had obviously been holding on for somebody. As I shut the door behind me, I heard him say into the phone: "Hello, Senator."

I never did learn what it was that Mankiewicz was so keen on talking to me about. Nor do I have any knowledge of what he said to McGovern in the phone call—which I have to assume had to do with Jones and me.

Late that night in Gainesville, McGovern and I sat together in his suite for more than an hour. We talked about all sorts of things. I told him Tuck had been telling reporters that if Muskie had had three more days of campaigning we would have won New Hampshire. That reminded McGovern of a story his friend Senator Gaylord Nelson, of Wisconsin, told about a candidate who was "so bad he didn't even win where they didn't know him."

I said I thought he was a little down in the dumps about New Hampshire. He nodded. "I don't care what anybody says," he

116

said. "You don't win anything with 37 per cent. To my mind Ed Muskie won that fucking election."

I offered him a chance to discuss what was on my mind—and, I imagined, on his—by observing that Kirby Jones had seemed out of sorts all evening. "Oh," he said, refusing the bait, "you know how these young kids are, Dick. They're not old pros like us." That was as close as we got to our conversation of the previous day.

Clearly the Mankiewicz phone call had done its work.

I was puzzled. Not by McGovern. Obstacles had been thrown in the way of my returning and he, obviously, wanted time to appraise the obstacles. My puzzlement was with Mankiewicz. Was he still angry with me for quitting? I could understand his being out of patience with me, resentful even—but not all that resentful. It couldn't be my unwitting lack of tact in handling the news conference. I knew Jones was a favorite of Mankiewicz's but the "*He* wants you to go" comment antedated any knowledge Mankiewicz could have had about the conference contretemps.

It seemed more likely that McGovern, subsequent to his chat with me the night before, had told Mankiewicz that he'd asked me to take over the press job again. But if that were so, why should Mankiewicz object? Not on the grounds of competence surely; he might find me an unremitting pain in the ass but he could not regard me as incompetent. Maybe he thought Jones was adequate to the task. That was hard to believe but possible. Maybe—and this seemed more like it—Mankiewicz simply didn't like me. I had over a long and checkered career encountered people—not many—who found my charm resistible.

But what argument against me might he have used? Well, if I were in his shoes, and I think I'm as inventive in such matters as anybody, I'd have argued that Dougherty was a slender reed on which to depend: I'm not saying he's not good, Senator, when

he's around. When he's around. Fine! Sure. You know? But I
mean there is the Irish temperament, hmmm? The sinus attacks,
the too-old-for-the-game bit? A little neurotic maybe? Or commitment, if you want to put it that way. Is he working for us
or is he working on a book? Sure he has friends in the press.
Who doesn't, hmmm? Whether you want 'em or not. Yeah.
That's right. He may even have got us some space when it was
tough to get space. But now we're up and away. What we need
now is somebody dedicated. You know, who's there when we
need him. Kirby can learn. I can help him over the rough ones.
It's not all that tough anyway.

It wasn't a bad case actually. Certainly if I'd been McGovern
it would have given me pause—as apparently it, or something
kindred, had.

Ordinarily such a development would have dismayed and depressed me, but this left me only bemused and fatalistic. The
reason for that was the book, more precisely a newly born vision
of the book I wanted to fashion out of my adventures with Mc-
Govern. That vision had risen in my mind in the midst of my
recent melancholy as I sat staring at the wall one night on
Seventy-second Street. It was a very different conception from
the original one, in which I'd seen a book largely as a kind of
literary hedge bet against the waste of several months in the
event McGovern got nowhere.

I should admit to a certain literary snobbishness here. Over
the years as a novelist I had always looked down on nonfiction
writing. Even though fame and fortune eluded me, even though
I knew I belonged to a novelistic tradition which was out of
fashion, I never considered writing a *fact* book. To do so would
have seemed a surrender, an admission that the creative impulse
had been stilled by a succession of defeats. But did this make
sense? Wasn't the real world as rich, challenging, amorphous,

as subject to interpretation and shaping, as the imagined world? To stand in awe of Homer needed one to scorn Thucydides? My thought now was to write my McGovern book as I might write a first-person novel. "Art," Tolstoy said in his down-to-earth way, "is a human activity consisting in this, that one man consciously, by means of certain external signs, hands on to others feelings he has lived through, and that other people are infected by these feelings and also experience them . . . [thus realizing] the mysterious gladness of a communion which, reaching beyond the grave, unites us with all men of the past who have been moved by the same feelings, and with all men of the future who will be touched by them."

Yeats, in a tribute to Paddy Flynn, commanded more colorfully: "Let us go forth, the tellers of tales, and seize whatever prey the heart longs for, and have no fear. Everything exists, everything is true, and the earth is only a little dust under our feet."

What better counselors than these? What better counsel for a minor novelist as he—the longing heart wheeling above the just-discovered prey—attempted to turn fact into art, to hand on to others the feelings he has lived through so that they too might experience them?

And what novelist, at least of my nineteenth-century tastes, would not delight in the cast of characters? George McGovern? In fact a Tolstoyan figure. Perhaps an element of Trollope in certain similarities to Phineas Finn. But mostly a creature out of Tolstoy: a Levin, I'd think, full of dreams for the betterment of society; at one time awash with affection for the common man and at another irritated by his ignorance and cupidity; full of love of country and yet impatient with it for failing to meet his own lofty standards of Christian decency. Had serfs labored around the McGovern parsonage in Mitchell, McGovern-Levin would have freed them. He would have set up a classroom and taught them to read and write. He would have despaired of this in time and tried other things. He might have prepared himself for the ministry; then quit the ministry and gone into university teaching; then quit teaching and, seeing the light at last, entered politics. That was the way to bring the simple message of justice, charity, tolerance and compassion to the people. He would have organized a political party in South Dakota, breathed life and hope into the moribund Democrats there; he'd have run for Congress—and won; he'd have run for the Senate—and lost; run again—and won. He'd have risked the displeasure of a President he revered to sound an early alarm against a lunatic war. But the war would go on, and in the end what could he do but to run for President himself?

Eleanor McGovern? That was almost easy: Jane Austen. Pretty, bright, lively, proper but not averse to shockers kept within bounds. A figure to be painted on china—in a garden, perhaps at tea or strolling, hoopskirts, parasols, handsome men in the background. A little lost perhaps, a little less worldly than the intelligence and the heart might have wished for, a little more self-denial in favor of a husband than the self sometimes wished it had allowed. Very strong, very weak, very feminine.

McGovern wouldn't have blamed her if she'd taken a lover, he said. How did he know she hadn't? There was about her that shy, fleeting touch of promise which one finds in every attractive woman. But he was doubtless right. She was a good woman in the old-fashioned sense, and thus one saw in her a hint of, if not waste, then diminution.

Mankiewicz? Stendhal. And a rich Stendhalian serving at that. A Julien Sorel out of Beverly Hills and cut from much the same cloth as me. That was amusing: the two of us as fictional brothers. What antagonists. The cunning Levantine versus the wily Celt. No face-to-face confrontation: oblique advances, oblique retreats, generally to the accompaniment of jokes.

There was Gordon Weil—ever present but moving toward the middle distance. One would have to say Dickens. Far too thin a soup, indeed too upright, for Heep, and yet Heepish, an excellent "heavy," as he liked to say. Obnoxious to live with and yet a creature to lift the storyteller's heart. I could love him. I could love Mankiewicz and his friend, the brooding Jones. I could love whoever entered the parade from now on. The only way this crowd was going to get rid of me was to fire me. The only man who could do that was George McGovern. If I knew nothing else I knew he never would.

At the end of our first full day in Florida McGovern asked me if I'd mind peeling off and going to Wisconsin. There was, he said, "a morale problem" with Pokorny and his lieutenants and it would be helpful if I were to appear and lend a hand in gearing up for the primary. I said I'd be glad to go, and meant it. Florida in my judgment was a waste of everybody's time, although I granted that McGovern, having committed himself early—well before George Wallace entered the race—had to go through the motions of candidacy there. But Wisconsin, three weeks away, was the primary on which everything hung for us. Of course it was also an assignment which would detach me from the candidate. I wondered how much the idea was McGovern's and how much—if any—of it could be attributed to Mankiewicz.

As things developed it appeared more than likely to be the candidate's alone. I had barely arrived in Milwaukee when Pokorny unburdened himself with regard to Mankiewicz. Desperate for funds, he was tired of being told a check was in the mail and having the check fail to arrive. When checks did arrive he was tired of having them bounce. He was tired of the struggle to communicate. He had finally got Mankiewicz on the phone a few days earlier only to be told to be quick about it since Mankiewicz had a "money call" on another line.

Now, he was given to understand by Gary Hart, a crisis was brewing "over Frank's usurpation of all powers." Could I do anything about that? I said I didn't know, but that I'd think about it. Pokorny had been brought into the campaign back in its infancy by Hart and he was frankly loyal to Hart. My respect for Pokorny was unqualified, but I couldn't say the same for Hart. I thought he was intelligent and, to my limited acquaintance, a decent fellow. I thought he was probably *nicer* than my Machiavellian friend Mankiewicz. At the same time I had a strong hunch that Mankiewicz was doing things that needed to be done and which wouldn't get done if he didn't do them. With special reference to finances, ours was very much a shoestring venture. To get the maximum amount of money into Wisconsin over the next three weeks—and, hard pressed as Pokorny was, that was being attempted—we needed a carnival operator in charge. Mankiewicz, I knew, was conning creditors, bouncing checks, soft-soaping contributors with all the skill of a riverboat gambler. This was not an occupation for which Hart, as I judged him, had either stomach or talent, no matter what his abilities as a political organizer. I thought I'd do well to keep away from any Mankiewicz-Hart showdown if I could.

Pokorny pinned his hopes for a resolution of things in favor of Hart on a strategy meeting which was scheduled for the Thursday following the Florida primary. Florida came and went. Wallace walked away with everything as expected; Humphrey ran a poor second. McGovern ran behind both Muskie and Lindsay, but they were hurt more because they had ill-advisedly made more of an effort. Thus the mood of the strategy session at the Red Carpet Inn, near Milwaukee's airport, was confident. We had slipped through Florida, now we had only to get by Illinois and into Wisconsin where the outlook improved daily. However, if the meeting related in any way to the power struggle between Mankiewicz and Hart it escaped my notice. Property taxes and the discontent of the working people in general, it was agreed by all, would be the theme of the Wisconsin campaign's final days. I tiptoed out before the meeting ended in order to get a plane to New York where I had a fund-raising chore to do with Dick Wade. There was no opportunity to say anything to Pokorny, whose young face across the room wore a melancholy look. He called me at home the next morning and confirmed my suspicion that nothing had been settled either at the meeting or in a private session following it. He was very down on Mc-Govern.

"You know," he said, "I'm beginning to think that the candidate may, at least unconsciously, want to have a star like Frank up at the top. That way he has somebody else to share responsibility for his failure if we don't make it." I said that might be a possibility, although I didn't really think so.

"Well, anyway," he said, "I just won't work for Frank. I'm quitting the day after the primary." I said: "Don't do that, Gene. I'll talk with McGovern."

I was now in precisely the spot I'd hoped to avoid. I either had to do a little knife work on Mankiewicz or watch Pokorny walk out of the campaign. There wasn't much choice. Mankiewicz could survive a light stab in the back; he was the type it took artillery to stop. But the campaign could ill afford the loss of Pokorny.

Eleanor McGovern was in town that day for an interview with *Women's Wear Daily* and some kind of dinner in the evening. I tracked her down and took her for a late lunch in the Palm Court of the Plaza. I had no idea how she felt about either

123

Mankiewicz or Hart, but I knew she shared my opinion of Pokorny. She was duly shocked when I told her of his determination to quit and the reasons for it. Did George, she asked, know anything about this? I said I intended to tell him. She said she would make sure he called me Sunday.

"I see," said McGovern when we talked. "Frank's been sort of after me to put him in charge of everything. Now I doubt the wisdom of it. I've heard other complaints from people in the field."

I said I didn't see anything greatly wrong with the way things were. "When it comes right down to it you are your own campaign manager." There was a chuckle of acknowledgment at the other end of the line. I went on: "And the practice of giving autonomy to the state co-ordinators—the Pokornys and Grandmaisons—seems to work. Frank's a gifted fellow. His main problem is that he won't let anything go and he's oversubscribed. What good is a boss you can't get through to on the phone?" I suggested he put someone strong, like Pokorny or Grandmaison, in as chief deputy to Hart. Then there would be somebody at headquarters to stand up to Mankiewicz and conceivably stiffen the Hart sinews a bit. "That sounds like a good idea," said McGovern. I told him I was sorry to burden him with such stuff and that I didn't enjoy putting the knife to Mankiewicz, but I was convinced Pokorny meant what he said. "No," he said, "I'm grateful. I appreciate your nailing this thing for me."

Later on I was gossiping with Dick Wade and I said how puzzled I still was about the relationship between Mankiewicz and me. "I thought you and he were my rabbis when I took the job," I said.

"Oh, heavens, no," said Wade with a cackle. "Frank was never too keen in the first place."

I said: "It's a fine time to tell me."

Later in the week Hart was in town and came up to the apartment to see me. He looked more gaunt and ravaged than usual. I had only just learned that he was suffering some thyroid difficulty but refused to undergo surgery because he was afraid, as I'd been told, that "Frank would steal the keys." He knew, through Pokorny, that I had talked with McGovern and that the threatened coup had been thwarted. My impression was that he had come to thank me, but nothing direct was said. He observed that he had been through "this sort of thing" before, a reference which I took to be to Ted Van Dyk who had ridden rather high a year earlier. "People tend to think I'm as dumb as I look," said Hart. He added that from the time he had taken the campaign manager's job two years before he had frequently told McGovern he'd step aside when somebody better came along. "But so far," he said in his soft voice, "nobody better has." I told him of my bewildering experiences with Weil and Mankiewicz and how they had contributed to my decision to quit the press job. "You ought to be traveling with the senator all the time," he said. "We've got to get you back into this campaign."

Thereafter I went through another period of sitting around the house—putting down notes for the book, drafting a couple of speeches, making phone calls. The Illinois primary passed with blessed speed—fifty-nine delegates for Muskie, fourteen for McGovern, less than half we'd originally hoped for.

At some point I got a call from my daughter reporting that she'd found a job as a waitress in a Cambridge place called Barney's Pub. "That's terrific, Lisa," I said, thinking: twelve years of private schools, two years of college, thousands of dollars in preparation for waiting on table in a saloon. Less than a week later I received a note saying she'd been fired. "I lied about my experience," she said. She thought, however, that chances were good for a better job. A friend of hers had just been hired as "an

125

advertising executive" for an underground paper and she was certain he could find her a spot. At another point I received confirmation of reports that the movie *Madigan*, which was based on my novel *The Commissioner*, would give birth to a television series in the fall. That meant a few dollars and was cheering news for a man on the brink of bankruptcy.

McGovern called me from Milwaukee late in the evening of March twenty-eighth. "How about going to California with me the day after Wisconsin?" he said. I said that was fine. "Just us," he said. "I'm going to leave these other characters behind for a little rest." I asked how things looked in Wisconsin. He said: "There's no doubt in my mind: I'm going to win it."

As indeed he did. Out of a field of a dozen candidates, half of them serious, McGovern won 30 per cent of the vote—exactly as Pokorny had predicted. Wallace was second with 22 per cent; Humphrey third with 21 per cent. Muskie was a bad fourth with 10 per cent. The polls had hardly closed when Lindsay, who ran far back, announced that he was withdrawing from the race.

I flew out from New York late in the afternoon and tried to be helpful in the triumphant aftermath when, it seemed, every newsman in the country was in Milwaukee writing rags-to-riches stories about the quiet man from South Dakota. Almost the first reporter I saw was Jack Germond who said: "I just filed my apology, Dougherty. What did you know that I didn't?"

The Secret Service had moved in since I'd last traveled with McGovern, and so as we flew to Chicago the next morning and then on to San Francisco, the party included a dozen agents. Exhausted but oddly unexcited, McGovern slept a good bit of the long flight to the west. But he had a couple of drinks instead of his usual single vodka martini before lunch, and at one point he said: "I don't want to tempt fate, Dick, but it really has worked out exactly as I thought it would." I said I had no doubt but that he was going to go all the way now. "Neither do I," he said.

"Unless this new flareup in Vietnam beats you out," I said. "You're going to make the covers of *Newsweek* and *Time* next week." He smiled. "No, I won't," he said. "We'll see Ed Muskie's picture with a banner across it saying 'Muskie fades.' I figure I'll get on those covers around about Inauguration Day."

A little later he roused himself to ask: "What about your coming back and traveling full time now? Do you feel up to it?"

"Sure," I said. "I'd like to."

"Most of these guys take it too seriously," he said, yawning and starting to laugh as he yawned. I said I knew that. After a moment, he said: "That's good. I hope you'll be able to stick with me."

"I will," I said. "That's a promise."

There must have been five hundred deliriously happy Mc-Governites at the airport to greet the hero, and a fund-raising dinner scheduled for the evening had burgeoned in twelve hours from seven hundred to eighteen hundred paying guests. In his suite at the San Francisco Hilton McGovern announced that the first thing he wanted was a nap, but he hadn't reached the bedroom door when the telephone rang. I answered it. The caller was a wealthy supporter who was convinced that unless we capitalized on Wisconsin immediately with a half-hour television speech, which included an appeal for contributions, we'd miss a historic opportunity.

I told him I'd check with the candidate but I suspected that —tired as he was—he'd be disinclined to do it. I said I'd get back to him and after ringing off passed the message to McGovern. "To hell with that," he said as he leaned against the door of the bedroom. "Can't these people raise any money themselves? I just won Wisconsin. What more do they want out of me?"

Mankiewicz appeared at the end of the afternoon, somewhat to my surprise. I'd never seen him in such high spirits before. The money was bound to come rolling in now, he assured the candidate. The days of scrimping were over. "Do you realize that we've actually been running a presidential campaign on a payroll of less than forty thousand dollars a month?" he said to McGovern and me. "That's unheard of."

"I'm coming back on the payroll, Frank," I said.

"Well," he said, "then make it forty thousand two hundred."

In less than a month McGovern had turned everything upside down. Thereafter, it seemed to me, the march of events bore the stamp of historical inevitability. Muskie dropped out before the end of April. On May 14, Wallace was shot by a lunatic and left paralyzed. By June, there was no one to stop us except Hubert Humphrey and he fought desperately—one could say viciously—in California. Still McGovern won California's 271 delegates by a solid if not overwhelming margin. New York, with 278 delegates, was already in the McGovern pocket and, with its June 20 primary ratifying the fact, the delegate-selection process was over. Our candidate would go to the convention with something like 1,400 of the 1,509 votes needed to win. A first-ballot nomination seemed assured.

There was cause for joy as those triumphant spring days fell away and the summer prospects brightened. But there was also cause for apprehension. It became evident that those who wanted to stop McGovern had, instinctively I thought, decided that the way to do it was to radicalize him. He was vulnerable to this attack: He was an admitted liberal, an admitted dove and Pentagon critic, and an outspoken advocate of tax reform and welfare reform. But radical? Only in the sense that Franklin Roosevelt was called radical by his haters in the 1930s.

Rowland Evans and Robert Novak, in a column which appeared on April 26, struck one of the opening chords of this theme. They predicted that party regulars, with Muskie fading away and Ted Kennedy still aloof, would turn to Humphrey as the only alternative to McGovern because "They fear McGovern as the Democratic Party's Barry Goldwater. The reason is given by one liberal senator whose voting record differs little from McGovern's. He feels McGovern's surging popularity depends on public ignorance of his acknowledged public positions. 'The people don't know McGovern is for amnesty, abortion and legalization of pot,' he told us. 'Once middle America—Catholic middle America in particular—finds this out, he's dead.' "

I've known Bob Novak and Rowley Evans for years and I like them, although they're mean as hell and somewhat to the right of McKinley. But I don't believe for a minute that any *liberal* senator, at least a Democratic liberal, told them McGovern was for abortion and the legalization of marijuana. And even if one had, they might have corrected him instead of investing him with absolute authority. They were able enough reporters to know that McGovern did indeed support a general amnesty once the Vietnam war was over, but that he did not, and never had, advocated abortion and the legalization of pot.

Still the rascals printed it and it did enormous damage around the country. It sounded like a fact even though it was attributed to an unnamed, and possibly nonexistent, source. It certainly sounded like a fact to a respected and sophisticated newspaperman like James Reston of the New York *Times*. Writing three days later, Reston observed:

"George McGovern has run an intelligent and determined campaign and has now got to the top of the greasy pole, but with a heavy load of promises: to slash the defense budget steeply, *legalize pot and abortion*, and grant amnesty to the Vietnam expatriates." (My italics.)

So McGovern, who had worked hard to enlarge his constituency by talking bread-and-butter issues, and who had, starting with Wisconsin, made steady inroads into the blue-collar vote, was increasingly portrayed as a radical and a rather kooky one at that. Few opponents made the outright charge that he wanted the lid taken off pot and abortion, but they relished saying that the public thought he did and, by so saying, they encouraged the public to think there must be something to it. It was pointless to try to get a retraction out of Evans and Novak. Reston, the target of immediate complaint from us, printed an apology of sorts in a later column. But the damage was done.

It was ironical. Now McGovern had two somewhat fanatical political entities to deal with—his own purists on the one side and, on the other, a sizable host of politicians and commentators who feared or disliked him sufficiently to falsify his positions. Under the pretense of fearing a Democratic Goldwater, they were engaged in creating one.

When I came back aboard following the trip to California there was no mention of the press job. McGovern simply wanted me to travel with him and I was happy to have it that way. I wrote speeches, particularly the short primary-victory ones; I scratched up quotations he might like. I talked to him when he wanted to talk. I hustled the newsmen, as Mankiewicz would say, and as diplomatically as possible, tried to be of assistance to Kirby Jones. I was hit by the sinus ailment once and had to go home for a few days in May. Otherwise life—granting the fundamental cruelty of campaigning itself—was pleasant. It became even more so as the traveling staff expanded a bit. Fred Dutton joined up in California and that was a considerable enrichment from both a political and personal point of view.

Dutton, in his late forties, is a man blessed with a zest for politics in particular and life in general. Balding, slight of stature, with a low-riding belly like a large egg, he is something of a gypsy—although not so much as his friend Dick Tuck—moving back and forth between the practice of law in Washington and politics. He is a respected scholar of American politics. More significantly for the McGovern cause, he is very practical and tough-minded. We—certainly McGovern and I and even Mankiewicz—needed toughness as a rein on the romantic liberalism, which was almost a part of the pathology of the campaign.

Bill Dougherty, the young lieutenant governor of South Dakota and no relation to me, was another welcome addition, although he could be with us only part of the time. He is very Irish, very talkative, boyishly handsome. We had a standing exchange. "Are you getting much, Dick?" he would say. I'd say: "No, Bill, but to you it would seem a lot."

Yancey Martin, one of the pioneer members of the McGovern campaign staff, was another pleasure: a dashing dude, black, bright, tough but kind, towering and powerful as a Zulu. There were others one saw for only a day or two at a time: Liz Stevens, the beautiful and highly capable wife of filmmaker George Stevens, Jr.; Charley Guggenheim, the civilized and intelligent producer of the television and radio spots; actor Warren Beatty, a smart and attractive rogue who put together the free talent for the concerts that raised hundreds of thousands of dollars; his sister, Shirley MacLaine, a fine and thoughtful beauty and an admirable bawd. We were visiting a Veterans Administration Hospital on Long Island when a dotty old fellow pointed a quivering finger at her and announced: "I fucked that girl once."

She greeted the comment with a laugh. "Well," she said, "maybe he did."

There was time, after the New York primary and before the convention, for a brief holiday. I joined Cynthia at our small summer house in Quogue, a village on the south shore of Long

Island about ninety miles out of the city. The town is an anachronism, a small bastion of WASPs and Irish Catholics. A few black families live in a settlement on the other side of the Montauk highway. Jews, in expensive houses, surround the place and, here and there, have extended lines into the heart of town. By and large, nothing changes and the community remains fixed in amber, as though time, moving out from New York, had stopped there to rest during the Harding administration and never moved on.

It has, for all of that—perhaps because of it—great charm. If you mind your business, people mind theirs. It is marvelous bird country. I can sit at breakfast on the kitchen porch and watch the traffic around my feeding station: towhees, cardinals, brown thrashers, catbirds, purple finches, mourning doves. Quail wander by like tourists. There is a justifiably vain cock pheasant who lives somewhere down the road. You often hear him before you see him; he has a bark that could shatter windows.

I stopped by at the hardware store and asked Charley Miller how the winter had been. "Long," he said. "Very long."

Peter Botsford, Cynthia's eldest, brought his charming children Jane and Blake, aged five and seven, to dinner one night. He and I talked vaudeville German to them much of the evening. They were amused.

One evening there were sudden tears in Cynthia's eyes. What was it, I asked. "I don't know," she said. "The great adventure seems to have priority over everything." I denied it. "I can't help it," she said. "I don't like uncertainties. What if he wins and becomes President?" I said we would stay in New York.

Later, as we were fixing dinner, I said to her: "That's enough chicken for me."

"I'm having some myself," she said. "There are more people in

132

the world than you and George." She smiled. "Put that in your book."

"I wouldn't," I said. "It might make you appear vindictive."

"I am not, you've got to understand, noble and long-suffering."

"You are not long-suffering," I agreed, "but you're noble. I promise. This is my last fling. I promise that we will not go to Washington even if he wins every state in the Union."

She said: "We don't have all that much time left, darling."

I said: "I know it."

CHAPTER *8*

BACK IN FLORIDA in March, only a day after Mankiewicz had blocked my return to the press job, Kirby Jones had been less than lucky and less than wise in the handling of an event involving Ethel Kennedy. She was visiting friends near Palm Beach and we made arrangements with her—as a keen but, for family reasons, unannounced supporter—to have a picture session at the airport before she took off for home. The idea was that a news photo of McGovern and Robert Kennedy's widow might, without much subtlety, convey her pro-McGovern sentiments to voters around the country. McGovern, talking to her by phone earlier in the day, assured her that all we asked of her was a picture. Given that assurance she said she'd do it.

The photo desks of the wire services accordingly were alerted to a picture possibility. The plan called for the candidate to walk her through the terminal to the airline departure gate, shake hands and say goodbye as cameras recorded the scene. What happened instead was that Jones bowed to protests from a local television crew who had set up their equipment in a small room off the lobby under the mistaken impression that they were covering a news conference. Thus he guided the unwary Mrs. Kennedy and McGovern into a cul-de-sac complete with microphones, lights and a little group of reporters with pencils at the ready.

We had a press conference whether we wanted one or not. A

startled Ethel Kennedy was the immediate target of questions as to whether she was formally endorsing McGovern. The poor woman gasped something to the effect that she was no longer in public life. Well, if she wasn't for McGovern what was this all about? In seconds she was visibly trembling and close to tears. One reporter wanted to know, if the Kennedys were really for McGovern why weren't they contributing money to his campaign? McGovern—himself taken aback by what they'd been led into—finally moved in with some lame comment on how it was always an inspiration to see Ethel Kennedy, and thank you all very much but she must run for her plane. He took her arm and the two of them headed for the door.

It was, all in all, a textbook example of how not to do something in the strange world of press agentry, and it was directly attributable to Jones's inexperience. That much was understandable. What was not understandable was that Dick Tuck, who was along that day, had tried to save Jones from the error and been rudely rebuffed. In the aftermath Jones was quite shattered. He kept repeating how it was all his fault and I felt sorry for him. Still, in the light of Tuck's efforts to help him, and the brusque way he had rejected that help, it seemed evident that he was burdened with handicaps other and more worrisome than mere inexperience. Tuck thought so and minced no words about it. Within the week he was off the payroll at his own request. "I can't afford to be seen with people like that," he said.

I thought things would get better with Jones, and periodically they seemed to. Yet during the New York primary campaign, by which time he had been in the press job for three months, I had to prevent him from stranding four or five reporters at the Syracuse airport. They had been given filing time and were inside the terminal on the phone to their offices when he—doubtless under pressure from Gordon Weil or an impatient candidate—

called out to me that we were taking off. "Come, come on," he said, motioning me toward the chartered plane.

"Kirby," I said, "you can't leave these people behind."

"To hell with 'em," he said. "Maybe it'll teach them a lesson."

"No," I said. "We've got to wait."

To his credit Jones's judgment was usually better than that, and one could hardly fault him for not trying. He was anxious to prove himself and he worked hard. In his assistant, Carol Friedenberg, he had chosen a gem. But it remained that he did not know what news was or how the business of news worked.

Several things accounted for his survival. For one, we had an extremely nice group of press people assigned to us. They liked him and Carol, were patient with them. Jones almost never sought advice from Dutton or me; and when we volunteered suggestions they were received with irritable grunts. Nevertheless, we were there to intervene when intervention seemed necessary—as in Syracuse.

Finally, he had Mankiewicz to call on—and report to—as he did with regularity. I had long since concluded that one motive in Mankiewicz's support of Jones—quite apart from the Mankiewicz sentiments toward me—was that in him he had his own representative close to the candidate at all times. It was an arrangement which might have served Mankiewicz's interests, but I failed to see how it served McGovern's.

The arrangement, it was true, had seemed to work over the course of the primaries. But change was coming fast. Where, in the early days, it was unusual to have more than three or four newsmen traveling with us, by the time of California and New York the number had grown to fifteen or twenty. Competition among and between the writing and the electronic press was getting keener. Pressures for interviews with the candidate, for help in the development of stories, were increasingly strong.

137

They would be that much stronger, competition that much more savage, when the general election campaign got under way and the press corps became four to five times the size we were used to. I was convinced that Jones would not be up to it.

The Syracuse incident removed any doubts in my mind. A few days after it I wrote a memo to McGovern in which I offered my appraisal and volunteered to take the job myself. I said:

"The painful fact is that Kirby is beyond his depth and not, in truth, a press secretary at all. He is a surrogate for Frank whom he calls a couple of times a day for instructions. The rest of the time he is entirely subservient to Gordon whose judgment about press, or even human, relations approaches zero.

"Carol Friedenberg—bright, brassy, instinctively open and honest—is, at the age of twenty-one or so, the stronger pillar of the press operation. It is true that Dutton and I are in the background and can be helpful. Still, we are limited in the help we can offer by Kirby's refusal to communicate, with me specially, information about what's going on.

"It isn't that he isn't hard-working and dedicated. It is that he is innocent of what journalism is all about. There are really two kinds of press secretary. There is the Ron Ziegler type which learns procedures by rote and acts out the role of an information officer. There is, as you once mentioned to me, the Jim Hagerty type which knows how to create news and can envision what a story will look like on the tube or in the papers. Given the loose-jointed nature of the McGovern campaign, you'd be better served with the latter type.

"I am not, as you know, overwhelmed with Washington ambitions. But I want you to be elected President. If you want me to take over the press I'll do it. If you want me to stay where I am I'll do that. But the stakes are too high to go on with the press arrangement you have now."

It was harsh. I felt very mean—and vengeful, too, for which I suppose I should have been ashamed but I wasn't. I was fed up with the young man's ill-concealed hostility. I was offended by his attempt to make our frictions look like a rivalry of equals. It was something I could almost—but not quite—accept in my weird relationship with Gordon Weil who, after all, had considerable experience and competence.

It was something I could welcome in Mankiewicz. One should be as snobbish about one's enemies as one's friends and Mankiewicz—friend or foe—was always first cabin in my view. But in Jones, I found it bizarre. Related to this, no doubt, and as difficult to comprehend, was his failure or refusal to take a sensible measure of me as either a foe or a possible friend. I am as easily seduced by good manners as I am repelled by bad ones. I could have, and would willingly have, been useful to him. I was, after all, the press officer of the New York Police Department when he was still in knickers and Mankiewicz in law school.

The whole juvenile business was, quite simply, self-defeating on his part. It brought him a predictable harvest within two days of my putting my memo in the mail when McGovern called to say: "I got your letter and I agree with you. I'd like you to take over after the convention."

I couldn't help but wonder whether he had said anything to Mankiewicz. Nor could I help speculating about what the next Mankiewicz move would be.

I knew it was childish, possibly a little demented to feel this way. We supposedly were adults engaged in trying to elect a President of the United States. We had better things to do than play Borgia court games. But the truth was that I had taken quite enough crap from all of these characters and I was delighted to give them a bit of their own back.

By now I had been a student of the McGovern personality for about seven months, in the uneven and frequently bewildering course of which a theory had evolved to help account for his idiosyncrasies as a political leader. It was a theory of the one-man band.

It required only a slight leap of the imagination to see in him the qualities of a Renaissance man, a kind of political Leonardo who was at once his own architect, writer, engineer, artist, whatever. He could do anything his staff did and do it as well or better. This was understandable in a way. When he started out as the poorly paid executive secretary of the South Dakota Democratic Party in 1953 he was his own speechwriter, fund-raiser, press secretary, organizer, typist, driver, mimeograph operator. Name any function in politics, and he had done it; put him in a room with a desk and a phone and you had a compact but complete political organization.

This may be said of a lot of self-made political men, but by and large most of them tend to cast off these skills as they rise up the ladder—turning them over to others, forgetting them almost as aptitudes connected with an impoverished and now somewhat embarrassing past.

Not so McGovern. Except for the grubby little chores that anyone would wish to be free of, he made a point of keeping his talents in working order. One could see that it was a matter of pride with him not to be too dependent on anybody, not to become too obligated to anybody. There was, one could imagine, an intoxicating liberation to be won out of this, and no doubt a comforting sense of solitude as well: one-man bands, on the face of it, being loners.

It followed from this, not surprisingly, that he was less apt to be concerned about the quality of his staff than an ordinary politician might be. If a fellow proved a disappointment as a

140

speechwriter, what did that matter to a man who wrote his own speeches anyway? If Frank Mankiewicz was all that keen on keeping Kirby Jones as press secretary, what difference did it make to a candidate who could talk with reporters as well as anybody?

This line of reasoning led me to other insights. A man for whom staff couldn't do much was likely to be not just undemanding of staffers but, implicitly at least, contemptuous of them. Weil once said to me: "The minute the man hires you his interest in you and respect for you declines." It was a reasonable observation. A one-man band is logically, I'd think, more apt to honor talent when it is independent of him than when it becomes just another klaxon on the rim of his drum. I thought I'd gotten a taste of that the day I was left to cool my heels outside his office. Moreover, it was quite possible that one element in the gradual improvement of my position with him over the spring had been that I was no longer drawing pay. Perhaps also —nature cherishing balance—there was a measure of self-hate hidden behind this quiet but towering vanity, a never-spoken judgment that if a man would work for George McGovern he couldn't amount to much. One thought of Groucho Marx saying he wouldn't want to join a club that would take a man like him as a member.

The one-man-band theory had application beyond the immediate traveling staff. McGovern had laughed when I'd said that he was his own campaign manager. But it was undeniably true. If Jones was a surrogate for Mankiewicz on the road, then so was Gary Hart a surrogate for McGovern in Washington.

That being so, how much importance would our candidate attach to power struggles between Mankiewicz and Hart, Hart and Van Dyk, to frictions between Mankiewicz and Dougherty, Dougherty and Jones, Jones and Dutton, Weil and just about anybody? The answer had to be: very little. These things were irritating and boring; they disturbed the private tranquillity. But they were not important because the people involved were, at bottom, not important.

News stories often referred to Mankiewicz as the campaign's chief strategist, Dutton was the theoretician, a few of us made up a so-called inner circle. The truth was there was only one strategist, one theoretician and one man in the inner circle— George McGovern. I suspected that he was surprised when the rest of us sometimes gave signs of not understanding that that was the way it was. Didn't we realize that we were around to take care of burdensome details and mundane chores—to help set up the drums, cymbals, horns and get him into the collar that held the harmonica? We could take tickets, distribute programs and sell popcorn during the intervals; but the musical selections and the performance itself were matters left to him.

It is probable that I exaggerate to make my point. But not very much. However, I have to say that, without belittling his proficiencies, he was not as good at everything as he thought. A good writer, yes, and an excellent speechwriter. But he was not on certain ground when it came to dealing with the press. He did not appreciate the mysteries of news nor the art of reporting, and this was a weakness.

Understandably, the one-man-band phenomenon and the attitudes stemming from it caused a good deal of frustration and grumbling within the staff. Now and then some of us—fresh victims of a McGovern failure to consult us, or having done so ignored our counsel, or having told us one thing had gone and done something else—sat around in rebellious humor and dared to ask: If this was the way he ran a campaign, how good would he be at running the country? To raise the question at all was to manifest doubts. Yet it was a reasonable, and not a disloyal, question. The nation has had great Presidents—Franklin Roosevelt comes to mind—whose executive gifts were, to say the least, eccentric.

My view—not so paradoxical as it may seem—was that the same qualities which humbled and outraged his staff could serve to make him a good and possibly great President. I thought this because, as a significant corollary to his cordial and kindly contempt for staff, he maintained a high regard and respect for the operational managers in the field—the people who ran their own affairs and did their jobs without direct need of him. The Pokornys and Grandmaisons and the rest were, to him, different; they should be allowed to do their work with minimal interference from the staff in Washington. "You don't have to check a damned thing with anybody, Joe," I overheard him tell Grandmaison once. "If you want to do something go ahead and do it." So much for chains of command and tables of organization. So much for Hart and Mankiewicz. So much, more to the point, for staff of any kind and rank.

I had little doubt but that McGovern would be guided by these attitudes if he became President. And I had reason to hope he would. For one thing, he had done time as a White House staff man himself when he ran the Food for Peace Program for President Kennedy, so he knew what the game was about. For another, he had read and taken to heart the counsel offered by George Reedy in his perceptive *The Twilight of the Presidency*.

Reedy's book is a sober yet passionate warning of the dangers inherent in a too-powerful White House staff because of what it does both to a President and to the functioning of government as a whole. It is not, one might assume, a book which was ever read by Richard Nixon, whose embrace of staff-dominated government—with its Haldemans, Ehrlichmans and Kissingers—seems almost total.

McGovern was convinced of the need to reduce the ridiculous size of the White House menage—grown to something like two thousand under Nixon—and to put a tight rein on its exercise of power. He planned to restore the Cabinet to its earlier and proper status and give the heads of all departments and agencies who are answerable to Congress the authority and power to meet their stated responsibilities. He was set on ending the practice by which ambitious young men in cubicles in the White House basement attempted to manage the enormous and complicated bureaucracies of the Executive under the shield of Executive privilege.

I believed this held promise of the revival of effective government on the level where the art of government is practiced day to day. People are forever complaining about bureaucrats and of all critics none speak with more scorn than bright and aggressive members of the White House staff. But the truth is that the ill-considered leadership policies of recent Presidents—which have been put to a gallop by Mr. Nixon—have accorded our career civil servants a treatment similar to that which the nation has traditionally reserved for the American Indian. Encouraged by staff people pretending to serve and protect his interests, President after President has whittled away at the power and prestige of the heads of our great departments, has, in effect, stripped these chieftains of their pride and made them figureheads. This has done grave injury to the pride of the agencies themselves. If our chief is demeaned and degraded are we not demeaned and degraded as well?

The bureaucracies—it is noteworthy that strong leadership agencies like the military and the FBI are never called bureaucracies—critics tell us, are lacking in spirit, vigor, enterprise. They are lumbering, listless, hidebound and obstinate. But what should one expect? Is such criticism very different from the line that Indians lack get-up-and-go, that black men are lazy, Latin-Americans childlike? I don't think so. Steal a man's pride and there is little left of the man.

There is a fine irony in this. The long-standing assault on the line officers of government and their troops by the staff officers of the Commander in Chief has ostensibly been fueled by the desire to have a strong President. Perhaps the illusion of that has been achieved, but the reality is a President weakened by the demoralization of his legions in the field—a strong President in a diminished presidency. If a President McGovern did nothing more than correct this he would earn high marks in the history of the Republic. He would doubtless also win praise and gratitude from the Congress to which—through the perversion and abuse of Executive privilege—the rise in staff-dominated government has brought reduced access to the actual managers of the nation's affairs.

There were, it was true, flaws in a man so readily identified as a one-man band and so content to be one—the ancient and tragic flaw of *hubris*, most notably. But the other side of this vanity and self-confidence was an absence of envy, an absence of fear that one might be outshone, and minimal tendencies toward the tough-guy posturings of Mr. Nixon. These were not bad qualities to have in a President. I have often felt that in Nixon we had a President who was living out fantasies born in the mind of a substitute football player on the Whittier College bench, who was now forcing us to live out those fantasies with him. The Nixon appetite for the "tough decisions," the hard and hardening line on welfare and amnesty—issues which begged for a measure of mercy—suggested that even if peace came in Indochina he would still feel the need for someone—something—to, as he might put it, "kick around." Whatever youthful fantasies awaited fulfillment in the head of George McGovern, it was safe to say that none stemmed from the frustration, shame, envy of an intense young man who had failed to make the varsity.

McGovern's abiding concern as the selection of delegates ended in the states and the nomination appeared certain was to be a good winner. He, and all of us, worried that the purists within the campaign would ride roughshod over the opposition at the convention and leave an already divided party irreparably split for the general campaign. There was reason to worry. David Broder, in a column which appeared in the New York *Post* the day after the New York primary, cited two examples of the problem: a burly, bearded McGovernite in Michigan roughing up a reporter because he didn't like the reporter's questions; a McGovern-dominated caucus in Minnesota passing a resolution sanctioning homosexual marriage. This sort of thing led Broder to speculate that the Miami Beach convention "may prove to be the disaster for the Democrats that the San Francisco Cow Palace was for the GOP in 1964. . . . The prospect of this poses more of a clear and present danger to McGovern's candidacy against President Nixon than the coolness of many elected Democratic officials or the leadership of organized labor." None of us, McGovern least of all, would have taken issue with that comment at the time.

I had, at the candidate's request, drafted a letter to our delegates and alternates—a letter he rewrote slightly but not much—and it said in part:

"We cannot afford to let a single delegate or group of delegates leave the convention embittered and alienated by the nomination of George McGovern. To do so would be to add to the already enormous campaign resources—public and secret—of Mr. Nixon and his special-privilege crowd in Washington.

"This means that we—all of us in the McGovern camp—must

be good winners throughout all the business of the convention. We need not sacrifice our convictions nor am I suggesting we do. But we must be considerate of the views and feelings of others, and generous in our dealings with them. This leaves no room for ill-will, ill-temper or discourtesy within our own Democratic ranks. It demands instead a genuine spirit of tolerance and a new sense of fraternity among Democrats of all shades of opinion."

This attitude of the candidate—this policy, in effect—was already being applied out among the states in the formation of the convention committees and the selection of committee members. It found expression chiefly in the composition of the Credentials Committee where, as gestures of good will, McGovern forces made seats available to Humphrey, Muskie, Wallace and other delegates. It must be said that motives were not entirely pure in this. In the eyes of reform-minded McGovernites the Platform Committee seemed more important, so they strengthened their hand in it at the expense of representation on the Credentials Committee. Still the give-and-take, the professionalism in a word, was genuine. It was not repaid in kind by the so-called professionals. Little more than a week after Broder termed the McGovern zealots a more "clear and present danger" to the candidate—and by extension to party unity—than the regulars and union leaders, our opposition under the leadership of Hubert Humphrey took advantage of a temporary majority on the Credentials Committee to strip McGovern of 151 of his 271 California delegates.

It was a shameful stunt on the part of the former Vice President. It violated his previous pledge to abide by the winner-take-all terms of the California primary for one thing, and it was an utterly negative action for another. There was no way, given the character of the majority of delegates, for a Humphrey nomination to come out of the convention. The move could only be read as a spiteful attempt to deny McGovern what he had won.

The "incredible, cynical, rotten political steal," as a furious McGovern labeled it, brought quick retaliation as McGovern forces—back in control of the Credentials Committee—bounced no less a figure than Richard Daley and fifty-eight of his regular-organization delegates from the Illinois delegation. This was not merely an act of revenge. As a result of California, we now needed the roughly fifty additional votes the Daley ouster brought to our side of the ledger. But it was all ugly and harmful and the people responsible were not McGovern and his purists but the solid citizens of the old line. One delegate from the ranks of labor was quoted in the New York *Times* as saying of McGovern: "I wouldn't work for him if the alternative was Adolf Hitler." One had to ask: Who were the professionals and who the amateurs in this internecine nonsense?

It must be said that Muskie covered himself with something less than glory over this period, standing aloof, being neither a candidate nor a noncandidate, declining to help prevent or even to denounce the California steal in the vain hope that, in the end, he might pick up the pieces of a fragmented convention.

Meanwhile, McGovern people on the Platform Committee, led by Ted Van Dyk, Shirley MacLaine and others, put together a liberal, yet moderate platform to the satisfaction of virtually everybody. "What surprised many experts," wrote Warren Weaver, Jr., in the New York *Times* "The Week in Review," "was that the McGovern majority, including most of the so-called 'crazies,' here again turned out to be political realists who made an effort to achieve a consensus and unity."

So the whole thing was ironic, and it augured ill for the future. It kept the divisions unbridged and the battle raging right up to the opening of the convention. It made it impossible for McGovern to act on his desire to be quick in healing the wounds of the primaries. Twelve days were lost between June twenty-ninth and July tenth as practically all the attention of the McGovern people centered on getting the convention as a whole to return the California delegates the Credentials Committee had taken away. The effort was successful, but the victory was not lacking in Pyrrhic undertones. An attempt by us to restore the seating of Mayor Daley and his regulars under a compromise giving each of them half a vote was snubbed by Daley and rejected by the convention. A tricky parliamentary problem relating to California led us to a rather shabby abandonment of a women's challenge to a South Carolina delegation that was short on female representation. Worst of all, in the loss of those twelve days McGovern lost the time and opportunity to work with other leaders—former foes as well as friends—on the single important piece of business left to the convention—the selection of a candidate for Vice President.

Once California was won again, the nomination became a *fait accompli.* Thus there was nothing odd about the anticlimactic quality of the moment when, in the early hours of Thursday, July 13, the vote of Illinois put McGovern over the top. He was sitting in his shirtsleeves off to the side of a large television set in the living room of his suite. He was holding a cigar in his long fingers and rolling it idly between them. The roar of the convention crowd filled the room. I saw no change of expression on McGovern's tired face as family and friends moved in to kiss him or shake hands. The absence of drama, of the electric shock of victory, was, as I say, natural. Yet it seemed somehow unjust. He had worked so hard for so long. He had been mocked and slighted. He had literally shaken American politics to its foundations. More was called for than handshakes

149

and kisses. The earth ought to have trembled under Miami Beach. Comets should have shot across the sky.

Hubert Humphrey's was the first congratulatory phone call. Ted Kennedy's was the second, and McGovern took the opportunity to ask him formally to be his running mate. McGovern had always—despite repeated statements by the young senator from Massachusetts that he wanted no part of it—clung to the hope that he could talk Kennedy into joining the ticket. But Kennedy, citing family responsibilities, was adamant, and it was hard to press a man who had seen two brothers lose their lives in presidential politics.

At eight-thirty that morning, after very little sleep, about twenty of us gathered in a conference room just off the Doral's lobby on the main floor. Our assignment from the nominee was to go through a winnowing process of likely, or unlikely, vice presidential possibilities and come up with a list of four or five names. Gary Hart presided over the meeting while Mankiewicz, I suppose one could say, subpresided. I was directly opposite the two of them at the enormous round table. I can't remember everybody there but it was a mixture of staff and important early supporters. Everyone—in the wake of three convention sessions which had gone on until the morning hours—looked exhausted.

A day or two earlier McGovern, through Gordon Weil, had asked us to put down on slips of paper the names of our preferences for the second man on the ticket. I had no particular choice beyond Ted Kennedy, and I had shared McGovern's belief that confronted with the no-longer abstract invitation Kennedy would come aboard. I'd also thought Governor Reubin Askew of Florida was an interesting possibility; but, like Kennedy, Askew had requested that he not be considered.

My concern was that we come up with the names of a few men who would be most likely to hasten the unification of the party behind McGovern. It was immediately evident that this was the concern of everybody. The purist factor was conspicuous by its absence, although all the major elements of the McGovern coalition—the women, the blacks, the Chicanos—were represented. This was serious business, our first since victory had been won, and it was going to be seriously pursued.

At the same time I don't think any of us harbored delusions of grandeur about our function. We knew that our task was to help McGovern to the best possible choice of a running mate— not to make it for him—so initially we cast a rather wide net.

The first batch of names was a potpourri: Leonard Woodcock, president of the United Auto Workers, who had been suggested by Eleanor McGovern; Senators Hart, of Michigan, Eagleton, of Missouri, Ribicoff, of Connecticut, Nelson, of Wisconsin, Mondale, of Minnesota, Bayh, of Indiana, Stevenson, of Illinois, Hollings, of South Carolina, Church, of Idaho; Governors Lucey, of Wisconsin, Gilligan, of Ohio, Bumpers, of Arkansas.

Also Representative Wilbur Mills, of Arkansas, Representative James O'Hara, of Michigan; Mayor Kevin White, of Boston, and Mayor Moon Landrieu, of New Orleans; Sargent Shriver, Larry O'Brien, Walter Cronkite and two university presidents: Theodore Hesburgh, of Notre Dame, and Kingman Brewster, of Yale.

The bulk of these were soon gone from consideration. Ted Van Dyk's reaction to the New Orleans mayor was crisp: "Make a good headline anyway," he said. "Moon over Miami."

At the end of the first winnowing, done by show of hands, the names remaining were: Lucey, Eagleton, Woodcock, Shriver, Cronkite, Church, Nelson, White, O'Brien and Mondale. There were two, maybe three more rounds of voting and some names which had been dropped were put back. Ultimately, on what would have been the fourth or fifth—and final—list, there were six names: Shriver, White, O'Brien, Lucey, Ribicoff and Eagleton.

Except for Sargent Shriver and Pat Lucey none of these had any obvious advocate in the room. Pierre Salinger made a pitch for Shriver as a Democrat of accomplishment, an attractive personality, and as, if not an actual Kennedy, a Kennedy in-law. Bill Dougherty felt that Shriver might be just a bit too well born and eastern for our so-called people's campaign: "I mean he may just not be crappy enough for us," he said, to considerable laughter. Dougherty's candidate was Lucey, and he argued his case with vigor but to little avail. My feeling about Shriver was that he had stayed on too long as ambassador to France in the early part of the Nixon administration. My feeling about Lucey, shared by others I thought, was that he was too closely identified with our side, having worked hard for McGovern in the days following the Wisconsin primary.

At one point I found myself speaking for Mayor White—not so much as a partisan but as the one person in the room who had any familiarity with him. Two or three times, while working for the Los Angeles *Times,* I had covered White and had been favorably impressed. He was personable, young, sensible, with a good record on the big issues and—in contrast with our man from the prairies—the mayor of a big city. The more we went on the more he emerged, not only to me but to Gary Hart and several others, as a happy choice.

At the same time there were some who expressed reservations about him on the grounds that he was apt to invite a tacit veto from Ted Kennedy as a potential competitor from the same turf. I felt that might be a problem but doubted that it would be insurmountable. I found it hard to believe that Kennedy, having himself rejected the McGovern appeal to run, would have the cheek to try to veto another Bostonian. I said as much to Dutton who laughed and said: "Don't kid yourself."

I remember that Rick Stearns, the clever young fellow who had managed the caucus states operations prior to the convention, surprised me by praising Larry O'Brien. But then I thought it wasn't surprising after all: It was the young, however idealistic, pro paying tribute to the old pro. O'Brien, as convention chairman, had indeed earned universal praise for his fairness, firmness and good humor.

So far as I could tell no one was seriously advancing Walter Cronkite. He had been put forward originally by Mankiewicz as an example of the sort of person to consider if McGovern should decide to reach outside the political world for someone of distinction. When his name was dropped, Mankiewicz said softly: "Good night, Walter."

Ribicoff stayed on the list not because anybody was pushing him—indeed the word was that he was as firm against running as Kennedy—but because McGovern had told Gary Hart he wanted the name offered to him. So out of the final six only two —Shriver and Lucey—had hearty supporters, in Salinger and Bill Dougherty; White had mild advocates in me and in Gary Hart; O'Brien, beyond Stearns, had no apparent partisan; neither did Eagleton.

Eagleton regularly came through the winnowings as White did—on form. He was young—forty-two or so—a Catholic, a city boy from St. Louis, a former prosecutor, a liberal but a regular, too, with good connections in organized labor. He was from a border state. He could be a bridge to the disaffected in the party.

Early on in the meeting someone—I think Stearns again— brought out that there was gossip about a history of alcoholism and mental illness in Eagleton's family. A reporter had told

153

Stearns about it, but Stearns was unable to recall the reporter's name.

It was something which, no matter how absurd it sounded, had to be looked into. Gordon Weil volunteered to check into it with Tom Ottenad, of the St. Louis *Post-Dispatch* Washington bureau. Weil said that while he was about it he would also make inquiries about Kevin White—not because of any gossip but because the mayor was so little known to most in the room. Yancey Martin, McGovern's adviser on minority matters, said he wanted to know more about White's record on civil rights, although I assured him that it almost had to be good in view of the fact that White had run against and defeated Louise Day Hicks, the Boston busing queen.

I can only speak for myself, but it seemed impossible that there could be substance to the rumors about Eagleton. He was, after all, a man who had been in the spotlight of public office for a good while. He had won election as Missouri attorney general at the age of thirty-one in 1960, and as lieutenant governor in 1964. He had defeated the incumbent Senator Edward V. Long—a tough character—in the 1968 Democratic primary and then gone on to win the general election. He had, that is to say, been subjected to public scrutiny—and more pertinent still—to the private investigation of opponents in at least three hard-fought primaries and general elections over a period of eight years. I could believe he might be a drinker, but I could not believe that he had suffered mental difficulties.

The meeting broke up around noon and the list went up to McGovern. Time was growing short. Under the rules of the convention, nominating petitions for Vice President were to be filed no later than four o'clock. No one would have held the presidential nominee to a rigid interpretation of this, of course,

154

but McGovern, with his innate courtesy, did not want to delay proceedings if he could help it.

In his suite he moved from one phone to another, placing and receiving calls. He made one more, absolutely final appeal to Kennedy and was turned down again. I don't remember the order of calls after that. At some point both Humphrey and Muskie were asked—not with great passion—if they might be interested. Both said no. Ribicoff also was asked and said no. It was clear that McGovern, while personally fond of Pat Lucey, was not going to ask him, and I assumed this was prompted by the same reservations I had—that Lucey was too much within the family. It was one of politics' crueler junctures where the course demanded of a winner was to punish his friends and reward the enemy. It was equally apparent that McGovern was shying away from Eagleton. He offered no outright explanation for this beyond saying at one point: "I really don't know Tom very well." I took that to mean that he knew his young colleague well enough not to like him.

Shriver and O'Brien excited no apparent enthusiasm in him either. Ultimately there was left—both from the list we had brought to McGovern and his own list—one name: Kevin White. A call was put through to the mayor who had to be tracked down at his summer place on the shore somewhere. The conversation, as I recall it, was confined to McGovern's inquiring if White would accept if the offer was made to him, he being one of a few under consideration. White said he'd be honored to. McGovern, showing what was for me his first smile of the day, asked the mayor to sit tight and said he would get back to him in a few minutes.

It seemed settled. I imagined that the reason McGovern had not made an outright offer was because he wanted to check with the senator from Massachusetts to make certain that there would be no Kennedy objection. I don't know that that call was ever made, however, because not long afterward McGovern took a call from Harvard's John Kenneth Galbraith, a Massachusetts delegate. Galbraith, no White admirer—along with much of the Cambridge academic community for reasons obscure to me—reported that the Massachusetts delegation was in a rage at rumors of White's selection. White, after all, had been a Muskie supporter and one of the stars of the Muskie slate which the McGovernites had defeated in the Massachusetts primary.

The Massachusetts delegates would, Galbraith said, walk out of the convention in a body if McGovern chose the Boston mayor.

A doleful McGovern thanked Galbraith for the information and put down the phone. He related the substance of the conversation to Mankiewicz, Weil, Dutton and me. My comment was that White had never enjoyed warm relations with much of the Cambridge establishment and had made a career quite independently of it. But I did not suggest making a fight. If it was true that the delegation from a man's own state would leave the convention in protest against his nomination, then the reasonable thing was to forget him. Subsequently, Weil told me he had talked later to someone from the Massachusetts delegation who said Galbraith's report wasn't so. In any case it spelled the end of White.

There appeared to be nobody left except Eagleton. Even now McGovern held back. He turned once more to his closest friend in the Senate, the witty Gaylord Nelson. Nelson, who had from the start told him that an inviolable pact with Mrs. Nelson —known to be a lady of strong will—prevented him from saying yes, said no regretfully once more. But Nelson also, as he had apparently done earlier, recommended Eagleton highly. Other senators had done the same—Kennedy for one, Majority Leader Mike Mansfield for another.

McGovern then asked somebody to put a call through to Eagleton. When the Missouri senator came on the line, he said: "Tom, I'd like you to be my running mate." There seemed to be a pause at the other end. Then Eagleton said something about how flattered he was and that he accepted "before you change your mind, George." There was a little more chit-chat, then McGovern said he wanted to put Mankiewicz on to ask a few questions and discuss details. Mankiewicz took the phone. I was standing nearby and heard him, after making some congratulatory comments, ask Eagleton in the breezy Mankiewicz style if there was anything about him we didn't know that we should know. Hmmm? Like, was he in the habit of beating his wife, or chasing girls or boozing? Had he ever been arrested for pranks or general cutting-up? Hmm? You know? Was there, in short— and I am paraphrasing all of this—anything in the Eagleton past which could hurt or embarrass the ticket? Eagleton, it was obvious from Mankiewicz's manner, assured him there was not.

A few minutes later McGovern walked up to me and said: "Dick, I know you're disappointed about Kevin White."

"No, I'm not," I said. "I think Eagleton will be fine."

I meant it. Gordon Weil's inquiry into the Eagleton rumors had included to my knowledge a talk with Tom Ottenad, and Ottenad had told him the St. Louis *Post-Dispatch*, responding to the rumors during the 1968 Eagleton Senate campaign, had conducted a thorough investigation and come up with nothing. That left me satisfied that if there was anything wrong with Eagleton, it had to be that he got loaded once in a while. I couldn't, as a relatively hearty drinker myself, see much to worry about there.

Somewhere further along in the evening, however, Bob

Anson chased down Weil and me in the corridor a few doors from McGovern's suite. Anson, author of McGovern's unusually straightforward campaign biography and a good newsman, was in considerable agitation. "I tell you there's something to those rumors," he said. Weil and I assured him that there couldn't be. "Well," he said, "I'm telling you there is." I don't remember if Anson urged any action on us, but I think I said something about its being too late to do anything even if he was right. Weil said much the same. And it was true: The choice had been announced, the convention was beginning to assemble and the nominating machinery was in motion. I left Anson with Weil and went on about my business, thinking that the young man was a decent fellow but a little excitable. One tends to believe what one wants to believe.

The purists and hairsplitters among the delegates—not having had enough of sunrise sessions apparently—dragged things out that evening so ridiculously that Eagleton's nomination didn't come until after midnight and the speechmaking of the new nominees for President and Vice President, plus Ted Kennedy, got underway about three o'clock in the morning. By then two thirds of the nation had gone to bed. The speeches were good and so were the speakers' performances. I was impressed with Eagleton as almost everyone seemed to be. McGovern's speech sounded the come-home-America theme with eloquence and freshness. He had, after looking through drafts from a dozen different writers, written it himself.

As I had done throughout, I stayed away from the convention hall. I watched it all on television while lying comfortably in bed. I was pleasantly drunk on a mixture of booze and fatigue. Cynthia, in the next bed, went to sleep in the middle of the speechmaking.

Earlier I had taken her and her daughter, Kathy, who'd come

down to work as a volunteer in the so-called VIP suite, to a late dinner at the roof restaurant of the hotel. Kathy was drooping with exhaustion; Cynthia was losing a battle with a cold; I was feeling and doubtless acting like a zombie. But we celebrated and spirits rose. We had something to celebrate. My adventure had over the long months been transformed from a pitiful thing into a thing of glory, from a grub into a resplendent butterfly. That strange, introverted, cocky character from Mitchell had worked a miracle. For Cynthia, a sensitive woman, it had not been easy over those months to walk through the world and have people inquire about me in tones suggesting she had married a dunce. Now, even in the misery of her cold, she was feeling saucy. She was proud of me, and that was a treat because while I always hunger for her praise, she is generally stingy with it.

We talked about the prospects of beating Nixon. I assured my audience of two that nothing could stop McGovern now. The gods, I said, could not in one's wildest imaginings be so unkind as to deny him a November miracle equal to that of July. I told them about Bill Dougherty's so-called McGovern Law which was based on intimate involvement with the nominee's Algeresque career in politics, a career in which on one occasion a favored Republican opponent had been so considerate as to die not long before election.

"There's one thing you got to remember," Dougherty said of his friend. "George McGovern is the luckiest son of a bitch you've ever seen."

CHAPTER *9*

EARLY IN THE course of our postconvention holiday in the Black Hills of South Dakota I received a phone call from Teddy White in New York. "Tell me," he said, "is there any point in my coming out there? Is anything going to happen? Is there a chance I might have a talk with him, or does he want to be left alone?"

"It really is a vacation," I said. "He's dead tired. He wants to sleep, to think and—yes, to be left alone." I described the routine which had quickly established itself in the rustic setting of Sylvan Lake Lodge where the candidate and Eleanor, with an assortment of young McGoverns, occupied a number of rather primitive log cabins. Late in the morning we served up a none-too-willing presidential nominee for some visually interesting activity which would provide the network camera crews and the still photographers with pictures to justify their presence with us. Later, at noontime, I held a briefing in which I tried to give the writing people something to write—whom the man had talked to by phone, when such-and-such might be expected to happen, what he had had for breakfast, what his plans were for the next day. It was dull stuff, but the writers, like the cameramen, needed to justify their existence—and their expense accounts—to editors at the home office.

On a good day stories were written and filed, still pictures and film set en route via courier, by one or two o'clock. The working day was over, and the Black Hills country, in all its considerable rough beauty and limited entertainment, lay at hand. One of the reasons, probably the chief reason, this awe-inspiring but Godforsaken neck of the woods had been picked for the vacation, indeed, was to give the Black Hills' tourist business a shot in the arm. Tourism was second only to agriculture as a source of revenue for the seven hundred thousand citizens of South Dakota and McGovern, presidential nominee or no, was still a United States senator with a constituency to cater to. In June, two hundred people had died in a flash flood in Rapid City, at the eastern edge of the Black Hills. (One of the posters in the crowd when we flew into the Rapid City airport was: "First the Flood, Now McGovern.") Publicity about the flood and resulting devastation had brought a sharp decline in tourists. The thought was that the publicity attendant on the McGovern holiday would get the cash registers ringing in the souvenir stands once again.

We visited Mount Rushmore where the cameras caught the McGovern profile juxtaposed against the massive stone faces of Washington, Jefferson, Theodore Roosevelt and Lincoln.

"We're here for a fitting," I said, reaching for a laugh and not getting it from Dick Stout of *Newsweek*. We got the man from Mitchell—a town boy after all—up on a dejected-looking gelding named Big Red and he appeared quite as unhappy as the horse. We got him into a cowboy hat, which he wasn't much at home with either. Other pictorial riches were planned for ensuing days—buffalo herds, canoes, trout streams, Wild West parades and Indians, although of the latter the candidate said: "Remember, no feathered headdress."

Also on the schedule was a day-long strategy session with Hart and Mankiewicz and a raft of others who would fly out from Washington; and a one-day visit by Tom Eagleton.

"But that," I said to Teddy White, "is about it. If I were you I'd save the money." White said he'd take my word for it. "I know that you, old buddy, would never let me down." I rang off feeling I'd done a good turn for a friend and went on with my chores. The holiday had turned out to be anything but that for me. Hardly an hour passed that I wasn't phoned by some special-audience periodical—ranging from the sacred to the profane—wanting to spend a day, half a day, "only an hour or two," interviewing McGovern. The political rewards to be reaped by us in such exercises were held to be rich beyond counting and—the other side of the coin—punishments in the event of refusal would be dire. "He is not, to be frank, all that strong with the gay people, Mr. Dougherty. . . . I needn't tell you that he's in real trouble with the Jews. . . . The blacks don't even know him yet, man. . . . With Catholic families it's not busing, Mr. Dougherty, it's aid to parochial schools. If you could just . . ." So it went.

Meanwhile, in the piny woods outside my cabin, and in the brush along the mile or so of road to McGovern's cabin, the foreign press lay waiting. Camera crews from German television moved over the forest floor like an advance party of Algonquins. Japanese photographers sprang like Shinnecocks from dappled glades.

No more than a couple of days of this—in combination with the more routine dealings with the sensitive types who were permanently assigned to us—had led me to call Cynthia and tell her to forget about flying out to join me. She was disappointed. "It looks so beautiful on the news," she said. "I thought I might even do some riding."

I said it was indeed beautiful but not all that beautiful and sketched a picture of living conditions as something less than de luxe. "This isn't your dish of tea," I said. "This is a bunch of cabins with furniture out of a thrift shop and lumps like rocks in the mattresses. The view from the cabin windows is of scraggy pines and the walls of other cabins."

"What about that marvelous lake?" she asked with a suspicious note.

"The whole layout was designed so nobody can see the lake," I said. There was silence at the other end. "It's true," I said—as it was. "Also," I added, knowing my woman, "you have to walk a couple hundred yards up to the main lodge for breakfast."

"No room service?" There was horror and disbelief in her voice. I knew I had her.

"That's right," I said.

"Forget it," she said. I assured her I was as disappointed as she was. She knows how to hurt though. "Well," she drawled, "that's something, isn't it?"

With all this, there was much to rejoice in. Even before we left Miami Beach McGovern had decided who was to travel with him and who was to stay at headquarters in Washington. Gary Hart was to continue as campaign manager. Mankiewicz was to join the traveling party as a kind of chief of staff. Gordon Weil was to leave off traveling and run the research operation. Or was he? Ted Van Dyk was involved in that too as head of an investigating and position-paper section. Kirby Jones—Mankiewicz had looked after his friend—was to head up the press office in Washington as a deputy press secretary, presumably reporting to me. It would be interesting to have a deputy who didn't speak to me, but frankly I didn't give a damn. The pleasant part was that Weil would be making life miserable for people at home base rather than on the road, and that the basic traveling staff of rank would be Mankiewicz, Dutton and me. Dutton, who had known Mankiewicz since college days and

164

been associated with him closely in the Robert Kennedy presidential campaign, said that Mankiewicz was a homebody who hated to travel. His guess was that Mankiewicz would come aboard for three or four days, then think of some reason to go to Washington for a week. Thus the Dutton vision of the future was of him and me and a few other congenial types occupying central positions in the traveling court.

That sounded fine. It sounded fine even if Mankiewicz was to prove Dutton wrong and stay on the road. One could never charge Mankiewicz with being bad company. Last, but far from least, Polly Hackett had joined Carol Friedenberg and me in the press section. She was one of those young but battered veterans who heretofore had worked as an advance man. She was blond, handsome and a fierce worker. Her selection—a suggestion of McGovern's—left one more spot which would be filled as of Labor Day by Jackie Greenidge, my old friend from the Los Angeles *Times* bureau in New York.

Beyond this I had, with the support of George Cunningham —now the deputy campaign manager—hired Christine Camp Turpin to be the press deputy in charge of administration in Washington. She was a veteran of John Kennedy's White House staff. Having her at headquarters meant that I'd have at least one deputy to talk to now and again.

McGovern was fifty on July nineteenth, three days after our arrival at Sylvan Lake. It appeared—at least to my eyes—to depress him disproportionately. Having gone through the experience myself I assured him there was serenity and happiness to be found in the sunset years. He looked at me and said: "You're a mean bastard, Dougherty."

We celebrated the occasion with a party at the main lodge at which we all stayed too long. We had to be up at three o'clock the next morning, into cars and on our way to the Rapid City airport for a flight to Washington and an important Senate vote on an increase in the minimum wage. There had been considerable argument both in the Black Hills and Washington about whether McGovern should return for the vote. Some vote counters on Capitol Hill advised that his vote wouldn't be necessary for the legislation to pass; others contended that it would be crucial. The latter, however much we may have cursed them for forcing us to make the trip, proved right. McGovern's was the vote which put the measure over.

This was specially gratifying because the day before the executive council of the AFL-CIO had met and, under the pressure of George Meany, voted not to endorse the Democratic nominee. This was the first time since the merger of the two huge labor organizations in 1956 that the candidate of the Democratic Party had failed to secure their endorsement. Thus the headlines crediting McGovern with having saved the minimum-wage bill amounted to a riposte to the bullheaded vindictiveness of Meany and his associates, and made the disruption of the holiday worth-while.

McGovern also held a news conference that day with Senator Eagleton and Larry O'Brien in which he announced that O'Brien had agreed to be "chairman" of the campaign. In this new, rather ill-defined post O'Brien, who had struggled to keep his job as national chairman but been dropped to make room for Jean Westwood, would act as "a foremost consultant" on the over-all policy and strategy of the campaign. He would not, McGovern made clear, have administrative authority over Gary Hart at campaign headquarters or Westwood at the National Committee. In actual fact, the chief O'Brien task was to start mending our fences with the old-line party types and the disgruntled barons of organized labor.

The new title was McGovern's idea and he was proud of it.

A nice man but with a tendency to swell with self-importance, O'Brien had suffered a badly wounded pride at the loss of the National Committee job and it was essential—given his long and cordial relations with the old guard—that he be brought around and put to work. The move was calculated to help solve a personal McGovern problem as well. The diminutive but strong-charactered Eleanor had been highly disapproving of the way O'Brien had been fired as national chairman. "She told me I acted like a shit," McGovern said to me at the time. "She's never used language like that to me in her life. She hasn't spoken to me for two days."

There was an embarrassing and rather silly moment during the news conference. After a flowery McGovern explanation as to how O'Brien would fit into the campaign, the new "chairman" rose to straighten out the presidential nominee on one or two matters.

"Far be it from me to correct the candidate," he said and proceeded to do precisely that. His operation would not, O'Brien said, be located in the same building as the Hart and Westwood operations. It would be quite separate and he had made that virtually a condition of his coming aboard. I assumed the old redhead from Springfield, Massachusetts, was taking a tiny revenge and didn't blame him in a way. Still, it was an odd performance and suggested that O'Brien was not going to fit too happily into the scheme of things.

We stayed overnight in Washington and flew back to South Dakota late in the morning with a full complement of Harts, Mankiewiczes, et al, who were coming along for the strategy meeting scheduled for the next day. In the meantime the nominee's mood—cheered earlier by the O'Brien ploy—had gone a little sour. An interpretive piece by Bill Greider in the morning's Washington *Post* had warned the somewhat holier-than-thou McGovern enterprise that care should be taken to preserve the credibility of the candidate and the campaign.

Greider had chided us about three or four incidents in which he felt we had been lacking in candor. He was on weak ground with a couple of these but not on the principal one—the South Carolina women's challenge at the convention in which we'd pulled the rug from under the ladies in order to be sure of winning the vital California challenge. Greider didn't object to our having done this—like most observers he thought it had been a smart maneuver. What he objected to were the subsequent denials by Mankiewicz, Hart and others—including McGovern —that we had been conscious of doing any such thing.

I alone, alas, was singled out for praise because of my "blunt" comment: "You might say we lied." I squirmed when I read that. I had in fact said it but I'd been under the impression that I was off the record. In any case, at some point in the flight McGovern came across the aisle to where I was sitting with Dutton and said: "Dick, I've half a mind to tell Bill Greider I think he's a son of a bitch." I said I wouldn't recommend that. "Damnit," he said. "Half the things in that piece are wrong. That business about the Secret Service and the guy with the gun—that's just not true." I said I knew it wasn't but I still thought he should let it ride; and, muttering to himself, he went back to his seat.

I wanted to add that Greider was in my judgment one of the ablest, and at the same time more sympathetic, reporters we had assigned to us. But I reckoned that might be ill advised in view of the small tribute Greider had paid me. Indeed, I assumed that part of the candidate's just-expressed ire was intended to serve as a Chinese reprimand for me.

I was not, needless to say, tempted to offer the opinion that while Greider may have been wrong on some facts he was right on principle. I believed we had, in fact, been too clever by half in denying what we'd done in the South Carolina challenge. I had to grant that the temptation had been strong and that the caper had even had amusing aspects. I had laughed as hard as anybody that night when, sitting with the McGoverns and some others, we'd seen Mankiewicz offering deadpan denials of hanky-panky to television newsmen. All of us had roared as an admiring McGovern said: "Frank's an even better liar than Bill Dougherty."

Yet, for all of that, our lies had been gratuitous and that was bad. I think the Lord allows for only so many lies in politics and thus to waste even one is unwise.

The Greider piece was not the only news item bothering Mc-Govern. High in the lead of Jim Naughton's O'Brien story in the morning New York *Times* was a paragraph which, following on McGovern's glowing description of the new O'Brien post, read: "Senior advisers to Mr. McGovern made it clear privately, however, that Mr. O'Brien's campaign title would be largely honorary."

The world was being told, in other words, that McGovern had not meant what he said, and had in fact led O'Brien down the primrose path. One could imagine the reaction this raised in the hypersensitive O'Brien over whose ruffled feathers the candidate had labored so hard. McGovern was still furious about it the next morning and made it the first order of business at the strategy session. We assembled in the so-called auditorium of the lodge, an elongated cabin down the rocky slope from the main building near the edge of Sylvan Lake. McGovern, wearing a suede jacket, with a silk scarf tied dudishly around his neck, stood at the bottom corner of a U-shaped table arrangement. Gary Hart, waiting to take over after the candidate's opening remarks, stood beside him. I think everyone was startled by the anger in McGovern's voice as he said: "I want this stopped. I don't know who all these 'senior advisers' are who know what's in my mind better than I do myself. I don't want to know. I'm just telling all of you that I'm not going to put up with any more of it."

He proceeded to reaffirm his view of O'Brien as a senior adviser and chief liaison with labor, elected officials and the like. Throughout all this—so obvious as to be embarrassing—Hart, tall and cadaverous, stood with his unbarbered head lowered in the manner of a schoolboy caught in a shameful act. Looking at him I thought back to the time he told me of his willingness to step down whenever "somebody better" came along. Clearly O'Brien, with all his credentials, failed to meet that criterion, and this was tantamount to saying that no one ever would. Hart was more of a scrapper than one might think.

McGovern, winding up his lecture, said: "So from here on out nobody is to talk to the press for this campaign except myself and Dick Dougherty, and that's that."

There was an extended and uneasy silence. I knew I was already in the doghouse because of the Greider column, but I thought this directive had to be qualified a bit. I risked the candidate's wrath by observing that I thought it would be difficult to impose such a restriction on our relations with the press. "Like it or not," I said, "this has been an easygoing and open operation for them. They've always talked to anybody they wanted to and to clamp down now will surely be reported. We'll get stories to the effect that McGovern has ordered aides not to talk to reporters, and I don't think we want that, especially since we've boasted, and properly, about running an open campaign as opposed to the secret and furtive Nixon operation."

I couldn't say that the candidate was pleased, but he did start to nod as I made my point. He replied: "Well, of course, I don't mean to put gags on responsible people talking about what they're personally qualified to talk about. All I mean to say is that I'm fed up with this damned gossip and if there's any more of it people will be invited to leave this campaign."

He turned the meeting over to Hart then and took a seat where, through both the morning and afternoon sessions, he sat unobtrusively, making only an occasional comment or suggestion. I was puzzled at his being quite so disturbed over the O'Brien business. It was annoying; it had probably required that he make a call to O'Brien to smooth things over. But, granting that, it seemed to me that something else must be troubling him.

I got at least a hint of what that was late the following day—Sunday. The hint came out of the curious manner and activities of Mankiewicz, who had moved into Dutton's cabin next door to mine. Mankiewicz was up to something involving Robert Boyd, chief of the Knight newspapers Washington bureau, who had appeared with a young colleague, Clark Hoyt, out of nowhere late Saturday night.

"Something's up," I said to Dutton. He looked unusually grave.

"Yeah," he said. "I think it has to do with Eagleton."

I had all but forgotten the brief Eagleton conversation Gordon Weil and I had had with Bob Anson. Now it came back to worry me again, although I still refused to make much of it. Bob Boyd, whom I knew well, was an excellent investigative reporter but not, I assured myself, any better than the investigators on the St. Louis *Post-Dispatch*.

Eagleton had originally been scheduled to fly in for a meeting with McGovern on Monday, but we had learned that a Senate vote of some sort would prevent his doing that. Now he and his wife, Barbara, were supposed to arrive very late Monday night. The meeting of the two candidates would thus take place Tuesday morning and would be followed by a joint news conference. I had seen to it the press corps was duly notified of these changes. In the meantime, Dutton and I waited to see if either Mankiewicz or McGovern was going to tell us anything.

Finally, Monday evening as I wandered into their cabin I broke in on Mankiewicz telling Dutton the news. He beckoned me in and said. "As I assume you've guessed, Richard, there is more than a little truth to those Eagleton rumors."

"Unbelievable," I said.

"But true, alas," he said wearily. "At least true enough to hurt. You know? A little shock treatment."

I looked at Dutton and shook my head. "Jesus Christ, Fred," I said.

He laughed that crackly, at times faintly maniacal Dutton laugh, and said: "That was exactly my response." Then he too shook his head and repeated: "Oh, boy, oh, boy, oh, boy!"

I asked Mankiewicz what we were doing about it. "We don't know yet," he said. "The Eagletons won't get here until one or two o'clock in the morning. Too late for any meeting. They're to have breakfast at the cabin with the McGoverns around eight. The senator wants you and me to join them at nine or nine-thirty. He'll alert me and we can go up together."

I said fine, and again: "Jesus Christ!"

"Hmmm?" said Mankiewicz, regarding me with sympathy. "Something, isn't it? I'd have told you before, but . . ."

"Glad you didn't," I said.

Dutton said: "I'll tell you one thing. If he'd pulled this on a Kennedy, we'd find his body at the base of the cliff in the morning." This time when Dutton laughed it really did sound maniacal, and appropriately so.

The McGovern cabin was the prize cabin of the Sylvan Lake establishment, which owed its existence to the New Deal's Works Project Administration, and the largest of the twenty or so which ranged around the hill-topped main lodge in no particular order. Set on a slight rise about sixty feet back from the macadam road which led to Custer, it had a small front porch to which one ascended up five rickety steps. The door opened directly into the living room, which had on one's left an opening into a tiny kitchen and, against the wall next to the opening, a nondescript dining-room table. Four matching straight chairs went with the table. At the back of the room—perhaps all of fourteen feet square—was an opening into a little hall from which one walked directly into the bathroom or into one or the other of the two bedrooms. Across the living room from the table was a low wooden-armed sofa. In the corner to the sofa's right was a fireplace made of oversized chunks of stone. Next to the fireplace was an easy chair of the old Morris rocking-chair variety.

There was a window over the sofa and one at each side of the front door. They were draped with curtains of a fruit-and-vegetable pattern which reduced the already limited flow of light from outside. It was a setting which might seem delightful to a couple of sportsmen, in red-and-black checked shirts and half full of booze, at the end of a day's hunting—the fire crackling in the fireplace, the canned stew bubbling on the stove, the wives three hundred miles away. But it was an unlikely meeting place for the candidates for President and Vice President of the United States, specially such a meeting as this.

Already with the McGoverns and Eagletons when Mankiewicz and I arrived at around nine-thirty the next morning were Doug Bennet, Eagleton's young administrative assistant, and Mike Kelly, a young former newsman who was the Eagleton press secretary. Introductions were made and hands shaken. Mankiewicz and Barbara Eagleton gave each other pecks on the cheek. She—blond, sun-tanned and pretty in an athletic way—wore a pink dress and was of the type which suggests money, good schools and a big house in the suburbs. I had not met her before. I thought as we said hello that her pale blue eyes were the eyes of a very frightened woman.

Breakfast dishes had been cleared from the table except for a cup and saucer at Mrs. Eagleton's place. She sat in one of the straight chairs at the side of the table next to the kitchen entrance with her hands on her lap and her ankles crossed. The McGoverns, side by side in the matching chairs, sat at the opposite side of the table. All three were turned to face Eagleton who took a place in the center of the sofa. I could read no expression beyond seriousness in the McGovern faces. Mankiewicz took the easy chair next to the fireplace. I sat to Eagleton's left on the sofa. Bennet and Kelly were in chairs to my left.

When we were all seated and the small talk had trailed off awkwardly, Eagleton, putting out a cigarette and starting to light another, looked toward McGovern and said: "Shall I, George?" McGovern nodded and crossed his long legs. He was holding but not smoking a cigar. Eagleton, turning slightly in my direction, thereupon addressed himself to me as presumably the one person in the room least familiar with what he was about to say.

"Dick," he said, "I'll repeat what I've just been telling Eleanor and George about problems with my health in the past. Then I guess we can proceed from there.

"I have, on three occasions, put myself into a hospital and on two of the occasions received treatment for nervous exhaustion, fatigue, depression—whatever you want to call it. I have, or used to have, a tendency to push myself too hard. The first time this happened was after the campaign in 1960 when I ran for state attorney general and won. It was my first statewide campaign and it wasn't easy, particularly with a Catholic heading the national ticket."

He looked toward McGovern and said parenthetically: "You know, George, I was the only Democrat on the state ticket who actually went out and campaigned for John Kennedy in Missouri that year." Switching back to me, he returned to his story. "I worked eighteen or twenty hours a day, day after day, week after week, and in the end it was too much. I went into Barnes Hospital in St. Louis."

Mankiewicz interrupted: "You went in on your own?"

"Yes, entirely of my own volition," he replied, and went on to say that he had spent around four weeks in Barnes and received psychiatric counseling and electric-shock therapy. The second hospitalization had been a brief one at the Mayo Clinic in Rochester, Minnesota, during the Christmas season in 1964, which was prompted by what he called "a nervous stomach." It had consisted largely of an exhaustive physical examination and had lasted four days. The third time occurred in September of 1966, when he went back to the Mayo Clinic and stayed about three weeks. That had included electric-shock treatment and psychiatric counseling again.

Mankiewicz asked if he had continued to see a psychiatrist or saw one now. Eagleton said no to both questions.

"Do you take any pills or medication now?"

"A sleeping pill once in a while, Frank."

I was impressed and, I confess, touched by Eagleton. His talk, in his pleasant baritone, was well ordered, candid, unadorned with self-serving touches. It was an apologia, of course, and he was contrite, but it was a contrition which made no overt request for sympathy. His hands trembled slightly as he lifted an ever-present cigarette to his lips. Now and then he took a white handkerchief and patted his brow. These were the only signs of the enormous tension he must have been under. He wore a pair of gray flannel slacks, which were in need of pressing, and a dark blue polo shirt under an obviously new, ill-fitting blue-and-white checked sports jacket. He had, there was no doubt, a boyish appeal and a certain undefinable vulnerability. The anxious eyes of Barbara Eagleton never strayed from his face as he told a story she knew as well, perhaps better, than he.

Mankiewicz said that a memo prepared by Bob Boyd and Clark Hoyt, summarizing questions raised by their investigations, mentioned alcoholism. "There's no truth to that at all," Eagleton said, "and there never has been." Mankiewicz said the memo also made reference to a tentative diagnosis of Eagleton as a manic-depressive with suicidal tendencies. Eagleton said: "I don't believe that; I can't imagine where that came from, Frank. I've never had any impulse to suicide. Never. And God knows I can get depressed, but I don't think anybody who knows me would call me manic."

Looking at me again, Eagleton said: "I've told George and Eleanor that I know I was wrong not to speak up about this before, Dick, but the reason I didn't was that I'd put it all so much behind me. To me it was something over and done. I knew my health was sound, that I'd had no trouble for the last six years, and I guess I'd just wiped it from my mind. I've also told George that if he wants me to I'll get off the ticket this second, this minute, this hour, today, this week—any time that he concludes that my presence on the ticket is an embarrassment or a hindrance to his chances of election. I'm prepared to do anything, anything at all that he decides I should do."

Speaking for the first time, McGovern said matter-of-factly: "I've told Tom I'm prepared to stand by him in this. I think we can ride it through."

So the decision had already been made. I was both surprised and not, relieved and not. I looked at Mankiewicz but his was a poker face. I asked Eagleton if he had ever been questioned about any of this in Missouri—meaning, as I saw he understood, had he ever lied to anybody about it.

"No," he said. "The closest it ever came to that was when I was running for the Senate in '68 and some editor at a meeting with the editorial board of the *Post-Dispatch* asked how my health was. I said: 'Fine.' And it was. The times I was hospitalized for any length of time my office put out notices to the effect that I had a virus or something, but nobody ever questioned me about them."

"This is everything? This is the whole story, Tom?" asked Mankiewicz.

"The whole story, Frank."

As I had from the start, I wished that Dutton was present. Mankiewicz was doing his best but he isn't a tough man. Neither am I, and neither, God knows, is McGovern. Dutton, a far less sentimental and seducible character, might have put some kind of brake on McGovern's instant forgiveness. He might have suggested, however politely, that the situation called for reflection, for some hard thinking about what was more than a problem of personal relations—of kindness or unkindness—for time to consider what the political impact of this extraordinary development might be and what should be done about it.

Talk of that kind might not have changed McGovern's mind, but it should have been heard in the room and it hadn't been. Why, I wondered, had McGovern not thought to have, or not wanted to have, Dutton there? Why hadn't Mankiewicz—or I for that matter—suggested he join us? I suspected the reason was that in the back of my mind—and doubtless the same was true of Mankiewicz—I had simply assumed that we would all,

Dutton included, meet again after Eagleton's departure from the cabin and talk about what to do.

If I hadn't been so surprised, if my head had been working as quickly as it should—and again the same was doubtless true of Mankiewicz—I might have had a try at the role of devil's advocate. But the opportunity, if indeed there was even a momentary one, had clearly passed as the subject turned to how the news should be made public. No one suggested that we attempt to keep it from being made public. So the question was when and how. Would it be better to wait until next week when both senators would be back in Washington? Or ought it to be done immediately at the news conference already scheduled?

Mike Kelly urged that it be put off a week and so—rather less passionately—did Mankiewicz. Kelly was concerned that not enough time had been taken to think about the best way to make the disclosure. The Eagletons were en route to Hawaii where Eagleton was to speak at a labor union convention. Breaking the story now meant that he would be questioned at every stop along the way, going and returning—Los Angeles, Honolulu, San Francisco, St. Louis and Washington. Kelly's point was that a Washington news conference some days hence would place us in a situation more easily controlled. McGovern and Eagleton could break the story and then make themselves inaccessible for a few days until the weather calmed. Mankiewicz said he thought that made sense. I thought, however, he must have something else in his mind—the hope that delay would bring a reconsideration of the McGovern decision perhaps; or at least provide an opportunity to examine the Eagleton medical records.

Kelly's reasoning was sound enough except for the unpleasant fact that it was no longer applicable. The story was already out of our control and, to prove it, we needed only to go out on

178

the porch and see Boyd and Hoyt standing on the other side of the road waiting to talk to Mankiewicz and me. They had to know they were sitting on one of the biggest political stories ever. Short of Mankiewicz and my going over there and piling lie upon lie to stay them, there was no chance of their sitting on the story any longer. They were aware—I'd learned from Mankiewicz—that *Time* magazine was onto the story too, and had a team of reporters assigned to it. Mankiewicz had told me there was even a rumor that our old right-wing critic in New Hampshire, the Manchester *Union Leader*, had somehow been alerted to the story.

I said: "I don't see how we can do anything but unload this right away. If we're going to have a news conference this morning—and we can't very well not have one after the vice-presidential candidate has visited the presidential candidate—and we don't reveal it, the judgment later on will be that we tried to bottle it up.

"Boyd and Hoyt are going to break the story this afternoon or tonight for sure; and if they break it before we do ourselves it is going to look thereafter as if the press forced us to be honest; that otherwise we might have kept the thing under wraps. We can't afford that. If we drop the story ourselves we at least have that much as a position."

Eagleton said promptly: "I agree with that."

McGovern leaned forward in his chair and turned to Mrs. Eagleton. "What do you think, Barbara?" he inquired. She looked startled at being asked. She said: "I don't know. I just don't know. I have no objectivity about this."

Eleanor said: "Of course, you don't. How could you?"

The argument went back and forth awhile longer with Kelly and me using different words to say what we'd said before. Bennet seemed to lean to my view. Finally McGovern said: "I think we'd better do it now. Are you prepared to, Tom?" Eagleton nodded vigorously. "Well," McGovern continued, "why don't I open up with something about how we've discussed over-all campaign strategy—which we will have done by then—and how we view the major issues? Something on that order. And when I've done that then just say that now Senator Eagleton has a statement he'd like to make. Is that all right?"

Everybody seemed to think so. McGovern's calm through all of this—granting that his was hardly a volatile personality—continued to astonish me. I wondered if he was really staring the monster in the face. It was hard to do, and one could hardly expect him to welcome with an unblinking eye the frightening possibility that all his labors had been brought to nothing by the ambition of this tightly wound young man from Missouri.

Mankiewicz brought up a problem in relation to Boyd and Hoyt, explaining that he had gotten them to agree to hold off writing the story until their facts—some of which were wrong —could be checked and the matter discussed directly with Eagleton. They had been responsible and decent. Now we were, by breaking the story ourselves, robbing them of their exclusive. Mankiewicz's question was whether we couldn't offer them something as a consolation prize—an interview with Eagleton following the news conference perhaps. He asked: "Would it be all right with you, Tom, if they rode to the airport with you?"

"If that's what you want, sure," said Eagleton, although he didn't look happy with the idea and neither did his two sober-faced, business-suited aides.

"We can tell them that the Manchester *Union Leader* is hot on the story too. Hmmm?" said Mankiewicz to me, and for the first time it occurred to me that he might have invented the *Union Leader* out of whole cloth.

Eagleton got up from the sofa, wiped his brow, and said to

no one in particular: "It'll be a relief to get this over with. I've been carrying this thing on my back for twelve years." It was a peculiar comment from a man who had only just told us how over and done his medical history had become to him, and how wiped from the mind.

I don't know how much Boyd, a small, finely made man with a gentle manner, believed our story when Mankiewicz and I walked down from the cabin to meet him and Hoyt. I think if I'd been in his shoes I'd have given the two of us a quick Italian gesture and run for the phone, but whatever his thoughts he took the news with good grace. Mankiewicz let me be the bearer of ill tidings. I said: "We're sorry, Bob, but we understand the Manchester *Union Leader* has the story and you can imagine how they'd handle it. We've got to break it ourselves, and right away." Mankiewicz then offered the Eagleton interview and we made arrangements to see that someone would follow along in their car so they'd have it available at the airport. Our largess thus distributed, Mankiewicz and I beat a retreat.

"I wonder if Boyd wouldn't like to kill us," I said as we pulled away.

"I wouldn't be at all surprised," said Mankiewicz.

McGovern followed his script to the letter at the news conference, held at noontime in the auditorium where we'd had our strategy meeting three days earlier. He droned on at some length about the approach to the campaign as he and his running mate saw it and how confident they were of success in November. The newsmen were polite but not too attentive. They knew the conference was being held mainly as a matter of form, and as a device for getting pictures of the candidates and their attractive wives onto the tube and into the papers. The last thing to expect out of anything like this was real news.

It was a blue, crystalline mountain day. Sunlight poured

through the windows of the auditorium, breezes ruffled the blue surface of the lake, less than a hundred feet away. All a reasonable man would want was to get the conference over quickly, get his story in and then relax over a pleasant lunch.

Eagleton sat on a folding chair to the right of the microphone-burdened podium where McGovern stood. Barbara Eagleton was on his left, and Eleanor was next to her. Eleanor's mouth seemed drawn tight and turned down at the edges. Eagleton, beginning to sweat heavily under the television lights, wore the same clothes as earlier and his wife remained in her Scarsdale pink.

McGovern's comment that Senator Eagleton had a statement he'd like to make before questions were taken provoked no special reaction among the twenty-odd press people. McGovern stepped back from the podium. Eagleton stood up, clearing his throat as he made the two or three steps up to the microphones. I stood behind and to the right of him some twelve feet away. I noticed a considerable trembling of his hands, and there was a slight tremble in his voice as well. But he spoke without notes and, I thought, spoke quite well.

A few pairs of eyes showed interest as he opened with the observation that rumors about candidates were "part and parcel" of political campaigning. The show of interest heightened as he went on to say that there had been "some rumors circulating as to my health," and thus he wanted to "give you as complete a picture as I possibly can, as a layman, about my personal health."

He charged no one with malice in spreading these rumors, but he thought: "It is a legitimate question the press has to ask me about whether my health is such that I can hold the office of Vice President of the United States."

The room was growing quieter. Puzzlement was obvious on some of the faces in front of me. There was a discernible leaning forward of bodies. Eagleton cleared his throat again. Then he said: "On three occasions in my life I have voluntarily gone into hospitals as a result of nervous exhaustion and fatigue. . . ."

That did it. In an instant the only faces directed at Eagleton were those of the still photographers and camera crews. The heads of the writers were down over their notebooks. Pencils were racing. The quiet deepened to a library silence broken only by the flow, now steady and measured, of Eagleton's voice, and by the click of the still cameras and the soft whir of film in the reels.

Eagleton went through his story in much the same way he had told it at the McGovern cabin. Then, having described the "third and final" hospital episode in 1966, he continued:

"One could ask and should ask, well, in the light of that history, have you learned anything? All of us live our lives, I guess, in the attempt to learn more about ourselves . . . in many respects we are our own worst enemies, and it took these experiences, these tough experiences, for me to learn a little bit about myself.

"I still am an intense person. I still push myself very hard. But I pace myself a great deal better than I did in earlier years. The past six years, from 1966 to date, I've experienced good, solid, sound health. I make it a regular practice to be as idle as I can on Sundays . . . in the winter months that's my day to lie on the couch and watch the Redskins and the St. Louis football Cardinals and the Kansas City Chiefs, the last two being my favorite teams.

"So I believe, and I have every confidence, that at age forty-two I've learned how to pace myself, and learned how to measure my own energies, and know the limits of my own endurance. Insofar as this campaign is concerned, I intend to give it all I have but on a measured basis, and not to repeat the experience that I have experienced as heretofore mentioned.

"So as far as the initial exposition is concerned, I've said about all I can, and now I'll take any questions from the press on any matter that they feel pertinent to what I have just said."

He didn't have to wait long. The first question was whether Senator McGovern had been "aware of these things" before he "decided on you as a candidate?"

A solemn-faced McGovern, who had stood off to Eagleton's side throughout the statement, moved up to be next to him at the podium. Eagleton answered: "No, he was not. He was made aware of it on the weekend or the Monday after the convention." This came as news to me and I wondered if Eagleton knew what he was talking about. My impression, gained from Mankiewicz, was that it wasn't until the previous Friday—when Mankiewicz and Hart had briefed him on the flight from Washington to the Black Hills—that McGovern had learned the rumors were more than mere rumors.

"How did Senator McGovern react to it?" Eagleton was asked by David Schumacher. McGovern himself answered: "Well, let me say, Mr. Schumacher, that when I talked to Senator Eagleton about my decision to ask him to go as my running mate, I asked if he had any problems in his past that were significant or worth discussing with me. He said no, and I agree with that.

"I am fully satisfied on the basis of everything I've learned about these brief hospital visits that what is manifest on Senator Eagleton's part was the good judgment to seek out medical care when he was exhausted. I have watched him in the United States Senate for the past four years. As far as I am concerned, there is no member of that Senate who is any sounder in mind, body and spirit than Tom Eagleton. I am fully satisfied and if I had known every detail that he told me this morning, which is exactly what he has just told you here now, he would still have been my choice for the vice presidency of the United States."

Oh, no, I thought to myself. Down, McGovern. Leave yourself a way out.

"At the risk of being indelicate," Eagleton was asked as McGovern again stepped back and off to the side, "did you find during these periods of exhaustion that it affected your ability to make rational judgments?"

"No," was the reply. "I was in a position to make rational judgments and decisions. I was depressed. My spirits were depressed. This was one of those manifestations along with the stomach upset, of the exhaustion and fatigue, that I heretofore described."

He was asked if alcohol was "at all involved?" He said: "Alcohol was not involved in any iota, in any way, shape or form whatsoever. I can assure you, categorically and without hesitation, unequivocal, there's been no trace, no hint, not one iota of alcoholism as part of these rumors—as part of the actual facts."

Did he receive any psychiatric help during these periods? Yes, he had. "As I entered the hospitals, voluntarily as I have described, my physician was an internist, Dr. William Perry of St. Louis. He's still practicing in St. Louis and he's no longer my physician since I moved to Washington. I use the services of the Senate, which is Dr. Pearson and his staff. Parenthetically, not to avoid your questions, I have received a Senate exam and another one at Bethesda Naval Hospital and all the doctors have found so far is that I'm two pounds overweight, and have half a hemorrhoid . . . I was treated by a psychiatrist, Dr. Frank Shobez."

"Can you tell us what type of psychiatric treatment you received?"

"Counseling from a psychiatrist," Eagleton said, then hastily, as though to get it over with quickly, "including electric shock."

"Any drugs?"

"Sleeping pills."

"Was the electric shock treatment at all three hospitals?"

"No. Barnes in 1960, and Mayo's in 1966, not at Mayo's in 1964."

"What were the purposes of the electric shock treatment?"

"At that time it was part of the prescribed treatment for one who is suffering from nervous exhaustion and fatigue and manifestations of depression."

Did he intend to make the documentation of this history public? One assumed from the answer that he didn't. "Medical reports are matters between one doctor and another doctor. They're not written in laymen's language . . . I know of no situation where any candidate for any office has made public records of any communication between doctors and other doctors pertaining to a particular patient."

"Would you release your doctors from the traditional doctor-patient relationship?"

"I'm sure Dr. Perry will make a statement. I haven't talked to Dr. Perry but he'll make a summary statement of what his findings were. He is not really the most important one because I haven't seen Dr. Perry as a patient for, I guess, over four years."

Eagleton's early tenuous composure seemed to be eroding. Sweat was streaming down his neck. The handkerchief was now permanently held in his right hand. He was asked what doctors he had seen at the Mayo Clinic.

"I don't remember the names of the physicians. If you know how the Mayo operation is you're more or less treated by a group of physicians . . . you're sort of the patient of the entire group."

"Why did you decide to address yourself to the problem now when you did not decide to do so in your previous political career?"

"In seeking the second highest office in the land it is only natural that one's life becomes more and more of an open book. It's quite obvious that I haven't relished being under these lights before thirty or forty newsmen, describing my health. It isn't a joyous undertaking, and I think that it is natural that, until it is necessary to respond to rumors that were circulating, the natural tendency would be to keep one's peace."

"If you had this to do over again, would you have consulted Senator McGovern before you formally accepted the vice presidential choice?"

"Senator McGovern's staff was aware, I believe, the night before my name was put in nomination, of the rumors . . . that were circulating on the floor of the convention, and they were satisfied as to my health as to permit me to be the vice-presidential candidate."

McGovern stepped forward, took the last question—and painted himself even more hideously into a corner. Would he give the press his own assessment of his running mate's health?

"Well," he said, "I think Tom Eagleton is fully qualified in mind, body and spirit to be the Vice President of the United States and, if necessary, to take on the presidency on a moment's notice . . . I know fully the whole case history of his illness. I know what his performance has been in the Senate over the last four years, and I don't have the slightest doubt about the wisdom of my judgment in selecting him as my running mate, nor would I have any hesitancy at all trusting the United States Government to his hands. I wouldn't have hesitated one moment if I had known everything Senator Eagleton said here today."

The stampede for the phones was on. Chairs toppled in the rush. A crude tribal courtesy gave the wire services and afternoon papers priority for use of the limited number of phones. But, even in that context, there were not enough instruments to go around. Moans came from the throats of the unlucky.

"That was bravely done," I said to Eagleton. He thanked me and we shook hands. It was a very wet hand. As the room cleared I looked around for Dutton and found him talking with *Newsweek*'s Dick Stout. When Stout moved on, I said: "Well?"

"Disaster," Dutton said. "Complete disaster." I asked if he thought there was any chance Eagleton might be kept on the ticket. "Not if we want a prayer of winning," he said.

"Well, we have to see what the public reaction is," I said. "That shouldn't take more than four or five days."

"One will be more than enough," said Dutton. We drove back up the hill to our cabins. My phone was ringing as I came in the door. I thought about my friend Teddy White and wondered if he would ever forgive me. I knew he couldn't be on the phone so soon, but I didn't answer the thing anyway.

The era of the jolly press briefings at Custer's Hi-Ho Motel was over. Next day the questions came at me like dumdums. How had this happened? How could we explain picking a vice-presidential candidate who'd undergone electric shock therapy not once but twice? Who was responsible for this incredible sloppiness?

We, I insisted, had no apology to make for the Eagleton selection or the way it came about. We had made what had appeared to be adequate inquiry into the rumors about his health. He was, after all, a member of the United States Senate. He had been in public life and high office in his own state for a good many years before being elected to the Senate. He had been recommended highly to McGovern by any number of Senate colleagues including Senator Kennedy, Senator Nelson, Majority Leader Mike Mansfield and others. Of course, we had no investigative unit—no FBI—at hand to examine his background for us, but then no nonincumbent presidential nominee ever had such units at his disposal. We had been assured that the St. Louis *Post-Dispatch,* an eminently responsible newspaper, had put a team of investigative reporters to work on the Eagleton rumors in 1968 and had found there was nothing to them.

Well, who did what little investigating we ourselves had undertaken? Members of the staff, I said. What members of the staff? I said I didn't think it necessary or proper for me to name individuals. Was Gordon Weil one of them? Well, I said, yes. Who else? I repeated my disinclination to name anybody in particular; all they needed to know was that the McGovern staff had looked into the rumors and found them to be without foundation. Where was Mankiewicz now? I said he'd gone back to Washington last night.

What reactions were we getting around the nation? Mixed, as might be expected, but heartening, I said, lying in my teeth. Was McGovern standing firm in his pledge to keep Eagleton on the ticket? He had no intention of anything else now, I said.

Now. They sent the word back at me like arrows.

"Now . . . you said *now*. . . . What do you mean: *now?*"

"Did I say that?" I said.

"Yes, you did, Dick. You said *now.*"

"Well, I didn't mean it that way. . . ."

"Well, you said it though. . . ."

"Please, please! Don't put that construction on it. Let me repeat: He's standing firm with Eagleton. Period!"

I cut and ran for it as soon as I could, my heart pounding, my head aching, Dutton drove us back up into the hills to the relative safety of the cabin. He chuckled as I said: "They're going to do me in, Fred. I'll have a heart attack. They're friends of mine too."

"Now you know why politicians hate you press guys," he said.

"Why do you suppose McGovern's painted himself into such a corner with this nut?" I asked.

"I don't know," Dutton said. "It beats me. I just can't figure the guy out sometimes."

The day's troubles were not over. In the afternoon Carl Leubsdorf, of the Associated Press—suspicious that Tom Ottenad of the St. Louis *Post-Dispatch* had gotten an exclusive interview with the candidate—tracked McGovern down in Custer where he was playing tennis. The result was hardly an interview, but Leubsdorf got a couple of questions answered. The lead went something like this:

"While vowing to stand firm with his running mate Senator Thomas Eagleton, presidential nominee George McGovern said today he would have to 'wait and see' if the controversial Missouri senator should remain on the Democratic ticket."

While I never saw the story myself it was relayed to me a few hours later by a highly indignant McGovern, who hadn't actually read it either. He was calling from his cabin and I was in the press room at the motel in Custer. I was also surrounded by a half-dozen reporters, one of whom had answered the phone and recognized the voice that asked for me. I barely had time to say hello when McGovern said: "Dick, I'm Goddamned mad at Leubsdorf. He's written a story—Gary Hart just called and read it to me—saying that I'm waiting to see if Eagleton stays on the ticket. I want you to get out a denial right now. I want you to say the story is absolutely false."

"Oh, Jesus, I wouldn't," I said, wishing my big-eared audience would go away. "He's a good reporter. . . ."

"I don't give a damn," McGovern said. "I never told him any such thing."

I was in no position to put up an argument. Even that—so hot an item had we become in the world of news—would have been turned into a story. Trying not to groan, I said: "All right, I'll get something out. I'll say the story's misleading. . . ."

"False," he snapped. "Say it's false; say it's just not true."

"All right," I said.

He hung up and I made my way to a table to compose a statement which could satisfy the outraged candidate without insulting a capable reporter. I silently cursed Gary Hart for not having called me about the story instead of McGovern. Then I could have had a word with Leubsdorf and, if the story was misleading, have gotten him to modify it somewhat. Even so, I was not going to put out a statement in the harsh language of the candidate. I wrote something to the effect that an AP story then on the wires conveyed an unfortunate impression etc., etc., and wound up reiterating McGovern's determination to stick with Eagleton.

I read the thing aloud to the reporters and gave it to Polly Hackett to type up for the bulletin board. I was about to leave and go back to Sylvan Lake when McGovern called again.

"Yes, Senator," I said, wondering what now, and beginning to get a bit angry myself.

"Dick, I want you to put in the statement that not only is that story wrong but that I'm a thousand per cent behind Tom Eagleton."

"Oh, no," I said. "Oh, dear."

"Yes, I do," he said.

"Are you sure?" I asked, looking around and lowering my voice. The ears were moving in on me again.

"You're damned right I'm sure," he said irritably. "A thousand per cent."

"Okay," I said. I put the phone down and announced: "The senator wants added to the statement that he is behind Senator Eagleton a thousand per cent."

It was a moment I would relive in my mind many times over in the course of the campaign. Should I have fought him? Should I not at least have asked for time so I could drive up and talk to him face to face? I could never really decide. He was the candidate after all. He was the one who had built all of this out of nothing and presumably what one builds one has the right to destroy. In any case I had rarely felt sicker at heart than I did as I drove back up into the hills.

I could understand his initial reaction to Eagleton's strange but sad story. McGovern was a kind and Christian man; Eagleton was an engaging, puppylike, troubled fellow. But now with a day and a half gone, with reaction storming in from all sides and 90 per cent of it bad, I couldn't understand at all. However unwillingly, I had to entertain the thought that my friend McGovern-Levin had, in a fit of Russian rage at the peasants of journalism, pissed everything away; that my friend the one-man band had struck up a tune bearing all the marks of a requiem.

CHAPTER *10*

I was slow in coming to it but it became my opinion that McGovern may well have meant his 1,000-per-cent statement when he made it. He was angry, of course, and anger tends to inflate one's rhetoric. But he also felt genuine compassion for Eagleton despite what the young senator had done. The McGovern intelligence, while of a high order, is not without great patches of liberal mush of the sort which allots sympathy equally to the rapist and the raped.

This was a guess, certainly. But, if indeed he did mean it, something happened very soon after to change his mind. One thing I know for sure is that the commitment to Eagleton had vanished by the time Dutton and I called on the candidate late the next morning prior to the midday press briefing. McGovern had just talked by phone with Henry Kimelman who was in a frenzy at the extent to which campaign contributions had dried up. As McGovern relayed this to us I asked straight out if he really thought we could keep Eagleton on the ticket. "No," he said, "I'm afraid we can't." On the one hand I was glad to hear this, but on the other I was tempted to ask why then had he forced me to tell such a whopping, inevitably damaging lie the evening before.

"For now though, until we can see what to do," he went on, "I want you to keep telling the press I'm staying with him."

Dutton and I then drove into Custer exchanging astonishments about the workings of our candidate's mind. "Things are getting worse instead of better," said Dutton as we wondered how McGovern could expect to get away with being a thousand per cent for somebody one day and planning to scuttle him the next. It was not until later, after I lied my way through a barrage of questions and fled back into the hills, that I began to think that something more than a McGovern conceit, or a bumbling deviousness, had to be involved in all of this. The suspicion grew that either the night before or earlier that morning McGovern had finally gotten through to a doctor who had actually treated Eagleton, and what he had learned was not good.

This was conjecture and could never be anything more. It was not something that McGovern—sworn to the privacy of the doctor-patient relationship—could ever confirm. But the more I thought about it, the more sense it made.

Eagleton had, I knew, been unwilling or unable to produce his medical records. Whether this was because his doctors would not release them for professional reasons, or because Eagleton himself thought they were too damaging, or whether they, in fact, had been removed from the files and no longer existed, one could not know. It was, however, certain that Eagleton had, in the light of his failure to produce the records, given McGovern permission to talk with his physicians.

Eagleton had not appeared to move with any haste in getting word to the doctors that they were free to talk to McGovern. So in the meantime, McGovern on his own had to my knowledge talked with four or five eminent psychiatric practitioners around the country, authorities who had admittedly no personal familiarity with the case. McGovern was really seeking sophisticated guidance from them and that, he indicated, had come in small quantities and a confusion of conflicting judgments.

If, at any rate, my guess was correct—that on Wednesday evening or Thursday morning he had at last talked with one or more of Eagleton's own doctors and the news was bad—then McGovern was in a terrible spot. He could not—and one didn't have to be a physician to realize it—call up a man whose emotional and mental stability hung by threads and say: "Tom, your own doctors say you're not as well as you think you are." Neither, obviously, could he make such an announcement to the world at large, for if doing so did not send Eagleton tumbling into the abyss, it would beyond question set him to fighting for both personal and political survival. He would deny it.

He would unquestionably refuse to resign from the ticket and, since he was as much a nominee of the national convention as McGovern himself, the only way he could be removed was through his own resignation.

Dutton did not share my view in this; his judgment of McGovern was less partisan than mine. But to me—given my perceptions of the man—the inferences drawn from the evidence at hand were legitimate and the conclusion inevitable. Putting it negatively, it was simply impossible to attribute what had happened to an innate McGovern stupidity and deviousness. Like any intelligent man McGovern was capable of moments of monumental stupidity, and like any honest man capable of lying. But he was not capable of sustained stupidity and deceit—as appeared to be the case over the next few days.

Let it be granted that it looked that way to the press—and thus to the world. But given what the reporters knew and what we were able to tell them, one couldn't expect otherwise. So it was that the following day—Friday—after we began dropping unsubtle hints that the situation had changed—(In Washington, Mankiewicz, unable to resist a line, said Eagleton support had dropped to around 400 per cent.)—we began to get harsh news treatment indeed. Reams of copy rolled out of the newsrooms to tell the public that "George McGovern, who on Wednesday said he was a 1,000 per cent behind Senator Eagleton moved to-day . . . appeared today . . . indicated today . . . etc." No matter what the operative verb the message was the same.

Meanwhile, Eagleton seemed to be straining harder at the leash with every passing hour, phoning bubbly reports to Mc-Govern about the wonderful receptions he was getting and swearing they were going to pull the thing off. By Friday morning, through the curious offices of columnist Jack Anderson, it looked as if he were off the leash altogether.

Anderson, in a radio broadcast the night before, announced that he had located photostats which proved that Eagleton—despite his disclaimers of an alcohol problem—had been arrested in Missouri a half-dozen times or more over a period of years for drunken driving. Eagleton immediately denounced the report as a "damnable lie," and in short order Anderson backed down, acknowledging that he could not produce the photostats a source was supposed to have had, and admitting he might have been premature in his haste to score a news beat.

A quick and alarming product of this development was a new Tom Eagleton. Suddenly he was no longer the naughty boy who had been less than candid with his party, his party's nominee for President, and the public and who was trying to make amends.

He was now a victim of injustice rather than a perpetrator of it and his determination to stay on the ticket hardened noticeably. McGovern called him sometime Friday morning and found him, as he put it, "in orbit." McGovern had a particular paragraph from a speech he would make the next evening to the South Dakota State Democratic Convention which he wanted to read to Eagleton. It went something to the effect that everyone was aware of the dark and stormy days he and his running mate were going through and asked for "prayers for Senator Eagleton and

196

me while we deliberate on the proper course ahead." McGovern asked me what I thought, and I said it seemed a clear enough signal to me.

"Do you know what he said when I read it to him?" McGovern asked with a puzzled expression. "He said: 'George, that's beautiful. I wish I'd written it myself.' "

I said: "He's not making it easy, is he?"

"He doesn't want to hear what I'm telling him. He tells me how I'd have to see his crowds to believe them. He says he can see everything turning around before his eyes; the Anderson thing was the best thing that could have happened, a blessing in disguise."

We were talking on the flat top of a huge boulder out back of the little cabin which had been fixed up as an office for him. He was in bathing trunks—a bony, outwardly relaxed holiday figure in a deck chair. It was a brilliant day and his hairy body glistened from generous applications of sun-tan lotion. It was then that I wondered aloud if we shouldn't try to raise the decibel count of the signals to Eagleton by dropping hints to the press. He thought that might be helpful.

"Would it make any sense if I had a talk with Jules Witcover?" he asked. Witcover, political writer for the Los Angeles *Times,* was a friend and a man of discretion. I said I thought that made good sense.

McGovern started to smile. He said: "I'll tell you why I'd like it to be Jules. A year or so ago when he was working on his book about Agnew he came to see me a couple of times to talk about the vice presidency. He was talking to me more as a historian than anything else. Anyway, I remember telling him that if, by some wild chance, I ever got the presidential nomination I would damned well avoid the messy way Vice Presidents had been picked in the past. I think Jules will remember that. I'll get hold of him and ask him up for a drink. If he wants to write something not for attribution fine, if not . . ." He let the sentence trail off. I assured him that Witcover would write something.

"It's our last night here, too," he added. "I was thinking we might have dinner at the lodge. What would you think if you were to pass the word about it to some of the fellows? I could just walk around and visit with some of them."

I didn't pick any favorites; I simply let three or four of them know and figured they'd pass the word on to whomever. A fairly sizable group showed up. David Schumacher was there with his wife and children who'd joined him for what had been thought a holiday. Theirs was the first table at which McGovern sat down as he began his table hopping. After that he ambled over to a group which included *Time's* Dean Fischer, *Newsweek's* Dick Stout, Bob Boyd and one or two others.

Doug Kneeland of the New York *Times,* a shaggy-haired, witty but dead-serious reporter—and a gentleman—was sitting with Dutton, Polly Hackett, Carol Friedenberg and me. He was in great anxiety. Courtesy seemed to require that he remain with us. But word was already out that McGovern had given Witcover a private audience and, there, only feet away, was the candidate apparently telling the others anything they wanted to know. Kneeland couldn't stand it for long. Suddenly he was up and away to the other table like something shot from a gun. He didn't really miss anything and his story the next day sent our signal out loud and clear:

"Tonight's casual conversations with newsmen by Senator McGovern, which seemed to have been carefully arranged by aides who dropped hints to a number of reporters that it might be wise to be on hand at the lodge for dinner, were interpreted by most of those present as designed to send a message to Mr. Eagleton that he might be a detriment to the ticket. . . ."

Noting, of course, that "only two days ago," McGovern had been behind Eagleton a thousand per cent, Kneeland continued: "Senator McGovern said there were three things he had to take into consideration in the Eagleton matter:

"First, the soundness of Mr. Eagleton's health; second, the effect that his candidacy would have on the outcome of the election in the fall; and third, whether the Missouri senator should have told him about his health record when asked before his nomination whether he had any problems in his past that might be a detriment to the ticket. . . .

"Senator McGovern also suggested in tonight's conversation that he had hesitated to appear to make a snap judgment on the Eagleton matter because he had not wanted to offend the many people in the nation who had family members who had suffered from mental illness.

"He said he thought there was a great deal of sympathy in the country these days for those who had suffered such problems.

"However, he said that even if a poll showed that 99 per cent of the people favored Mr. Eagleton and only 1 per cent were opposed to his continued candidacy, that might be enough to tip the scales in a tight election. In noting this he recalled the close margins of victory for John F. Kennedy in 1960 and Richard M. Nixon in 1968. . . ."

This story, which varied little from paper to paper and wire service to wire service, was thus prominent in every Saturday newspaper. It was hardly possible that Eagleton did not read it in one form or another, but if he did he gave no sign that the message had gotten through. If anything, he began to raise the ante, using words like "irrevocable" to describe his determination to stay on the ticket.

Late Saturday night, after McGovern had spoken to South Dakota's Democrats at Aberdeen, we flew back to Washington. The next morning McGovern enlisted the help of Jean Westwood and on his instructions she—seconded by National Vice Chairman Basil Paterson—said on "Meet the Press" that it would be "the noble thing" if Eagleton were to step down.

Somewhat earlier, meanwhile, Eagleton had appeared so adamant on "Face the Nation" that, as Johnny Apple wrote in the New York *Times,* "He seemed almost to be challenging Mr. McGovern to live up to the pledges he had made. The Missourian's stance was so firm . . . that some politicians foresaw the possibility of a standoff, with Senator Eagleton unwilling to accede even to a direct request from Senator McGovern to withdraw."

It all came to a head finally on Monday at a meeting of the two men in the Marble Room of the Capitol. With them through virtually all of the meeting was Senator Nelson, a friend to both and possibly the man most responsible for Eagleton's selection in the first place. Nelson was present, McGovern told me subsequently, on the advice of a psychiatrist, whom he didn't name, but who had warned that failure to have a third person present risked the creation of an adversary setting in which Eagleton's resistance would be heightened.

Even then it took almost two hours of persuasion and argument before Eagleton gave in; and when he did he made it a condition of the resignation that he write McGovern's statement as well as his own for the news conference to follow. Much later on in the campaign McGovern told me that Eagleton "made the writing of my statement—emphasizing that his health was not a problem—a condition of his stepping down. Otherwise, he said that he'd stay on the ticket and fight me right through November seventh."

When I arrived at McGovern's Senate office late that afternoon I found him sitting behind his desk waiting for the draft
he'd already prepared in the company of Eagleton to come back
down from the latter's office with its final revisions. It was a
small price to pay, probably, and the situation was not without
comic aspects; but it was frightening as well. In any case, the
announcement read a while later by McGovern to a hushed
audience in the packed Caucus Room of the old Senate Office
Building went as follows:

"Senator Eagleton and I have met to discuss his vice-
presidential candidacy. I have consistently supported Senator
Eagleton. He is a talented United States senator whose ability
will make him a prominent figure in American politics for many,
many years.

"I am fully satisfied that his health is excellent. I base that
conclusion upon my conversations with his doctors and my close
personal and political association with him.

"In the joint decision we have reached health was not a factor.

"But the public debate over Senator Eagleton's past medical
history continues to divert attention from the great national issues that need to be discussed. I have referred to the growing
pressures to ask for Senator Eagleton's withdrawal. We have
also seen growing vocal support *for* his candidacy.

"Senator Eagleton and I agree that the paramount needs of
the Democratic Party and the nation in 1972 are unity and a
full discussion of the real issues. Continued debate between those
who oppose his candidacy and those who favor it will serve to
further divide the party and the nation. Therefore, we have
jointly agreed that the best course is for Senator Eagleton to
step aside.

"I wish nothing but the best for Senator Eagleton and his
family. He is and will remain my good friend. Further, he has

generously agreed to campaign for the Democratic ticket this fall. I can assure you I welcome his strong support."

The phrase *health was not a factor* is of interest because of McGovern telling me a little later how much Eagleton wanted it stressed. "The way he had written it," McGovern said, "it read: 'health was not—I repeat not a factor.' I said to him, 'Tom, isn't that a little defensive? Isn't it enough just to say once that it wasn't a factor?' He agreed then that we should take it out."

Left to his own I daresay McGovern might have written a more convincing statement. Even so Eagleton served him better than himself—with a response that was almost sophomoric:

"As Senator McGovern has stated, he and I are jointly in agreement that I should withdraw as the Democratic candidate for Vice President. Needless to say, this was not an easy decision for Senator McGovern or me. Literally thousands and thousands of people have phoned, telegrammed or written to me and Senator McGovern urging me to press on.

"But ladies and gentlemen, I will not divide the Democratic Party which already has too many divisions. Therefore, I am writing to the chairman of the Democratic Party withdrawing my candidacy. My personal feelings are secondary to the necessity to unify the Democratic Party and elect George McGovern President of the United States. My conscience is clear. My spirits are high.

"This is definitely NOT my last press conference and Tom Eagleton is going to be around for a long, long time. I'm for George McGovern and I'm going to continue working to see him elected President of the United States."

It was over at last. Now, as fate would have it, poor McGovern was off on the rounds again looking as fruitlessly for a running mate as he had before he reaped the bitter harvest of the strange Mr. Eagleton's blind ambition.

Kennedy, Ribicoff, Humphrey and—after thinking it over from Thursday to Saturday—Muskie. It was a familiar litany of negatives. Finally McGovern turned to Sargent Shriver. The following Tuesday a special meeting of the National Committee formally nominated the former Peace Corps director and husband of Eunice Kennedy. It was two weeks to the day since the Eagleton press conference in the Black Hills, two weeks in which George McGovern had been transformed in the public mind from a possibly too radical, possibly too righteous, but interesting new political leader, who would be worth watching, into an undoubted bumbler and probable liar. Once so bright and sassy, so full of hope and life, ours was now a deeply—perhaps mortally—wounded enterprise.

Jim Naughton, writing in the August 6 New York *Times* "Week in Review" reflected the view of virtually all the media. What appeared to matter most, he wrote, was not that McGovern had dropped Eagleton but that "He had gone about the whole affair in such a way as to cast doubt on his ability or willingness to meet his own test of public performance. 'Truth is a habit of integrity,' he said in his acceptance speech at Miami Beach . . . [so] critics asked whether he could now expect ready acceptance of a pledge of, say, 'one thousand per cent,' support for Israel or tax reform. And whether his performance raised questions as to how he would go about making tough presidential decisions. The most Senator McGovern would say was that he had 'no alternative under the circumstances,' but to defend Mr. Eagleton initially and to back off when all the facts and the reactions were in. Those who might question his credibility just 'don't know much about the facts,' he said.

"Indeed the best available explanation for Mr. McGovern's handling of the Eagleton affair came from one of the candidate's associates whose defense 'He doesn't like to hurt people' was based more on an assessment of Mr. McGovern's character than on intimacy with the facts. But the assessment, some observers were quick to point out, might suggest either compassion, a political plus or timidity, a questionable leadership trait."

It was a tough appraisal but, given the information available to the press, not an unfair one. It became unfair only if one accepted the view that McGovern could not and would not divulge the facts which might have spared him such judgments. One has to believe, as I do, that McGovern risked the loss of his chances for the presidency in order to save the career and possibly the life of the man who had wronged him.

I am back with my view of McGovern as a Tolstoyan idealist sprung from simple and deep religious origins—as a missionary but still a profoundly private and Fundamentalist figure who saw politics and public service as means rather than ends, as, at bottom, expressions of the moral passion and the religious experience, and activities ultimately accountable to a plain, unyielding Christian conscience.

Let me quote at some length from a speech he made early in October at Wheaton College, in Illinois, a rather strict school affiliated with the Methodist Church. I think it is one of the most revealing of his speeches and I cannot but think that he must have had himself and Senator Eagleton in mind as he wrote it:

"I have no intention of giving you a political speech. I suspect, in fact, that you are far less interested in my politics per se than in how my religious convictions have shaped my view of America's difficulties and our destiny. My father attended Houghton College in New York State and was ordained as a minister in the Wesleyan Methodist Church, an evangelical, Fundamentalist faith. In our family there was no drinking, smoking, dancing or cardplaying. So you can see why I feel so much at home here at Wheaton. In all candor, I later came to regard that kind of strict legalism as somewhat beside the point, and not a necessary or totally positive part of a Christian upbringing. But that was not the whole picture.

"In our home the family gathered every morning to read Scripture. In fact, I remember how my father taught me to read aloud from the Bible before I was old enough to go to school. We spent all Sunday at church, at Sunday school, listening to my father's sermons, followed by a children's worship service and then a prayer meeting. It is from these experiences that I have some of the most vivid and vital memories of my past. Daily teaching from the Scripture, and a constant immersion in faith, made an indelible imprint on me.

"I went through a period of mild rebellion against some of the rigidity of my early years; but, then, after my service in World War II as a bomber pilot, a pattern started to unfold in my life. I felt called into the work of serving others. At first, I thought my vocation was the ministry and I enrolled in a seminary. During that year I served as a student pastor for a church in Diamond Lake, Illinois, north of Chicago. It was a year that left me with fresh insights about the demands of religious leadership, and a time when I grew in many ways. I thought about my vocation for I knew, as my mother told me, that a man should not go into the ministry unless he was certain God was calling him there.

"After a period of deep reflection I decided I should become a teacher. Yet, even in my teaching at Dakota Wesleyan University I still felt that there was something else for me to do—and that is what finally led me into politics. The Bible teaches that government is to serve men, not that men are the servants of government. When the New Testament speaks of 'honoring those in authority,' for instance, it points out that power is ordained by God for the purpose of doing good for the people. In this light I have come to understand the responsibility of political office, and the opportunities for service which it holds. But we must also recognize a central fact: All that we seek in society will not come solely from government. The greatest challenges of our age defy purely political answers. . . .

"For our deepest problems are within us—not as an entire people—but as individual persons. So Christians have a responsibility to speak to the questions of the spirit which ultimately determine the state of the material world. . . . Some Christians believe that we are condemned to live with man's inhumanity to man—with poverty, war and injustice—and that we cannot end these evils because they are inevitable. But I have not found that view in the Bible.

"Changed men can change society, and the words of the Scripture clearly assign to us the ministry and mission of change.

"While we know that the Kingdom of God will not come from a political party's platform, we also know that if someone is hungry, we should give him food; if he is thirsty, we should give him drink; if he is a stranger, we should take him in; if he is naked, we should clothe him; if he is sick we should care for him; and if he is in prison, we should visit him: 'For inasmuch as you have done unto the least of these my brethren, you have done it unto Me.'

"That is what the Scripture says. None of us can be content until all of us are made whole. . . .

"We must have a fundamental stirring of our moral and spiritual values if we are to reclaim our true destiny. . . . We must look into our souls to find the way out of the crisis of our society. As was so often true for the people of God in biblical days, we must heed the words of the prophets. The New Testament tells us: 'Be not conformed to this world, but be ye transformed by the renewing of your mind.' Some Christians have misused this passage as a pretext for isolation from the existence around us. But the point is that our thinking, our perspectives and our actions should not be molded by the world's view, and its tides of opinion; rather, they are to be rooted in God's vision. And we must carry the good news of that vision into the world. . . .

"The President can be the great moral leader of the nation. He can ask us to face issues, not merely from a political standpoint but in our conscience and our souls. By his words and deeds the President must witness to the values that should endure among our people. . . .

"Power cannot be his only purpose. There is no virtue in simply 'being President.' A candidate should seek the presidency to serve the nation and call it to a higher purpose. This is the meaning of true leadership. It is not expressed in power, fame and honor, but in the washing of dusty feet. We know that 'he who saves his life shall lose it.' And he who seeks the presidency should not be willing to pay any price. He must do so in allegiance to his principles and his faith: 'For what shall it profit a man if he shall gain the whole world and lose his own soul?' . . .

"So what then do we do? What is your responsibility and what is mine? Micah asked and answered the same question in a verse I have remembered since my childhood and turned back to ever since: 'What doth the Lord require of thee, but to do justly, and to love mercy, and to walk humbly with thy God.'"

I have no illusions about George McGovern. I have seen him with feet of clay that reached to his knees. But I submit that the man who wrote those words in the midst of a presidential campaign for the students of Wheaton College, who was "witness to the values that should endure," who believed that the meaning of true leadership was "not expressed in power, fame and honor, but in the washing of dusty feet," who cautioned that he who seeks the presidency "should not be willing to pay any price," but must do so "in allegiance to his principles and faith,"—I submit that this man sacrificed the high ambition of his own life so as not to destroy the life of another man. For: "He who saves his life shall lose it," and: "What shall it profit a man if he shall gain the whole world and lose his own soul?"

I've no wish to canonize McGovern, or even beatify him, in this. One must remember what a cocky character he is, with a pride more Greek than Methodist and a lucky gambler's taste for the long shot. I have little doubt but that he thought he could carry it off and win the White House anyway.

Let me move the narrative from the sublime to the ridiculous now, and a report on the impact of my having identified Gordon Weil as one of the staff people involved in checking on the rumors about Eagleton's health at the convention. When I came into my office—our Washington headquarters having moved during our Black Hills sojourn to a dumpy building on K Street which had formerly housed the Muskie movement—on the morning of the day of the McGovern-Eagleton meeting, I was told by a nervous receptionist that Mr. Weil had been in to see me. Chris Turpin was at her desk in the inner office which she and I shared. She too was apprehensive.

"Gordon's on the warpath, I'm afraid," she said. "He wants to be notified the minute you come in." I told her to go ahead and notify him and asked if she knew what was bothering him. She didn't. I, making no connection with the Eagleton business, sat down at my desk and awaited the unknown.

In minutes he strode in, eyes narrowed, pipe in a grim mouth, fist clenched around the bowl of the pipe. I greeted him and received a quick nod in response. "Would you mind?" he said to

Chris Turpin and held the door for her as she, not minding at all, hastened from the room.

He closed the door behind her; then he closed the door which led into an adjoining room. That done he began to pace with long and heavy steps up and down in front of my desk. At length he wrenched the pipe from his mouth as though it were the pin of a hand grenade and, lifting it high in the air, said: "You! You! You have ruined my life!"

"Oh, Gordon, come on," I said.

"You have destroyed me." He kept pacing. "I'll never be able to get another job after this. My reputation, which is all I have, is literally in ruins. Thanks to you."

At last I understood. I said: "Gordon, that's not true. . . ."

He raised the pipe hand again to stop me. He left off pacing and planted himself, legs apart, in front of the desk. "You singled me out," he said. "Out of all of us in that room, you singled me out. Now, I want to know only one thing from you: Did you consult with the senator before you did it? Was it done with his approval? If that is the case . . ."

"No, I didn't," I said. "I never had a chance to. And I didn't single you out. I was asked specifically if you . . ."

"No other name was mentioned. Only mine."

"That's true, but Jesus Christ, Gordon, you have to realize what it was like . . ." His hand stopped me again.

"You had no right. You had no right in the absence of Mc-Govern's approval to do that to me. Oh, I can understand your trying to protect the candidate at the expense of staff. But why me? Why only me?"

"Gordon, you've got to understand. Questions were coming at me like missiles. Of course I had to think of McGovern first. He's the one who's running for President. But I argued that our investigation was adequate, that we had no apologies for it. I

209

didn't try to fix blame on anybody including you, and if it looked that way I'm sorry."

He started pacing again but in a calmer way. I began—my initial amusement at the operatic character of the scene fading—to sympathize with him.

"Time was the worst," he said. "Did you see what they did to me?"

I said I had, even though I hadn't. I was thinking back to some time in June when Weil had abruptly, and at a late hour, canceled a McGovern lunch date with the editors of *Time* in New York. A deeply offended Dean Fischer had called me and said: "What's wrong with that fellow? He was almost gleeful about it." I didn't think it unlikely that somebody with a memory at *Time* had tasted revenge. As we sow, so shall we reap.

"Would it help, Gordon," I asked, "if I were to draft a letter to *Time* for McGovern's signature, saying you were ill used in their story?"

"Yes, frankly it would," he said. I said I'd get right at it and repeated that I was sorry.

"You know whose fault it really is, don't you?" he asked. I said I didn't. The hand and the pipe shot toward the ceiling again and, in a voice that rose in volume, he said: "McGovern! McGovern! That man is the most selfish son of a bitch I've ever known."

When he was gone and Chris Turpin returned to see if I was alive—"You could hear him clear down the hall," she said—I reflected on the oddities of my sentiments toward him. I had become fond of him in a way, although admittedly it was a fondness which increased with the distance between us. There was something gutsy about him in his continuing battles with the unappreciative and unmalleable world around him.

I suspected he was probably right to hate McGovern. Mc-

Govern seemed to value him highly at some moments but he also frequently treated him like a servant. I supposed the thing that had finally gotten through to me about Weil was that he concealed so little of himself. His virtues and faults, strengths and weaknesses, were there for all to see; and while he lacked many of the qualities which attract me to people, authenticity was not one of them.

CHAPTER *11*

As a running news story we were no longer McGovern, presidential nominee; we were McGovern-in-trouble. One could imagine managing editors everywhere sitting down with their colleagues to make up the front page and saying: "What went wrong today? What's he done now?" Hard news is a creature without emotion or bias, but once one is labeled and locked into it there is no escaping. Had things gone the other way, had Eagleton never seen the inside of a hospital but been the attractive young politician he appeared to be, the story would have been entirely different. News leads would have dealt with McGovern, the party unifier, as he went about making peace with Richard Daley, calling on Lyndon Johnson, bringing Larry O'Brien into the campaign, wooing George Wallace and George Meany, embracing old-line leaders like Meade Esposito of Brooklyn, announcing that he'd be joined on the campaign trail by Hubert Humphrey, Ted Kennedy, Ed Muskie, Eugene McCarthy. Positive elements in the campaign would have been more newsworthy: the new-voter registration effort, the direct-mail fund-raising operation, the joining together of most of the big unions in a McGovern committee independent of Meany. The Restons, Reasoners, Broders and Brinkleys might have commented on how McGovern was clearly moving to the center as he modified his economic views and how this was the traditional way of presidential candidates who mean business and know what they're about.

The journalistic *Weltanschauung* would have been hospitable
to possibilities. Nixon, it hardly needed saying, was in a strong
position as an incumbent and he had played cleverly on the
meaner instincts of the people. But he was not a specially popu-
lar President; he had not ended the war he was committed to
end within his term; the cost of living was skyrocketing; crime
was up 30 per cent; unemployment was high; scandals—as in the
ITT and Watergate cases—were juicy; the budget was running
deficits of thirty billion dollars a year; the nation was experienc-
ing a balance-of-trade deficit for the first time in the twentieth
century. One could envision a Reston writing: "It could be; it
wasn't likely but it could be that we were in for a horse race."

But, alas, the constructive labors of McGovern, the tangible
accomplishments—and there were many—had no place in the
running story of McGovern-in-trouble. And, alas again, there
were several developments which did.

A week and a day after the nomination of Sargent Shriver
when, one could hope, things had no way to go but up, we were
in Springfield, Illinois, at the St. Nicholas Hotel.

It was late in the morning. I was in my room preparing to go
with McGovern to a Democratic rally at the State Fairgrounds
when one of the reporters called from the press room downstairs
to say that United Press International had a story out of Paris
about Pierre Salinger having met secretly there with the North
Vietnamese. Salinger had, according to the report, conveyed a
message from McGovern urging them not to let American politics interfere with efforts toward a peace agreement; if they
could, in other words, negotiate an accord with Nixon they
shouldn't wait around hoping for a better deal out of a Mc-
Govern administration. I jotted down the bare bones of the story
and went across the hall to McGovern's suite to ask him about it.
I knew that Salinger had gone to Paris after the convention,

presumably on personal business, but I knew nothing about an assignment to see the North Vietnamese.

I knew it was a sticky story. We have statutes forbidding private citizens—including presidential candidates—from trying to conduct the nation's foreign policy. But beyond that the story was hardly a hurtful one, showing as it did that McGovern was willing to put peace above his own political ambition.

So I was surprised at his reaction when I told him about it. He was in front of a mirror in his shirtsleeves and starting to put on a tie. "There's no truth to that," he said irritably as he yanked the necktie into position. I didn't believe him. I said: "Well, we better think what to say about it. You're going to be asked."

"I'll say there's no truth to it," he said. "I never told Pierre to tell them to go ahead and make a deal with Nixon. I never told him to tell them anything."

"Let me get Dutton and Mankiewicz in here," I said, thinking that the best device to use in such circumstances was the old one of not wanting to comment on a story you haven't seen yourself. It is a dodge which gives one time to think, if nothing more. As I started out of the room, I said: "Hold on a minute, will you? Let's see what they think."

He grumbled something in reply, which I took to be yes. I hurried into the room next door where Dutton was pecking away at his typewriter and Mankiewicz, as usual, was on the phone. I gestured for him to get off. When he did I told them about the story. They were slightly unnerved. Mankiewicz said that all McGovern had asked of Salinger was to inquire about the possibility of more and bigger releases of prisoners of war.

"He promised the POW wives he'd try to do something about that at Miami Beach," Mankiewicz added.

"Pierre must have leaked the story himself," said Dutton. I suggested that perhaps we should say there was some substance

215

to the story but . . . "No, no," they said in one voice and proceeded to tell me about the Logan Act's prohibitions on private foreign-policy dealings.

"Well, whatever," I said, "he's going to have to say something. Let's talk to him before the reporters get at him." I led the way as we came out into the corridor, getting there just in time to see McGovern and two of the Secret Service agents step into the elevator. "Oh, no," I said and started to run. Then the door closed and he was gone. The press swarmed over him in the lobby as he came out of the elevator and he testily denied having asked Salinger to convey any messages to the North Vietnamese. He was already in his car by the time I got to the lobby and I had to run to get aboard one of the cars.

We drove to the fairgrounds. It was so hot there that heat waves shimmered above the heads of the crowd. McGovern made a speech which was wisely short but even then he looked as if he might faint from the heat. As he came down out of the bandstand I moved ahead thinking I'd get him a lemonade at a stand down near the cars. While I was doing that, damned if the reporters didn't come at him again and damned if this time he didn't declare that he had given Salinger "no instructions whatsoever."

Back at the hotel the four of us finally sat down for a rational discussion. It was evident that he couldn't go on denying what was fundamentally true so eventually we got out a statement, after talking with Salinger who'd just flown into New York from Paris, saying that Salinger's only mission had been to make an appeal for prisoner releases and that he had volunteered on his own—as restatement of a known McGovern public position—the peace-above-politics message.

In hours, McGovern-in-trouble was again in the news and the credibility strain was up at the top of every story: "McGovern denied today . . . later reversed himself in a statement saying . . ." McGovern argued that he was getting a bad shake in this, that the question first put to him had been worded in such a way that he thought the story had Salinger telling the North Vietnamese they could get a better peace agreement out of Nixon than McGovern. Well, maybe. But it was a niggling, lawyer's argument and I don't think anybody believed it. I didn't.

I could sympathize with him. The air conditioning in the old St. Nicholas left much to be desired; he was grouchy after a hot, sleepless night. His immediate thought when I brought him the news had obviously been that Salinger had deliberately leaked the story and that made him angry. But, granting all that, it was an asinine performance and he had one-man-banded himself into another pretty pickle. I must add I didn't feel free of blame myself. I should have, at the least, urged him to use the no-comment-till-I've-seen-it technique before I ran off to get Dutton and Mankiewicz. Knowing my man, I should not have assumed that he would wait for staff to come and advise him what to do.

Nor did I think he was wrong to infer, as had the rest of us, that Salinger had dropped the story for purposes of self-gratification—possibly even for a little unconscious revenge. Salinger had asked to be national chairman at some point as the primaries wound down and the nomination loomed on the horizon. McGovern, so Salinger had thought, appeared to regard that as a reasonable request. I daresay McGovern didn't. My hunch was that Salinger got one of those Chinese answers on the order of "That's a good idea, Pierre," which any sensible McGovern observer would translate to: "No, Pierre, and I think you're out of order to ask." The fact was that McGovern had committed himself to the women in general and to Jean Westwood in particular, and she was his first choice to succeed O'Brien.

Mrs. Westwood had, in due course, gotten the nod from Mc
Govern, and Salinger—as a consolation prize—had been chosen
for vice chairman. However, that blew up in everybody's face
when the National Committee met on the last day of the convention. Presumably the committee would give the nominee what
he wanted. But Joe Crangle, the wily little New York State
chairman, seeing a weak spot, had proposed Basil Paterson, a
distinguished black lawyer and former state legislator from New
York City for the vice chairmanship. Who was McGovern to
scorn the idea of a Negro vice chairman? He stood up to say
that either Salinger or Paterson would be fine with him. Salinger,
smelling not only treachery but public humiliation, was on his
feet a second later to withdraw in Paterson's favor. Thus, out
of all his labors on McGovern's behalf—and they had been considerable in terms of traveling, raising money, making speeches
—Salinger wound up with nothing but disappointment and, one
could suspect, disillusionment.

I like Salinger, whom I've known off and on for years. I think
he is extremely able and an honorable man. But he is something
of a celebrity—a star, if you will, which has faded a little as the
memory of the Kennedy Camelot has faded. I think he wanted
to get back into the limelight, to have a place and title from
which to command attention from the press and public. There
was nothing wrong there and certainly he wasn't alone in it
among the major McGovern lieutenants. Gary Hart was never
loath to see his name in the headlines or his face on the tube,
and one might in all kindness say of Mankiewicz, as Murray
Kempton once wrote of Bernard Baruch, that he could hear the
film moving in a camera at a distance of up to three city blocks.
This too should be said, that if Salinger had leaked the story—
and it was impossible to see why either the North Vietnamese
or our State Department types would have done so—it was a

good story for McGovern. It told the world that he was concerned for our POWs and that he'd like to see peace come quickly no matter what its effect on his election chances. What was wrong with that? Salinger must have been as astonished as anyone when McGovern turned the thing into a fiasco.

We picked ourselves up and pressed on. Things went well enough for a couple of weeks when suddenly another old pro did his bit for disaster. Larry O'Brien, nursing new wounds to his vanity as the result of seeing Shriver picked over himself in the vice-presidential selection, let it be known to political writers that if the campaign didn't straighten itself into some recognizable organization by Labor Day he would quit.

That was a lively stimulant to the McGovern-in-trouble story, even though O'Brien quickly professed that he had no intention of resigning. A week after that, Representative Frank Thompson of New Jersey, who was heading the voter registration drive, resigned in a huff. This was after a losing battle with Hart who had siphoned money away from registration into the operations of the campaign. Headlines again.

Nor was the end yet in sight. On the same day that O'Brien dropped his ultimatum, Hart circulated a memo at headquarters announcing that Gordon Weil was now the executive director of the campaign and as such would be clearance officer for any and all written material coming out of headquarters. This was unsettling news for most division chiefs and specially for Ted Van Dyk. Van Dyk, a good but haughty man, was grossly offended that speeches and papers coming from his issues-and-research section should require the imprimatur of Weil. The following day—a Saturday—Van Dyk reached me in my room at the Jefferson as I was washing my socks and said he was quitting. If the press asked me about him I should simply say that he had left because of the demands of his business.

"The truth is," he said, "I'm fed up. It's a second-rate, amateur operation and that memo was the last straw." Which memo? I asked, there having been two or three odd ones in recent days. "The Gordon one," he said and hung up while I was still urging him to reconsider. It happened that he did reconsider as the result of a call which I suggested McGovern make to him, and, to my best knowledge, his was the only resignation, real or aborted, which didn't make the papers. Even the usually serene Mankiewicz was nettled by the Weil development. I was getting out a couple of press releases the day the memo appeared and Mankiewicz asked teasingly if I'd cleared them with Weil. I said no. He nodded approval. "Shall we throw down the gauntlet?" he asked rhetorically.

As might have been predicted, Weil managed to get locked in combat with someone who knew how to fight back. I didn't know the man, and don't remember his name, but he was a newcomer from the world of agriculture who knew McGovern well enough personally to call him up and get a Weil decision overruled. With that, Weil resigned and McGovern-in-trouble had a fresh news lead.

Reporters asked me about it as we were flying somewhere or other and I tried to minimize it. I said: "Gordon's just having a little tantrum. He'll be back tomorrow."

In point of fact he was back at work the next day after a long late-night phone conversation with McGovern. ("Who let Gordon get through to him?" Mankiewicz wanted to know.) And he was, I was duly informed, sore at me for my "tantrum" remark.

That, so far as I can recall, was the end of the resignations season. But it too had made its mark. A resentful McGovern said: "Why's the press making so much out of these petty things? It's ordinary shakedown stuff you might get at the start of any campaign. What's it amount to compared to Nixon's campaign? We haven't had a John Mitchell quit as head of our campaign. We haven't had his wife telling about security men ripping her phone out and sticking hypodermics in her ass. We haven't had our people arrested in the dead of night with their rubber gloves on burglarizing and bugging the Committee to Re-elect the President." He was right, of course, but in the world of hard news there was no running story called Nixon-in-trouble. Quite the opposite. Nixon was so little in trouble that negative Nixon stories were as reduced in terms of news value as positive McGovern stories. This was a hard concept to get across to McGovern, however, as he grew increasingly paranoid about the press.

I felt sorry for him. At some point in the midst of all the resignations he and I were riding into the NASA space center at Houston and he said: "You know I'm beginning to feel like an astronaut in space would feel if all these people here"—and he made a sweeping gesture toward the big complex of buildings— "were to get up and walk off their jobs. Here I am knocking my brains out and those bastards in Washington can't think of anything but themselves."

By and large, however, he remained amazingly unperturbed through it all. He had—and this was part of the Phineas Finn I saw in him—a blissful faith in life's ultimate kindness and his own ultimate good luck. I was reminded at times of the old story about the father with two sons, one an optimist and one a pessimist, who decided to put them to a test at Christmas. He set a gleaming fire engine under the tree for the pessimist and a box of horse manure for the optimist. When he came downstairs Christmas morning he found the pessimist sitting morosely beside the fire engine expressing fears that the wheels wouldn't stay on. Meanwhile, from out in the yard he heard whistling and singing. He went out to discover the other child searching the grounds and explaining that "with all the shit there must be a pony."

I am no mean optimist myself and I confess that I was not convinced all was lost. Nixon, no matter what his posturings, was an unappetizing piece of work; the American people were a more perceptive people than politicians gave them credit for; Election Day was still two months off. Anything could happen. I remembered Bill Dougherty's "McGovern Law." I knew that the image of McGovern had suffered terribly from the Eagleton affair all the way through to the resignation of Gordon Weil. I knew that the public McGovern which had emerged as a result was in fact a caricature of the real McGovern. I thought that could be corrected. I repeatedly told the newsmen that while the cause of McGovern-the-caricature was undoubtedly lost, the cause of the real McGovern—once he came to be known—might yet flourish. The response I got to this was mostly sad looks and reluctantly shaken heads, but I still held to the view and peddled it with vigor. One night talking to Cynthia from some far-off place she asked: "How are you really?" I said: "Heads up and spirits sinking." But that was not what I meant to say. I meant to say: "Heads up and spirits rising." So it seemed that somewhere in the subconscious a possibility had been embraced which the conscious mind yet spurned.

We were off on the campaign proper on the eve of Labor Day with a brief evening swing into the South to call on the Southern Governors Conference at Hilton Head, South Carolina. For this effort we were rewarded with nothing more than old-fashioned Dixie courtesy. We headed then for Ohio and the formal campaign opening next morning. Soon the creation of a small campaign world was underway. It was, for all our difficulties, a rather classy and cheerful world.

The heart of it, of course, was the McGovern compartment in the front section of the first of the two United Airlines 727s we had chartered. The plane was called *Dakota Queen II* after the B-24 bomber McGovern had captained in World War II. The compartment was pleasant and commodious with a large, almost regal easy chair covered in a dark red material, which suggested the royal purple. It would be nice to say that McGovern looked at home in the thing but he never seemed to—his manner about the whole setup always being a little like that of a man in a rented tuxedo. In front of the chair was a sizable table desk, on the other side of which was a banquette for two, covered in a blue-green material. It was usually occupied by Eleanor McGovern or Mankiewicz, or both. Along the opposite wall ran an oversized studio couch, of the same color as the candidate's chair.

It was easily converted into a bed and curtains could be drawn to shut off light and noise. Directly to the front, toward the cockpit, was a galley and a washroom and two seats which were reserved for the Secret Service—generally Larry Short and George Hollendersky, the chief and deputy chief, respectively, of the detail.

In the main section of the plane the first six or so rows of seats were for staff and distinguished transients—except for the two front seats on the left side directly facing the thin wall of the McGovern compartment. These too were for the Secret Service. The other pair of front seats belonged to Jeff Smith and me. Smith, who had worked for McGovern in a variety of roles since 1968, was an anomaly among the essentially rube types who had served the candidate longest. In his late twenties, he was conspicuously eastern seaboard and upper drawer. Thin and elegantly built, he seemed a throwback to another era—the era of speakeasies, straw boaters and green tennis afternoons in Southampton. His sleek dark hair was combed straight back and

223

close to his head so that in his well-cut but far from modish suits he looked startlingly like sketches of the young men who tangoed with flappers on the sheet music covers of long ago.

Smith was at once idealistic, snobbish and droll, and he was devoted to McGovern. This was a good and necessary thing because he had moved into the job of personal aide—a euphemism for valet—once performed by Weil. His mimicry of McGovern's speech and occasionally quaint speech mannerisms was uncanny:

"Je-e-ff, on yesterday I couldn't find my breakfast cereal. Do you know what might have happened to it, Je-e-ff?"

"Yes, Senator. It was in the refrigerator next to your milk where you asked me to put it."

"Ohhhh! Ohhhh, yes! Was that what that was next to the milk, Je-e-ff? I wondered."

"Yes, Senator. Would you like me to put it somewhere else on tomorrow, Senator?"

"No, thanks, Je-e-ff. On tomorrow it'll be better if it's where it was on yesterday. Don't you think, Je-e-ff?"

Behind Smith and me were Dutton and usually Yancey Martin. Behind them were the writers John Holum and either Bob Shrum or Sandy Berger—all pleasant and talented fellows. Holum, also in his late twenties, was the senior writer both in terms of service and hierarchy. Another South Dakotan, he had been with McGovern for eight or more years and, while I found him rather young now and then in guarding his jurisdiction, he was highly and warmly regarded by the candidate.

He also came closer than anybody to drafting speeches which McGovern would use without substantially rewriting them. Other regulars were McGovern's secretary Pat Donovan and her assistant Nancy Howard; Stan Tretick, the eccentric and immensely likable photographer. Dutton called him "Ten-watt Tretick," because of his habit of preparing McGovern's suite for the advent of other photographers by removing his own powerful light bulbs from the hotel lamps and putting back the hotel's weak ones.

When Eleanor McGovern was with us and not campaigning on her own—a role she played less and less as time went on—her aides and friends Mary Hoyt and Margot Hahn were also aboard. They were charming ladies of, one of my years may freely say, a refreshing maturity. At the extreme rear of the plane was a well-equipped office with electric typewriters, mimeographing and other such machines. That was the base for my press crew which now included, in addition to Polly Hackett and Carol Friedenberg, my dear friend from the L. A. *Times* bureau in New York, the beautiful and black Jackie Greenidge. However, at least one of these three was always aboard the second aircraft on any given flight.

That plane—also entirely first class but with no compartments —was called, in keeping with the tradition of campaigns, the Zoo plane. The name stems from the fact that the second plane is always heavily populated with photographers and camera crews, and it is obviously the invention of their natural antagonists, the writers. "Zoo" is a mean word, of course, but there is something faintly wild about people who take pictures for a living.

There were something like thirty-four seats for the press aboard the *Dakota Queen II*. Given first priority for them were those news organizations which covered us all the time. This group included the richer and bigger newspapers and newspaper chains, the two wire services plus Reuters, the weekly newsmagazines, the television networks and several radio news networks. The initial scurrying for seats by these ladies and gentlemen, the staking of claims through crudely printed, faintly threatening signs, reflected the territorial imperative at its most naked. I got

all but one of the organizations which had two reporters assigned to agree to have one or the other of them always fly the
Zoo plane. The exception was the New York *Times,* whose
writers tend to view themselves as above the journalistic herd.
Messrs. Naughton and Kneeland sat like fighting cocks ready
for the pit as I asked them to go along with the idea, and I finally
gave up.

When all the resident members of the club were accommo-
dated there was little room for transients, no matter how distinguished. Etched in my mind still is the image of Joe Kraft, a
friend from Columbia College days, walking angrily toward the
Zoo plane one night and complaining that his secretary had arranged everything with Mankiewicz's office weeks before. It was
a pique only Joe Alsop might have matched and, happily, I was
finally able to find him a seat on the candidate's plane.

Robert Novak provided a memory to be cherished. As I think
I said earlier, I've known and liked Novak and Rowland Evans
for a long time, and I continued to do so even though they were
vicious in their treatment of McGovern. I'm specially fond of
Novak who is an earthy, elemental man. He makes you feel that
if you were drowning he'd try to save you, something I wouldn't
say of Rowley, although he, one could depend on it, would be
properly outraged at the absence of the lifeguard.

In any case Novak joined us for a couple of days the first
week out on the trail and, on the day he did so, there was in
truth no seat available on the *Dakota Queen.* I put him on the
Zoo plane. Throughout the day he offered no complaint about
this profoundly *infra dig* situation. But that evening—in Dallas
I think—as he, Dutton and I were having a drink, he looked at
me with his huge, round, ageless dark eyes and said: "I get it,
Dougherty."

"You get what, Robert?" I asked.

"Never mind," he said, nodding gravely. "I get the message and I'm telling you: from now on no more Mr. Nice Guy."

Gradually, imperceptibly, the *Dakota Queen* and the Zoo plane became a pair of mother ships, jointly forming a world more and more removed from the world over which we flew endlessly to strike three, sometimes four, cities a day.

Home was not connected with the earth's surface. It was not the motel or hotel room into which we staggered late at night to sleep for five hours, to bathe and shave in, while half awake in the early morning, then lift our bags and stagger out of again. Home was our plane; it was the seat in which we ate, worked and napped. Family was not the wife and kids back in Washington or New York but the friends around you, the pleasant young stewardesses, the muscular characters of the Secret Service. It was a life divorced and the conditions of it were fatigue, the constant drumming of the jet sounds on one's ears, the blinding blue of the sky above the clouds, and a steadily heightening sense of detachment from everything, even sometimes from the campaign itself. I talked to Cynthia one night and she, half in tears, told me our friends Oz and Deirdre Elliott were breaking up. That ought to have been very sad news for me. The Elliotts as a pair were one of the stronger, happier pillars of our private world in New York. Yet I couldn't feel anything very much. The Elliotts, New York, even the divine Cynthia were very far away.

I was jolted back into the real world toward the end of the second week out by McGovern himself. We had just flown out of Des Moines. I was telling Jeff Smith about an exchange I'd overheard between McGovern and a man named Broderick, whose farm we'd visited earlier. The two were talking about farm problems and food prices as the cameras recorded them leaning against a fence. Broderick, speaking of the sharply rising food prices, said: "My wife is the mother of eight, Senator, so she's a pretty good consumer," McGovern said. "You could say she's a pretty good producer too."

Smith and I were laughing at this when the candidate called me into his compartment. I started to tell him what I was laughing about but the worried, even stern, expression on his face stopped me. I asked him what was the matter. He got up from his chair and, signaling me to join him, sat down on the sofa across the aisle.

"Dick," he said, "I don't know quite how to put this but some of us think we may have a saboteur in our midst." I asked what he meant. "Well, I know how fond you are of Fred," he said, "but I'm told that he is talking the campaign down all the time to people. I'm told—and I get this from people I trust—he is going around saying that 'the principal problem of the campaign is the candidate himself,' which I don't like much. Maybe I am, but I don't want my people saying so."

"I don't believe it," I said. "Fred is, God knows, candid when he talks to people—reporters, anybody. But he's not out to sabotage this campaign. He works his heart out."

"I know he does," McGovern said. "But still, what do you think we can do? This just can't go on if he keeps talking that way."

I was shaken and tried to do some fast thinking. Dutton, as I'd acknowledged, was nothing if not blunt about his assessment of our chances. But this was nothing new. I remembered back in June a Jim Naughton story in the New York *Times* which quoted Dutton as saying he thought McGovern had "no realistic chance" of defeating Nixon. Obviously a candidate could wish for a senior staff man who was rather more cautious and less bearish in his comments, but that was the way Dutton was and it seemed to me McGovern had always accepted him on those terms.

I had heard Dutton say something about McGovern being

our biggest problem, but he'd said it with an affectionate laugh and I don't think he was alone in saying it. He certainly wasn't alone in thinking it sometimes even among those as loyal as Jeff Smith. But these were the lamentations of people committed to electing McGovern President. They were not the calculated droppings of would-be saboteurs.

I couldn't but suppose that the knives were out for Dutton within our traveling court and at headquarters. Dutton, sophisticated as he was, did not suffer fools or foolishness gladly, and I had seen him on a few occasions give short shrift to some of the younger men.

I had an idea. "How would it be," I asked McGovern, "if I were to call John Douglas and ask him to get hold of Fred and tell him to keep his mouth shut?"

"Yes," he said. "Good idea."

"I can't think this anything but excessive candor," I said. "It sure as hell isn't sabotage."

"All right, Dick," he said, but I thought his reply lacked conviction.

I went back to my seat feeling as concerned and possibly as angry as he was. Somebody had taken a very cheap shot at Dutton and struck target. I was mad at whomever that might have been and mad at McGovern for taking the nonsense at face value. Dutton was a man of substance and accomplishment. He was a successful lawyer, a former Assistant Secretary of State under John Kennedy, a member of the Board of Regents of California. He wasn't, except for occasional expenses, getting a penny out of the campaign. He worked ceaselessly: One of the nearly comic sights on the *Dakota Queen* was Dutton, his small typewriter on his knees, pounding away at the keys with his latest idea for a speech, for a tactic, for a strategic move. He was a fountain of ideas and by and large they were good ideas. Early in June, as a kind of updating of his book *Changing Sources of Power,* published the year before, he had put together an eight-page memo which he called "The Determining Margin of Difference." In it he urged McGovern to invest most of the early money of the campaign in a registration drive for first-time voters. I can't remember the arithmetic of it, but twenty-odd million new voters would be eligible to cast ballots as a result of the reduction of the voting age to eighteen.

McGovern, the apostle of change and heir to the Bob Kennedy-Gene McCarthy constituency of youth, might, Dutton maintained, aim for a goal of eighteen million of these and count on 60 to 70 per cent of them being McGovern voters on Election Day. This new constituency introduced into the election process would drastically reduce the existing Nixon strength as shown in the polls, and to such a degree as to provide a comfortable margin of victory. We would have not just a new ball game, as Dutton put it, but would be playing in a new park. It was an impressive presentation and persuasive enough to have become the core of our strategy. What the fuss over Dutton came down to really, I thought, was that McGovern's mind had been poisoned against the man who had shown him the only way he could hope to win. It also occurred to me that the poisoning might have been going on for some time; and that I had, perhaps, stumbled on the explanation for Dutton's absence from the meeting with the Eagletons that fateful morning at Sylvan Lake.

As soon as I could I put a call through to John Douglas. I have not mentioned Douglas before, but I had found him from the beginning one of the more interesting and attractive of McGovern's friends and early supporters. A big, roughly handsome man, a son of former Senator Paul Douglas, and a former Assistant Attorney General under Robert Kennedy, Douglas has a sense of humor and a cheerfully suspicious mind.

He liked Dutton too and his reaction, like mine, was: "Who's trying to get him, do you think?" I mentioned a name or two, and he came up with a couple more. Dutton had done his painting with a broad brush, it appeared. However, Douglas and I agreed that it didn't matter who the villain was. What mattered was to get word to Dutton to be on his guard and to keep his lip buttoned. I felt it would be awkward and embarrassing if I were to carry that message; Douglas agreed and said he'd get after it, which he promptly did. But from then on things were different and, for me at any rate, the ship a less happy one. Dutton, who was running a campaign against some proposed California constitutional amendment on the side—and for money—began to absent himself for days at a time. He never left altogether, but the chief reason he didn't was to spare the candidate still another news story about the resignation of a top aide. McGovern, I will say, tried eventually to bring Dutton back into the family, so to speak, but neither of them ever felt quite at ease with the other again.

The Dutton decline and occasional disappearances to California left the job of going over schedules with the candidate uncovered. This created an opening for Gordon Weil to return to the road and so he did, somewhat subdued in spirit and manner following his brief career as executive director and chief clearance officer in Washington.

There was still some fight left in him however. On the evening of Thursday, September 21, we flew into Detroit after a long and battering day. When we came off the plane at the airport there was a problem about getting the press buses into the motorcade. I was talking to a young Secret Service agent about it when Weil came up to offer his unneeded counsel. I was in no mood for him. I said: "Gordon, please mind your own fucking business. I'll handle the press."

He exploded. To the astonishment of the agent, and to my

own, he seized me by the shoulders. I thought his strong fingers were going to come through the material of my trench coat. He shook me a couple of times. I was too tired to offer resistance. "I know you have power over the press," he said. "But I have power too. And I will get you, you prick. You have cut me up for the last time."

It was not one of his more prophetic moments. I said: "Oh, buzz off." He released me, turned and strode away. "Jesus Christ," said the agent, who was new to the detail. I said: "Don't worry. It doesn't mean a thing."

As indeed it didn't. It proved to be our last dramatic clash and we went through the remaining weeks in relative harmony. Weil even provided me a good laugh a couple of weeks later as McGovern was being interviewed in Boston by one of those morning-television ladies. A faded-actress type, this one made cuteness her stock in trade.

Her opener, once she had settled—a lumpy figure in a cloud of chiffon—onto a small divan opposite McGovern was: "Now, this may surprise you, Senator, but my first question to you is: What's in your pockets right this minute?"

A sleepy McGovern looked as if he hadn't heard her. "Huh?" he said. "Oh! Yes! Well, I have a handkerchief, and a copy of a speech and a comb." She thought that was very interesting indeed. She went on to say that she realized how exhilarating it must be to run for President—the cheering throngs, the headlines, the pressure, the speeding motorcades, the constant spotlight and all. "But tell me, Senator, are you never lonely in the crowd?"

Some of us were giggling by then, not only at her but at McGovern's discomfiture and bewilderment. Weil was sitting directly behind me and in that rather metallic voice, which he made no attempt to lower, he said: "The next thing she's going to ask is: What's your favorite disease?"

CHAPTER *12*

Spirits began to rise toward the end of September and into October. A Gallup poll at September's end showed a gain of six percentage points in the McGovern column. That made us only twenty-eight points behind. "I've been almost that far back in South Dakota elections," said McGovern soberly.

Distinguished visitors came aboard to campaign with us. Ted Kennedy was the first. He was a superb warmer-upper of crowds —very Irish, beefy, charming and witty, a touch of bartender peeping through the lace-curtain veneer of what my father, who believed divine ordinances forbade the Irish to be rich, used to call Masonic Catholicism. Two Kennedy aides were along, Dick Drayne and Paul Kirk, and they were an amusing pair of smart alecks. Ed Muskie was next. I'd never met him and found him an interesting, humorful, sentimental man—feeling, I thought, a little lousy about having declined the vice-presidential thing when McGovern was on the spot.

Muskie had a story to encourage people to work hard for the cause. It was about a doting but economy-minded father who bought a horse for his daughter and then shopped around for a place to board the animal.

The first farmer he went to wanted twenty dollars a month plus the horse's manure for fertilizer; the next wanted fifteen dollars a month plus the manure; the next asked only five dollars a month. That sounded great but the owner of the horse was puzzled that at such a bargain price the fellow didn't insist on the manure. He asked why that was and the farmer said: "Well, because at five dollars a month there isn't any manure."

Hubert Humphrey, bearing his guilts lightly, bounced in next, acting for all the world as if he had been a McGovern supporter since New Hampshire. It is impossible not to like Humphrey. Fundamentally he must be a little mad, but the madness is appealing and infectious, and he is, beyond doubt, the Democrat's Democrat, so carried away with the thought of Democratic virtues, so excited at Democratic prospects that he could, in his own words, "wrestle alligators." Now he could not conceal his delight and pride at standing on the same platform with his old friend George McGovern and that beautiful Eleanor whom he and Muriel loved so much they could just hardly bear it. And he was there to tell the good folks of such-and-such not to pay any attention to what the Gallups and the Harrises were saying because the polls had been wrong before and, by golly, they were going to be wrong again come November seventh, and old Mr. Nixon, sitting there so smug in the White House and feeling he'd sold the people of America another bill of goods for another four years of naysaying to the working men and women of this country, well, that fellow was in for the surprise of his life.

Sure, he and his old friend and neighbor George had disagreed on a few things and he had even given George a pretty good fight for the nomination if he did say so himself, but that was all in the past now, ladies and gentlemen, and he was out working day and night like everybody ought to be for the McGovern-Shriver ticket because when it came down to the clinch, down to the basics, down to the old nitty-gritty, Hubert Humphrey was a dyed-in-the-wool, wrapped-and-labeled, all-time, full-time, double-time, triple-time Democrat. You could bet

234

your boots on that. You could accept that, like they say, as a "Fiat accompli."

The engaging Gene McCarthy joined us and amused himself with a ship-of-state metaphor. The ship was taking water and slowly sinking, but the Republicans were running around telling everybody not to worry because it was dry in first class. "If Nixon were the captain of the *Titanic*," McCarthy said, "he'd be telling the passengers that he had just stopped to pick up some ice."

No matter what the polls said it was apparent that crowds were getting bigger everywhere. We were in Boston on October 3 for a huge rally—some sixty thousand or more packed into Post Office Square for what the locals said was a larger turnout than a Kennedy had ever drawn. The New York *Times*'s James Reston was with us part of the day.

I found the following piece of discarded copy near the place he'd been working in the press room at the Sheraton Plaza:

> *New York Times*
> *New York, New York*
> *reston's wed. column for editorial, syndicate, salisbury &*
> *barzilay*
> *By James Reston*
>   *Boston, Oct. 3—George McGovern's problem in the last five weeks of the campaign*
>   *Boston, Oct. 3—George McGovern's*

That was it. It was comforting to suppose that, given the evidence of the polls on the one hand and the impressive crowds on the other, Reston wasn't quite sure what to make of things. It was also comforting to see that even the giants of journalism sometimes have trouble with their leads.

On October 6, we finished the day with a rally in Kansas

City's old Union Station that as an indoor event, matched the Boston rally. This was Eagleton country too. Looking at the crowd in which middle-aged and working people seemed to outnumber the young I began to think that something was indeed happening. I began to believe that the multitudes of Joe Six-packs and Archie Bunkers were having another look at McGovern, beginning to respond to the appeal of the underdog and say to themselves: "The guy's no quitter."

Later that night as he was preparing for bed and I was stealing a scotch from the bar in his suite, he said: "I think things are beginning to roll, Dick." I said I thought so too. He grew increasingly chipper over the next few days. When some Nixon-buttoned harridan in Philadelphia screeched at him: "Where's my thousand dollars, McGovern?" he paused before her and said with the right touch of amazement: "Is that what you charge?"

In mid-October a combination of fatigue and a sudden cold brought my sinus difficulties back on me. We were in San Diego at the charming old Coronado Hotel and goodhearted Bill Rosendahl, who had begun traveling with us to make sure McGovern made the "money" calls he was supposed to, was alarmed enough about me to find a doctor. A noble physician named Arvin Klein came and ministered to me at one or two o'clock in the morning and filled me with antibiotics. McGovern was concerned and later called me into his suite while he was having breakfast. "Why don't you go home for two or three days," he said. "Get some rest and get well."

"I can't quit when we're winning," I said.

I didn't get the response I expected. He turned and looked out the window for a moment, then turned back and with a long face said: "Well, do what you think best." The euphoria was beginning to ebb.

I suspected that the telethons were beginning to get to

him. The idea behind them was to give people the opportunity to see and hear the real McGovern as opposed to the caricature, to have him on the screen taking their questions by phone—any and all questions—while Nixon hid in the White House "resting on his Gallup poll," as McGovern liked to say. We were buying half hours—a full hour once or twice—on statewide television networks and the screening of questions was aimed at avoiding repetition only. By the end, I think, we'd done fourteen of the bigger states. But as one followed the other they began to seem like reruns: pot, abortion, amnesty; amnesty, abortion, pot; the one thousand dollars a year for everybody, the 1,000 per cent for Eagleton. McGovern explaining, explaining endlessly; correcting impressions; struggling to get out of the caricature and becoming bored and despairing at what little progress he made.

On October 19, we came into New York for the Alfred E. Smith Memorial dinner, a ponderous affair given every year by Terence Cardinal Cooke, Archbishop of New York. I left as soon as I could but not before seeing two Republicans I like: Vic Gold, press secretary to Spiro Agnew and an admirable Tory out of the old Goldwater crowd, and Happy Rockefeller. I got a peck on the cheek from her and a promise that "we'll see you when it's over."

I went home, kissed Cynthia and fell into bed where I stayed over much of the weekend. On Sunday somebody called and told me about the latest Harris poll. It gave Nixon 59 per cent to McGovern's 34. In the New York *Times Magazine* there was a thoughtful piece by Tom Wicker called "McGovern With Tears." We were no longer merely McGovern-in-trouble; we'd been written off. I confessed to Cynthia that I knew the cause was hopeless, but I made her promise not to tell anybody I'd said so.

Monday, when I rejoined McGovern there was news of progress being made toward a peace in Vietnam. He told the press he hoped the reports were true and said what a tragedy we had had to wait four years for terms that could have been agreed to when Nixon entered office. One Wednesday the Washington Post ran a story which said H. R. Haldeman, Nixon's chief of staff in the White House, along with John Mitchell and Maurice Stans, two other high Nixon minions, had administered the secret $700,000 slush fund out of which the Watergate burglary had been financed. The "chain of scandal and corruption runs to the very heart of Mr. Nixon's White House operation," McGovern declared. Within other contexts, one might have thought the Watergate business alone would topple an Administration from office. But not this time.

In the early hours of the next morning in Detroit I was awakened by a call from a local radio station. A young man with a rich voice informed me that Hanoi had announced an accord. He wanted a comment from McGovern himself at this historic moment. I said we wouldn't have any comment until we knew more about it. Why couldn't I rouse McGovern and have him answer one question at least, the fellow wanted to know? I said because the candidate was very tired; it was three o'clock and I was tired myself. I suggested he try get hold of the Republican candidate. "This is no one-lunger you're talking to, you know," he said sternly. "We are fifty thousand watts."

The following day we learned that Henry Kissinger had announced that peace was "at hand." Well, if McGovern had accomplished nothing else he had helped force the bully boys to stop the killing. "You know, Dick," McGovern said, "I never would have got into this if it hadn't been for that war." That afternoon we were at the University of Iowa in Cedar Rapids. It was an enormous, howling, cheering crowd of students ob-

238

viously bent on telling McGovern he was still all right with them. Off to the left of the crowd a not-so-young couple with a pair of teen-aged children held a big banner which read: "Help Us Be What We Can Be."

Sunday, October 29, brought the first report of the New York *Daily News'* poll of New York State and it forecast a Nixon landslide in that traditionally anti-Nixon constituency. McGovern was stylish that day on "Meet the Press" where his questioners were a group of slow-witted newspaper publishers and editors. Why, asked one of them from a Detroit paper, had McGovern in all his campaigning in Michigan never mentioned busing? McGovern could have asked in reply why the man never read his own newspaper since a McGovern busing speech had been all over the front pages less than two weeks earlier. But he forebore to expose the fellow for the ass that he was.

Monday, October 30, brought us into Pittsburgh where the off-lead story in the afternoon paper reported that McGovern "brought his limping bandwagon to the city today. . . ." Could a bandwagon limp, I wondered? Were writing courses available for political reporters in Pittsburgh?

Tuesday, October 31, saw us back in New York where, at the end of a murderous day, we held a surprise party at the Biltmore for the McGoverns' twenty-ninth wedding anniversary. Jackie Greenidge had called ahead and got Cynthia to go to Tiffany and buy a silver bowl with the $150 or so that the press corps had contributed.

One of McGovern's cornier speech closings was to quote himself in telling about when the first *Dakota Queen* was hit by flack over central Europe in the war. He, as the pilot and captain, had told his crew: "Resume your stations. We're going to bring this plane home." The idea was that he would, as President, do the same for America. So that was the legend the reporters wanted carved on the pretty head which Cynthia brought around. Dick Stout, Jim Naughton, David Murray of the Chicago *Sun-Times* and Pye Chamberlain of UPI Radio put on a little show in which they offered their versions of the column leads which might be expected from the Alsop brothers, Joe Kraft, James Reston and David Broder when the returns next week showed McGovern the winner. They were funny but I can't remember any of them; almost the only thing I remember of the party was the sight of Eleanor McGovern laughing—something I hadn't seen in weeks. She had begun almost perceptibly to droop. The day before she'd said to me: "I can't make up my mind whether I want it over right now or to let us have one more week to change it around." Rather less the Jane Austen figure now; more a Brontë.

At some point in the confusion of days Mankiewicz asked me if I'd "like to be kind" to a young fellow. I didn't know what he was getting at but I said of course I would. "I just think it'd be nice if we could have Kirby come aboard for the last week," he said. "Hmmm?" I said: "By all means. But please ask him to speak to me now and then, would you?"

"You bet," he said. As it happened, Jones never did appear, which I rather regretted since I held no ill will toward him. But I felt it was thoughtful of Mankiewicz and revealing of a genuine affection for his young friend. Mankiewicz, for all the curious skirmishings and unacknowledged frictions between us, was, I thought, a better man than most.

On Thursday, November 2, we did a morning telethon in Chicago, a noontime rally in Cincinnati, and flew into Battle Creek, Michigan, in the afternoon. The crowd along the other side of the airport fence was small but of a respectable size and the cheering as McGovern came down from the plane was loud enough. Not so loud, however, as to drown out the bellow of a fat kid who was yelling: "Go back to South Dakota, McGovern! Go home, ya bum!"

McGovern, after shaking hands with the welcoming committee at the foot of the steps, headed straight for the heckler. He was, I'd guess, eighteen or twenty, an unappealing specimen of 250 pounds, little of it muscle, and there were patches of unsuccessful beard on his pimpled face. His windbreaker was adorned with Nixon buttons of all shapes and colors, as was a shapeless denim hat. He continued his chant even as McGovern came directly to him: "Go back to South Dakota! Nixon's gonna beat you so bad you'll be sorry you left." McGovern leaned over the fence and beckoned him to come closer with a long finger. "Let me tell you a secret," he said as the surprised youth came up and bent forward. McGovern put his hand beside his mouth and whispered something in the other's ear. The boy jumped back in astonishment. "He said a profanity," he shouted. "He said a profanity to me."

McGovern was snickering as he started moving down the fence and shaking hands. I asked him what he'd said.

"I told him to kiss my ass," he said.

I laughed and so—in a fleeting loss of Secret-Service professionalism—did Larry Short and George Hollendersky. Saul Kohler, of the Newhouse papers, was the writing-pool reporter that afternoon. He must have heard McGovern tell me what had been said because the incident went right into the pool report and was on the news wires in no time.

I thought it was funny. McGovern and Dutton thought it was funny; so did Eleanor when she heard about it later. But we were obviously in a minority. Subsequently in Grand Rapids, at a motel called the Mr. President, Mankiewicz and Weil—bolstered by an apparently unanimous opinion at headquarters—pressed McGovern to get out a statement minimizing the business. He refused, but next morning, armed with the front page of the Detroit *Free Press*, and a headline reading: "MC-GOVERN SHOWS STRAIN BY CURSING AIRPORT HECKLER," they returned to the attack.

"This is not presidential! This simply is not presidential, Senator," said Weil in great perturbation.

McGovern, still only half dressed, was eating his bacon and scrambled eggs with gusto. "I don't care whether it is or not," he said. Eleanor, sitting across the table from him, asked: "What was it that Harry Truman said to that music critic who was cruel about Margaret's voice?"

"That he'd kick him in the groin," I said. "And that he was a son of a bitch."

"I don't remember that his stock went down after that," she said. Mankiewicz said: "Henry Kimelman called with an idea I like, probably because I was thinking along the same lines myself. He says we should get out a statement saying this was just a personal response to a personal attack."

"What good would that do?" asked Eleanor.

It was a good question. I said: "Frank, for Christ's sake, if you want a story to die you don't put a new lead on it. I happen to think we might have won more votes than we lost. Nobody likes hecklers but aside from that, as a simple news principle, what we have now is a one-day story, and if we open our mouths about it we turn it into a two-day story."

My point seemed not to get across. "It's just not presidential," said Weil again. "We have to do something."

McGovern stopped eating and pushed his plate away. He said firmly: "Well, I'm not. I'm not saying a damned thing and that's all there is to it."

I had to make a phone call and went into the McGovern bedroom to do it. Mankiewicz apparently gave up his efforts and left, but Weil remained long enough to give the candidate some kind of dressing down. An angry Eleanor came into the bedroom as I was putting down the phone and said: "Did you hear that Gordon trying to lecture George about offending people?"

I said I hadn't. She said: "I'm so mad I can't see straight. Really, when you think of all the people he has alienated over this campaign."

That was Friday, November 3. The same morning the New York *Times* carried an exclusive story that the reports of the Secret Service detail assigned to us had, throughout the campaign, been made available to members of the Nixon staff in the White House. The clear implication was that our agents had been spying on us and Short and Hollendersky were properly upset.

I'd have bet anything the story was false. I knew that McGovern, who thought as highly of Short and Hollendersky as I did, felt the same. It was conceivable that someone at Secret Service in Washington was politicking with their reports—harmless to us in any case and useless to the Nixon bunch—but I was inclined to doubt even that. Short, Hollendersky, Woody Taylor, Bob Knapp—the whole group of the forty or so men who rotated in and out of the assignment—were thoroughly professional. Beyond that they had lived in the most intimate association with McGovern since April and, while they were cops and endowed with the natural conservatism of cops, they liked and genuinely admired him.

There was, if I was any judge of character, no chance that they would turn themselves into informers against him. When I left Eleanor and came back into the sitting room I asked McGovern if he'd said a reassuring word to Larry Short. "I did it just now," he said, "even though Gordon warned me I should wait and see if there's anything to the story."

"Good for you," I said. "To hell with Gordon."

Late that afternoon we went to Gary, Indiana, for a so-called black rally. It was the final of a series of events over the past couple of weeks which had made no scheduling sense at all. We were within three days of the election and still campaigning within what should long since have been wrapped up and filed as part of our basic and dependable constituency. Were American Negroes going to vote for Richard Nixon? Hardly. Yet here we were in Gary—in Indiana of all places where we hadn't a prayer under the best circumstances—doing nothing except soothing the feathers of black leaders who didn't want to be taken for granted or felt McGovern needed to be nailed down in his commitments once more. It was the purist factor again, the thing that might have destroyed us even without Eagleton. "A typical black event," said Weil tartly as we looked around the partially filled hall. "Sixty per cent white and 50 per cent empty."

From Gary we drove through a cold rainy night into Chicago where Richard Daley, least of the purists and probably best of the old guard, was the McGoverns' host at a torchlight parade and rally. McGovern was coming down with a cold and had developed a hacking cough. The plans for the three-block parade along Michigan Avenue called for him to ride with Daley in an open car. It wasn't very wise but he insisted on doing it even when the mayor offered to use a closed limousine. When they started off the dark and misty skies exploded in a wonderful variety of lights and shapes and thunderings. It was a marvelous show. I rode with Eleanor in the car behind the open one and I noticed that as the parade began and the rain fell on the candidate's head—hatless as usual—our seventy-year-old host unostentatiously removed his own hat and also went uncovered.

Sometime in the course of that day I read a *Newsweek* piece by Peter Goldman and Dick Stout which constituted the last report of the magazine to its readers before Election Day. It bore the title "McGovern's Politics of Righteousness," and here are some excerpts:

"His eyes go flat and lifeless on television. His voice struggles for passion and sounds like grace at a Rotary luncheon. His mandatory candidate's tan . . . is fading toward vellum. He looks less the politician than the schoolmaster, an assemblage of bony angles and stray wisps of hair and ill-at-ease smiles. . . . But George Stanley McGovern, in the waning weeks of his campaign, has turned more furiously evangelical than any major party candidate since William Jennings Bryan. He is trying in his low-decibel style to preach his way to the presidency on the once implicit and now open proposition that this election is a contest between good and evil—and that if he loses evil will have won. . . .

"The issue in his campaign is no longer peace against war, or the people against the interests; it is a 'coalition of conscience and decency' against the 'most corrupt and immoral administration in history.' . . . He has moments of passion, even eloquence, in all this; moments when his leaden eyes borrow fire from the klieg lights and his voice rises to a hoarse shout: 'Give us back our country.' But more often his Billy Sunday evangelism is blunted by Billy Saturday style."

There was more. One had to grant McGovern had indeed taken the gloves off and started punching away at the Nixon gang. But why not? Had he any choice?

Was *Newsweek* suggesting that the Administration was not uniquely corrupt and immoral? What other Administration in our history had sent its paid agents into the national headquarters of the opposition party to bug its walls and tap its telephones? Was this standard procedure in American politics?

What other Administration had sent three quarters of a million dollars—to finance these criminal activities—into Mexico to be "laundered" so there'd be no tracing the money to its sources? Did this sort of conduct not represent, as McGovern maintained, "the total erosion of political and moral and public values?" And what of the Segretti Chaplin, and doubtless Haldeman, sabotaging of Democratic candidates in the course of the primaries; was the forged "Canuck" letter which ultimately brought an angry Muskie to tears in New Hampshire really the equivalent of just another Dick Tuck prank?

What was so out of order or proportion in what *Newsweek* called McGovern's "politics of the revival tent" in the face of assaults on the freedom of the press and the First Amendment which were without precedent? Could the magazine name another Administration which had sought and gained an injunction against the publication of news—as it had done with the Pentagon Papers?

McGovern was not some Messianic nut. He was an American historian with a sense of our fragilities. He was an alarmed citizen alerting us to danger. He was a religious man concerned for the spiritual quality of our national life. He was making an issue out of the moral character of Mr. Nixon and his cohorts because that character was patently deficient. If McGovern seemed hyperbolic to the liberal minds of *Newsweek* and of the press and the intellectual community in general, it was precisely because of his seeing—and their stanch disinclination to see —that the Nixon administration was different, not just in degree but in kind from any the Republic had known.

McGovern saw something new emerging in American politics and saw that it was ugly and frightening not only because of its burglars and saboteurs, its insensitivity to the delicate mechanisms of freedom, but for its profound deceptions of a troubled people which, if successful, would reduce and debase them as a people. Nixon offered no improvement in the life of the people but only empty and ersatz satisfactions to their angers and bewilderments. It cost the rich Nixonian oligarchs nothing, yet it gratified the lumpenbourgoisie to tell the poor to go out and get jobs, the black children to stay off the buses, the young draft evaders to stay out of the country, to make noises about permissive judges rather than hire more policemen.

Let 'em eat revenge.

That was the gimmick. Was not this sleaziness, this moral midgetry, this menace to the American character, proper stuff for a presidential candidate to raise as an issue?

It seemed so to me. I bore down on Dick Stout in something of an Old Testament rage myself. "That," I said to him, "is the most hate-filled, unfair, poisonous piece of writing I've ever read in the magazine. I want to tell you that, and to say that you and Peter Goldman ought to be ashamed of yourselves."

They should have been too. I was all the more incensed because I am fond of Stout; he's good company and a decent man. So is Goldman. So, for that matter, is my old friend Oz Elliott, the editor of the damned magazine. I tried to get him on the phone later and, I suppose fortunately, failed.

Stout, big and shaggy and looking like a blond bear, sat slumped in his seat as I laced into him. When I finished he had the gall to say: "What does this do to my interview request?"

"We're a tattered vessel," I said. "But we've got a few shreds of pride left. There'll be no *Newsweek* interview."

I felt better after that. I went back to my seat and asked one of the stewardesses to get me a drink. I recalled Russell Baker's having written early in the spring that "The swinishness season opened at Christmas this year and will continue through Election Day."

Saturday, November 4, found us in Texas where I made an ass of myself by correcting some reference McGovern made to an editorial in the Washington *Star*, telling him during a pause in his speech that it was the Newark *Star-Ledger*. A furious John Holum came up to me with a clipping showing beyond doubt that McGovern had been right in the first place. I passed the word to him and he recorrected himself, not without irritation, for which I couldn't blame him. I felt shriveled with embarrassment. That night we were in St. Louis, and Martin Nolan, pride of the Boston *Globe*, fell over a log in a dark parking lot and broke his arm badly. He got patched up at a local hospital and came in to say goodbye in the morning before flying to Boston for surgery. "St. Louis has not been the luckiest city for the McGovernites this year," he said to the candidate. McGovern said: "You could say that, Marty."

Sunday, November 5, I had time in the morning to check on my daughter whom I'd not talked to for weeks. "Oh, boy," she said when I reached her in Cambridge, "things look good here in Massachusetts." I said: "That's great, Lisa. Who knows, we may do it yet."

We plodded through the day. There were interviews with Frank Reynolds of ABC, John Dancey of NBC and Bruce Morton of CBS, and McGovern was in top form. They would make first-rate features on the news shows Election Eve. We flew from St. Louis to Moline, Illinois, for an airport rally, then to New York for a rally in Brooklyn. We canceled a rally in Queens so that McGovern could make one more television speech on the continuing war and ask what had happened to the peace Henry Kissinger had said was "at hand" only days before. Finally, leaden with fatigue, we headed for the Bronx and still another rally. I peeled off after that to go home. I planned to skip a flight to the West Coast the next day so that I could vote Tuesday

248

morning before heading for Sioux Falls and the moment of truth. I watched McGovern lift his long frame into the car at the end of the Bronx rally and remembered what Walter Mears, the Associated Press's chief political writer, had told me a few days earlier. Mears was not one to flatter and certainly no sentimentalist but he'd said: "I'll tell you one thing, Dougherty. Your guy has more guts than any politician I've ever seen."

That afternoon on the flight from Moline I had said to him: "You're going to win this thing yet." He looked at me with a sad face that seemed half again its normal length. "Do you think so, Dick?" he said. "I don't know. I'm psychologically prepared to lose."

He smiled then as he was reminded of a story some politician had told him years back about a mayor who won an election and called in his chief supporters for a victory celebration. "When they were all gathered together," McGovern said, "the mayor made a little speech in which he said: 'Our opponents stooped to every dirty trick in the books in this campaign. They bought votes. They voted the cemetery. They stuffed the ballot boxes. They lied and slandered and called us every kind of crook and criminal. But we stayed right in there every inch of the way. And we beat them at their own game!'"

"That's funny," I said.

"I've always liked that story," he said.

CHAPTER *13*

CYNTHIA AND I voted at a school on Seventy-fifth Street between Lexington and Third avenues in the morning. Then, toward noon, we took a taxi to La Guardia. There were only a few people at the departure gate for the flight to Minneapolis where we had to change planes to go on to Sioux Falls. Among them were Arthur Krim and his pretty, buxom wife, Mathilde. I was pleased and a little surprised to see them. They had done sturdy labors for McGovern once he had won the nomination but not before, and Krim was, however liberal, rather an obvious Establishment Democrat. He was an old and close friend of Lyndon Johnson's and had over the years raised millions for the party and its nominees. Owner of a big chunk of United Artists, he was extremely rich in his own right. On the short side, with an over-large, well-shaped head, he was also a very intelligent, rather courtly man of, I'd guess, sixty or so. It puzzled me that he and his wife should be going so far to be in attendance at what they knew would have to be a disaster. I could only assume that in the course of the campaign they had developed a genuine affection for McGovern and I liked them for that.

When we arrived at the Sioux Falls Holiday Inn the McGoverns had not yet returned from Mitchell where they had gone to vote and to attend a reception in their honor at Dakota Wesleyan. They finally appeared a little after five o'clock, both of them looking thoroughly bushed. They had not gotten to bed until after three, in the morning at the end of a day which had taken them from New York to Long Beach, California, and then back through two time zones to South Dakota. Eleanor went immediately into the bedroom of their suite to have a nap. McGovern wanted to have some supper before getting a little sleep himself.

I sat in a chair a few feet away as McGovern—jacket, necktie and shoes off—sat at a room-service table and hacked away at a large steak. With him, and only pretending to eat, was his eldest daughter, Ann Meade. Stanley Tretick was a silent presence in the room as he moved about taking pictures. The room itself was all somehow bluish with instant-antique furnishings of the Bronx renaissance style fancied by so many motels.

As McGovern ate he and I talked about how he saw his activities for the evening so that I could brief the newsmen. He thought he would sleep for an hour, or maybe two, then watch the returns with Eleanor and the family—the children and various other relatives being in adjoining suites and rooms on the eighth floor. He said I was right to think he would not want photographers or reporters covering him even on a pooled basis. He also said that no matter what happened he would not go to the Sioux Falls Coliseum, where a reception was planned, before ten o'clock at the earliest.

"I think this could turn out to be a long night, Dick," he said.

"So do I," I said.

"I wouldn't be surprised if we have another 1960 on our hands. Do you remember? It wasn't until almost noon the next day that Nixon conceded."

"Could be," I said. "Yes, I remember." I looked at Ann, a plumpish, pretty girl who favored her mother more than the other children. She had come from watching television in the adjoining sitting room. It was already after seven o'clock in the

East and the early, fragmentary returns were shattering. I was afraid she was going to burst into tears, but she didn't.

McGovern got up from the table, stretched and yawned, and said: "So, anyhow, I don't think I'll miss anything if I get a couple hours sleep." He said he'd see us later, went into the bedroom and closed the door quietly behind him. Ann excused herself and went into the other sitting room where a row of three huge television sets were lined up and aimed at the family like a firing squad. I went over to the bar, fixed myself a drink, and went down the hall to my room where Cynthia and Maureen Tretick, Stanley's attractive wife, were also having a drink and staring morosely at the news. Tretick came in right behind me.

"Did you notice how fast he headed for that bedroom?" he asked me. I said I had.

"He never even asked if the returns were starting to come in," Tretick said. "The poor guy: He doesn't want to know."

I went down to the press room off the lobby, briefed the reporters and told them they could take their time over dinner since he wouldn't be stirring until ten anyway. Then I joined Cynthia and the Treticks in the restaurant on the top floor of the hotel. Bill Dougherty and his pretty wife, Billy, were at a table across the room with a couple of their children. I sat down and ordered a drink. The next time I looked the Doughertys were only a few feet away from us. I realized then that our table was on an enormous turntable which revolved so slowly as to be imperceptible. They'd gone about as far as they could go in Sioux Falls. Dougherty joined us for a moment, his astonishingly young face wearing the look of the kid who just dropped the pass that would have won the game. "What ever happened to the McGovern luck?" I asked him.

"I don't know," he said. "It sure went when it went, didn't it?"

253

He was up for re-election as lieutenant governor and Cynthia asked how things were going for him. "Great," he said and winked. "I figure about 70 per cent." It was not an immodest estimate as time soon proved. "And McGovern?" I asked. Dougherty shook his head: "Not a chance, Dick. Not even in South Dakota."

I said I had a theory about that. "They're going to show him the folly of getting too big for britches, of puttin' on airs."

"That's part of it," he said. "Is that the way folks are in Bolivar, Dick?"

"That's why I left," I said.

"I still can't believe it," said Maureen Tretick. "He's such a nice man."

A little before nine o'clock I excused myself and went down to the McGovern suite. I saw John Holum hurrying in as I came along the hallway from the elevator. He was carrying some papers and I guessed the candidate was awake and had already asked for a draft of a concession statement. I followed Holum into the bedroom. Eleanor was not visible and I assumed she was in the bathroom.

McGovern was sitting on the foot of his bed. He was in pajama bottoms and an undershirt. He had a pen in hand and went immediately to work on the Holum draft. I gathered he must have told Holum what he wanted because he said: "The Stevenson reference works all right, doesn't it, John?" Holum, whose hands were shaking slightly, said he thought so. Holum sat down in a chair and I leaned against a chest of drawers. I heard a faint sound of sobbing coming from the bathroom.

Except for that there was no sound in the room for several minutes except that of McGovern's pen, crossing out something, adding something along the margins. When he was finished he handed the speech back to Holum, saying: "Would you read it

254

out loud, John? So we can see how it sounds?" Holum took the speech and started:

"Here among my friends in South Dakota . . ." His voice began to choke. He said: "I can't. I can't read it." I said that I'd do it and he handed the speech to me. McGovern asked: "Can you read my scribbling, Dick?" I said I thought so and proceeded to read:

"Here among my friends in South Dakota, where this campaign began twenty-two months ago, we bring it to an end tonight.

"I have sent the following telegram to President Nixon: 'Congratulations on your victory. I hope that in the next four years you will lead us to a time of peace abroad and justice at home. You have my full support in such efforts. With best wishes to you and your gracious wife, Pat. Sincerely, George McGovern.'

"The first presidential concession I remember hearing was that of Adlai Stevenson in 1952. He recalled the Lincoln story of a boy who stubbed his toe in the dark. When the lad was asked how he felt, he replied: 'It hurts too much to laugh, but I'm too old to cry.'

"It does hurt to lose. But we are not going to shed any tears about this campaign or over this election. All the joy we have found in these past twenty-two months cannot be washed away with the tears of one night.

"We have found the greatest outpouring of energy and love that any political effort has ever inspired. Eleanor and I and our family, along with Sargent and Eunice Shriver, will never forget the people of this campaign—those we have seen at countless meeting places, and those we know about on the telephones and on their feet, who have worked so hard for all these many months.

255

"The poet Yeats once wrote: 'Think where man's glory most begins and ends/ And say my glory was I had such friends.'

"The presidency belongs to someone else. But the glory of these devoted working friends, and their devotion to the noble ideals of this country, sustains me now and will sustain our country.

"We will shed no tears because all this effort will bear fruit for years to come. We have pushed this country toward peace. And we love that title 'peacemaker' more than any office. We will press on with that fight until the bloodshed and sorrow have ended once and for all.

"But I want each of you to remember that if we moved peace closer by a single day, then every hour of this campaign was worth it. And if we have brought into the political process those who never before experienced its joy and sorrow, that too is an enduring blessing.

"The question is: to what standard does a loyal opposition now rally? We do not rally to the support of policies we deplore. But we do love the nation. And we will continue to beckon it to a higher standard. I ask all of you to stand with your convictions. I ask you not to despair of the political process for it has yielded too much valuable improvement these past two years.

"The Democratic Party will be a better party because of the reforms we have carried out. The nation will be better because we never once gave up in the long battle to renew its oldest ideals and to redirect its current energies along more humane and hopeful paths. So let us play the role of the loyal opposition in the spirit of Isaiah:

" 'They that wait upon the Lord shall renew their strength; they shall mount up with wings as eagles, they shall run and not be weary; and they shall walk and not faint.' "

I handed the speech back to Holum. McGovern said: "What do you think, Dick?"

"I think it's magnificent," I said.

Eleanor had come from the bathroom and listened as I read. He looked up at her and asked: "Eleanor?" She was patting her eyes with a handkerchief. She nodded and said: "I think it's excellent."

He took the speech from Holum and lifted his pen as if to make an addition. It was never made. His eyes welled over and a tear fell that was so large it splashed when it struck the top of his hand. A terrible sound came from him that was like a giggle except that it was as much a sob as a giggle. He got up. He said: "I don't know why I do that when I'm sad—why I laugh." He moved quickly toward the bathroom.

Eleanor, beginning to cry again, said: "George always does that. He always laughs when he feels most badly." Holum picked up the speech from the bed and almost ran from the room. I put my arms around her and gave her a hug. She is so tiny; it was like comforting a child.

"Oh, Dick," she said. "He has always said he had more affinity with you than with the others."

McGovern was in full command of himself when he came back from the bathroom. He searched through some shirts for one he wanted to wear. I started to leave. "If the fellows ask why we lost, Dick," he said, "tell 'em because we didn't get enough votes. It's a stale joke but it's all I can think of at the moment."

Reporters clustered around me when I came into the press room. They wanted to know how he was taking it. "He's very disappointed, of course," I said, "but he and Mrs. McGovern are bearing up."

"Is there anything we can quote? Did he say anything when he realized?"

"No," I said. "He didn't say anything special."

"You say he's disappointed. How did he demonstrate that? Did he tell you he was disappointed?"

"I think that's an inference I could reasonably draw," I said. "Take my word for it. You can say he's disappointed."

"You say they are both bearing up. In what way are they bearing up?"

"With style," I said, temper rising and starting to leave. "They're a very classy pair."

Mary McGrory, a dear woman and a fine writer from the Washington *Star,* grabbed me before I got out the door. "Dick," she said, "can't I see him? Can't I go up for just a few minutes?" I shook my head. "The Washington *Post* had an interview toward the end. The *Star* has never had one," she said. She had written of McGovern with great sensitivity during the last Gethsemane weeks. And she looked as if she'd shed an Irish tear herself. But I had to say no. "Darling," I said, "I can't let anybody see him now. The poor son of a bitch is utterly crushed." She patted my arm. "All right," she said.

Upstairs, looking for Cynthia, I ran into Miles Rubin, a California businessman, an intense, darkly good-looking fellow in his forties, who had worked with great effect at everything from voter registration to money raising since before New Hampshire. We shook hands. "Three people did it," he said. "Bremer [George Wallace's would-be assassin], Eagleton and Humphrey." I said I supposed so. "Humphrey really radicalized us in California," he said. "Really radicalized us."

By that time the full extent of the defeat was evident. Nixon, helped by the monolithic endorsement of the George Wallace voters, had swept everything excepting only the heavily black District of Columbia and Massachusetts. Massachusetts, I thought, had remembered the real McGovern whom it got to know so well in the winter and spring as he came and went en route to New Hampshire and his long-shot challenge of Muskie.

Years ago I had a play on Broadway and on opening night the prop man forgot to put the props on the stage. The curtain went up on the first scene and the young actor and actress, finding themselves lacking a couple of things they needed, panicked and talked gibberish. The maid came on, looked around and said: "I'll leave you to your own deserts then." She thereupon fled the set. In the second scene the young man's bathrobe caught fire. It was all a nightmare. I sat and watched the work of over a year and the dreams of many more years than that come crashing down. The reviews next day were scalding and their target was the playwright. Eight million New Yorkers were told that the play was, among other things, "the most witless piece of writing" Broadway had seen in modern memory. For weeks, for months, friends lowered their eyes when we met as though I'd been picked up in the men's room of Grand Central on a morals charge. It took a year for the lump of lead in my stomach to go away.

This was admittedly a weak analogy to set beside McGovern's fate but to recall it gave me at least a sense of his humiliation as he stood examined and found wanting by forty-six million of his fellow citizens. I thought of that cheerful, rocklike, blissful faith he had that he was one of the Lord's lucky ones. What a shambles that must be now. I thought of that high and hawkish pride, its wings crippled and bleeding as it struggled and tumbled, falling through the regions of the upper air. What a fall was there, my countrymen.

Cynthia told me she didn't mind not going to the Coliseum for the concession speech; she would stay and watch it on television with Maureen Tretick, and, besides, I was "too busy to

have to worry" about her. I said I doubted if I'd be gone long.
When the McGoverns were in their car, a red-eyed Jeff Smith,
Gordon Weil and I piled into the spare car of the Secret Service
and followed along to the Coliseum, which was only three blocks
away.

We pulled around to the rear of the big, barnlike building.
McGovern, back straight and head up, was composed as we
waited in a small room off the stage for the rest of the family to
arrive. When they had assembled, he and Eleanor led the way
into such a roaring reception that one might have thought it a
victory party. I followed along behind Steven, a twenty-year-old
replica of his father, and the daughters Ann, Susan, Terry and
Mary. I took a position at the very rear of the stage platform. It
was a couple of minutes before the crowd would let McGovern
speak. He and Eleanor stood, arms around each other, at the
center of the family huddle while the television lights blazed and
the still photographers took pictures.

Sometime back in the spring McGovern, prompted by reasons
now forgotten, had told me how he and Eleanor had come by
train into Kansas City on their wedding night. It was in 1943.
He was in flight training at some air base in Oklahoma. He and
she had had a change of heart about not getting married until
he came home from the war, so he had gotten a three-day pass,
come home to Mitchell where they were married by his father,
and then hurried his bride onto a train so as to get back to the
base on time. They had to change trains at Kansas City. They
got on line before a ticket window in Union Station and waited
their turn. They had two pieces of luggage, which they moved
along on the floor until they got up to the window. They bought
their tickets and turned to pick up the suitcases, to discover
them gone.

"Somebody had just walked up when we weren't watching

and stolen them," McGovern said. "We didn't know what to do. Our other train was about to leave so finally we ran for it and got aboard. It was one of those old cars with the straight-backed wicker seats and we were going to be on it all through the night. We sat facing each other and we looked at each other and then we both just put our faces in our hands and bawled. It was everything we had in the world."

Now as I watched him speak, her standing at his side and looking up at him, there came into my mind the image of them in the alien vastness of the railroad station—stunned at the world's cruelty, bereft of everything, alone.

By the time we got back to the hotel a group including Mankiewicz and Henry Kimelman had arrived from Washington via a small chartered jet. Mankiewicz and I shook hands and he gave me a hug with his left arm. Nice, temperamental Henry Kimelman also hugged me. "Ah, Dick, Dick," he said. "Isn't it a shame? Isn't it a crime? If the people only knew."

I saw Joe Floyd with a rather dark drink in his hand. His pleasant wife, whom I'd met that time I dined with the McGoverns in December, had died in the spring and Floyd had been quite shaken by it. Now he said: "Even South Dakota, Dick. Even his own people." Bob Knapp, one of the senior Secret Service agents, came up to shake hands and say goodbye. "You guys did more good than you know," he said huskily.

I found Cynthia and we drifted from one crowded suite to another as the McGoverns had started to do. We saw and embraced Shirley MacLaine and Liz Stevens. Shirley asked about Dutton and I said he had dropped off in Long Beach the day before. "How many new voters did we finally register?" she asked. I guessed about five or six million. "A little short of eighteen," she said. In one suite we saw the McGoverns talking to the Krims—the former looking like hosts at a successful cocktail party. I heard McGovern say to Krim: "One of the nicer things about all this, Arthur, has been getting to know you and Mathilde."

George Cunningham appeared at my side, puffing his pipe and looking grumpy. He had a suite full of South Dakotans down the hall which he wanted to steer McGovern toward. He was thinking ahead to a Senate re-election campaign. "There's not a person in this room," he growled, "who's going to be useful in '74." At some point Gordon Weil came up and said: "Well, are you going to write a book?" I said I didn't know but I supposed so. I guessed from his tone that he was going to.

Next morning as we were about to leave I met Stanley Sheinbaum in the lobby. He is a gentle, full-bearded, wealthy McGovern supporter from Beverly Hills. He said: "What are you going to do when you grow up, Dick?" I said: "Stanley, I've been asking myself that for fifty years."

When the McGoverns came out of the elevator and into the lobby they were engulfed by people, most of whom were weeping. Eleanor, her head back, was blinking tears away. I started to walk them to the car. As we came to the entrance an elderly lady grabbed McGovern to shake his hand. He tried to say something to her, but choked up. He bent and kissed her cheek instead. "I'm all right if I don't try to talk," he said to me. "Darned Irish sentimentality."

A gallant Sargent Shriver was at National Airport to greet us, along with Pierre Salinger, Gary Hart and thirty or so others from headquarters. The last pictures were taken of the 1972 Democratic ticket. There were kisses and handshakes, tears and laughter, exchanges of phone numbers and addresses. The McGoverns—Redwood and Redwood II—were helped into their car and driven home by the Secret Service for the last time. The scramble for luggage and the struggle for taxis began. Tom Oliphant of the Boston *Globe* had a cab and kindly dropped Cynthia and me at the main terminal where we hurried to the shuttle.

There had been torrential rains and flooding in New York earlier in the day. Air traffic was piled up over La Guardia and it was more than three hours before we landed. I slept most of the time. Cynthia read a detective story. Now and then she reached over and took my hand.